The
21st
Century
Nonprofit

The 21st Century Nonprofit

Remaking the Organization in the Post-Government Era

Paul B. Firstenberg

The Foundation Center

Copyright © 1996 by The Foundation Center.
All rights reserved.
Printed and bound in the United States of America.
Cover design by Apicella Design.

Library of Congress Cataloging-in-Publication Data

Firstenberg, Paul B., 1933–
    The 21st century nonprofit : remaking the organization
in the post-government era / by Paul B. Firstenberg.
        p.   cm.
    Includes bibliographical references and index.
    ISBN 0-87954-652-2. — ISBN 0-87954-672-7 (pbk.)
    1. Nonprofit organizations—United States—Management.
2. Organizational change—United States. 3. Strategic planning—
United States. 4. Organizational effectiveness. I. Title.
HD62.6.F57   1996
658′ .048—dc20

96–3764
                                                                        CIP

To Jonathan—
child and friend—who got me going on this

CONTENTS

Executive Summary

The 21st Century Nonprofit is written primarily for people who manage or serve as trustees of nonprofit organizations dedicated to educational, cultural, scientific, and social objectives—organizations that meet the requirements of Section 501(c)(3) of the United States Internal Revenue Code and thus are exempt from income tax on income related to their mission. In addition, donors to such organizations receive tax deductions for their gifts.

The book's context is today's "post-government" America, where the government's ability to provide effective social, educational, cultural, and welfare programs is under challenge, and where sharp reductions in government funding for many nonprofits are unlikely to be offset by increased private contributions. Just as global competition has forced businesses to reengineer their operations, this tight-fisted environment will exert pressure on nonprofits to restructure theirs. At the least, in the coming Darwinian world, the managements of nonprofits need to gain tighter control over their organizations' performance and sharpen the quality and productivity of their work.

Nonprofits have been significant forces for change in American society and have the potential to be even more important agents for change in the future, as Part 1 of the book underscores. However, nonprofits cannot simply rely on their altruistic intentions or their past record of contributions to society in order to attract the support they require. As important as these factors have been to the generally positive reputation of nonprofits, in the future, organizations will have to define specific objectives and show that they have achieved those goals. Donors will increasingly insist on verifiable results, and nonprofits must take the initiative in accounting for the degree to which their performance matches their aims—and in documenting that they have operated as cost-effectively as possible.

To achieve a more effective, more efficient level of performance will, in many cases, require *remaking the organization.* This kind of fundamental rethinking has been taking hold in American business, which has had to become more productive to hold its own in the face of fierce global competition. Various methodologies—"total quality management," "reengineering," "downsizing," "benchmarking," and "restructuring"—have been designed to achieve this transformation. These varied conceptual formulations for transforming an organization share a common objective: to determine what the organization's purposes ought to be and then to identify how to organize the work of the enterprise in order to achieve those aims at the least possible cost. This book encourages nonprofit organizations to take the same hard look at their operations and how they can be made more efficient and more responsive to the enterprise's aims.

Such a reexamination will challenge nonprofit managers to increase productivity through better cost management. Productivity in the manufacture of tangible products typically increases steadily as capital investment in technology reduces unit labor costs. But in the case of "knowledge," artistic, and professional service enterprises, capital cannot be typically substituted for labor; this leaves managers confronting the problem of how to *restructure the work* of the enterprise in order to constrain the costs of its operation.

The catalyst for change will inevitably be a chief executive with a clear vision of where he or she wants to take the organization, the ability to communicate that vision effectively to all levels of the organization, and the force of personality needed to move people to implement the vision. In addition, the boards of nonprofits must provide active and unequivocal support for the transformation of the organization. Indeed, in the absence of shareholders prodding management to provide better returns, the board may be the only external force that can energize a nonprofit's management to address the need for change. Certainly, the board cannot remain passive in the face of controversy or conflict; it has to provide energetic, firm leadership.

The 21st Century Nonprofit thus has three principal themes: (1) Today's nonprofit enterprise has the urgent and no longer avoidable task of carving out a strategic position that advantages the enterprise relative to its competition, and of managing its day-to-day performance to maximize the effectiveness and efficiency of the organization. (2) While managing nonprofit organizations is a complex and demanding task with unique requirements, effective nonprofit management need not be a product of invention; rather, it can be the adaptation of the "best practices" that currently guide America's outstanding businesses and nonprofits. (3) The fund accounting system that governs nonprofits' financial statements typically does not provide in a user-friendly format the information that management needs in order to guide the performance of the organization. A specially crafted management information system, designed to illuminate the performance and financial condition of the organization for the benefit of managers and board members, must be at the heart of any nonprofit's financial management system.

Part 2 of the book shows how a series of management practices—restructuring, downsizing, performance management, and strategic positioning—can be applied to the management of nonprofits. It also explores mergers, traditionally not thought of in discussions of nonprofit management, as a means of remaking an organization.

The text takes the point of view that if the management of nonprofits is to improve substantially, grantmaking organizations must make a deliberate effort to look more closely into a grantee's management practices before making a grant and to exercise closer oversight concerning how effectively a grant, once received, is used. This more active stance toward the managerial quality of grantees is not only in the best interest of grantees, but also a fiduciary responsibility of grantmaking organizations. The text also proposes that one or more grantmaking organizations fund the establishment of a data base—accessible to nonprofits—containing those "best practices" of nonprofits and for-profit businesses that are applicable to the management of exempt organizations.

Part 3 addresses the issue of how exempt organizations can expand their present revenue base. It describes how a "marketing approach" can lead to increases in funds raised from foundations, corporations, the government, and individuals. It also presses organizations to consider how they can generate earned income, pointing to various successful models of such endeavors that have proved successful. It also discusses a heretofore relatively rare phenomenon: the conversion of a nonprofit corporation to a for-profit business enterprise, a type of transaction that we are likely to see more of in the future, particularly in the health-care and hospital industry.

Part 4 of the book focuses on maximizing the effectiveness of an organization's human resources, undoubtedly the most critical facet of the management of any enterprise. The section begins with a discussion of the changes that are taking place in the work world of executives and professional practitioners and how these changes affect not only the individual but also the organization. Then it describes actions that an organization can take to respond to these changes and to create an environment that will enhance the ability of individual members of the organization to maximize their contributions to the organization while also furthering their career options. Compensation policies that will attract and motivate first-rate talent, without having to offer salaries inconsistent with the basic value system of the organization, are essential. However, so are other actions that an organization's leadership can take to move people to perform at their best.

The section also discusses how boards of trustees can effectively fulfill their fiduciary responsibility for the destiny of exempt organizations. Significant changes are taking place in the behavior of boards of directors of public corporations under pressure from large institutional shareholders, the Securities and Exchange Commission, stock exchanges, and the media and others, not to mention the growing number of lawsuits aimed at corporate directors; there are lessons in these changes for the boards of nonprofits. The section identifies seven steps that establish the foundation of effective governance of nonprofit institutions: (1) giving trustees control of the nominating process, (2) shaping the agenda, (3) getting access to independent sources of information, (4) creating a committee on governance, (5) holding board meetings without management present, (6) establishing someone other than the organization's CEO as leader of the board, and (7) empowering the audit committee. The question is where will the pressure come from to move nonprofit trustees to take a more active and dynamic governance role.

The book's last section also focuses on human relations issues. It contains profiles of McGeorge Bundy as head of the Ford Foundation, William G. Bowen as president of Princeton University, and Joan Ganz Cooney as founder and CEO of Children's Television Workshop (producer of *Sesame Street* and other shows and products for young children). Although these three leaders ran these very different types of organizations and possess different personal characteristics, each of them is a model of an effective CEO. Their effectiveness derives not only from the direction they give their respective organizations, but from the force of their personalities.

INTRODUCTION

Rethinking Nonprofit Management

The pressure on colleges to be accountable to the public for their cost and educational quality has reached an all-time high.
> Arthur J. Rothkopf
> *President, Lafayette College*[1]

Accountability is the password to credibility.
> Margaret E. Mahoney
> *Former president and CEO, The Commonwealth Fund*[2]

Margaret E. ("Maggie") Mahoney is the consummate foundation professional. She is one of a core group of foundation careerists who established that foundation work is a profession, demanding its own special blend of skills. These foundation workers demonstrated by the quality of what they accomplished that foundations did not exist simply to enable people—prominent or otherwise—to take time off from their regular careers, or to provide sinecures for friends and relatives of the philanthropists who establish foundations. The people who work at foundations today owe much to Maggie and her peers.

Maggie has been a foundation professional since 1972, and no one knows more than she about the business of formulating foundation programs. She has a knack, essential in foundation work, for fashioning feasible programs out of broad-based ideas, as well as the wisdom and solid judgment that come from a strong sense of self-possession. Maggie is a woman of infinite curiosity and enthusiasms, with a vast reservoir of knowledge and a wide network of contacts.

At the Commonwealth Fund, where Maggie was named president in 1980, she applied her talents not only to every aspect of program design and policy execution but also to all facets of the foundation's operations. She traveled ceaselessly, searching for new program ideas and grant candidates. She mastered the principles of endowment investment, playing an active role in the fund's policy administration, and she built a strong, constructive board of trustees. She is indeed a model CEO for all types of nonprofits. At the end of 1994 she retired from the fund to move to her next challenge.

Maggie's president's essay in the foundation's 1994 annual report is devoted to the active role she believes a constructive board of trustees should play. The quotation from that essay is excerpted from her discussion of the duty of foundations to be "accountable for meeting acceptable standards in the management of finance and the quality of programs." She adds pointedly: "For foundations, the ultimate bottom line is their success in showing how improvements can be made in society."[3]

Maggie's reference to accountability applies to the entire nonprofit world. Thinking about how managers can realize this ideal on a daily basis provided much of the stimulus for this book.

More than 10 years ago I completed *Managing for Profit in the Nonprofit World.* I wrote that book because in teaching a course on nonprofit management at the Yale School of Organization and Management I could not find published materials that offered a systematic approach to the management of such organizations. While more has been written in the intervening decade about the management of tax-exempt nonprofit organizations, I have to agree with Peter Drucker's recent observation that "what constitutes performance for social-sector organizations has yet to be worked out . . . [and] . . . what precisely management means for the social sector is just beginning to be studied."[4]

Let me focus on terminology for a moment: There are several million nonprofit organizations that are not subject to federal income taxation; but throughout this book, the terms "nonprofit organizations" and "exempt organizations" refer to one category of such organizations, namely those which, under Section 501(c)(3) of the Internal Revenue Code, are not only exempt from taxation but also are entitled to receive tax-deductible contributions from donors. Under the code, the primary purpose of such organizations must be to further "religious, charitable, scientific, and educational" aims, and no part of the net earnings of such an organization "may inure to the benefit of any private shareholder or individual."[5]

The concepts and practices advanced in this book are intended to be applicable to the range of organizations that fall within the broad category of enterprises meeting the tests of Section 501(c)(3). The reader may wonder why the text's examples refer to universities, a television production company, a social service agency, and other types of nonprofits as if they were all the same type of enterprise when in fact there are significant differences in their operating dynamics and cultures. This book, however, argues that the "best practices" of businesses and nonprofits can be adapted to inform and shape the management of all nonprofit enterprises.

Furthermore, these practices can prove valuable to large and small, established and new enterprises. I had the occasion during the writing of this manuscript to consult with a relatively small-scale nonprofit organization engaged in promoting international educational exchanges. As the organization's president and I sorted through various matters, it became evident that the objective and action plan setting process outlined in Chapter 8, "Performance Management," would help the organization. The organization was considering an array of appealing projects but needed to determine, in light of the limited resources of its able but very small staff, which programs absolutely had to be implemented in order to meet the organization's highest-priority objectives, and how much time and effort such programs would require. The process enabled the president to decide whether the organization was in a position to pursue other projects that, while interesting, did not dovetail with the organization's immediate priorities.

Restructuring the Way Nonprofits Work

In *Managing for Profit in the Nonprofit World,* I wanted to convey a straightforward message: nonprofit organizations can be as well managed as enterprises formed solely to make a profit, and there is no inconsistency between trying to advance the public good and running a well-managed organization that is in healthy financial condition. The book underscored that sound management means effective direction and control of the entire organization, its finances as well as its humanitarian programs. The book encouraged nonprofit organizations to reduce their dependence on a single source of funding, be it grants (especially from the federal government) or other contributions, and to increase the revenues generated by their own programs or related business activities.

The 21st Century Nonprofit, building on the themes of the earlier volume, seeks to:

◆ Articulate the unique role nonprofits can play as agents of change. However, the ability of the nonprofit sector to become an increasingly vital social and cultural force depends on exempt organizations improving their overall management and, in particular, establishing *verifiable objectives* and accepting *accountability* for how well they achieve them.

◆ Describe techniques developed by American business for improving performance—downsizing, benchmarking, total quality management, teamwork, reengineering, and restructuring—and illustrate how nonprofit organizations can adapt these and other best practices to improve in fundamental ways the efficiency and effectiveness of their performance.

◆ Urge the nonprofit community to restructure the way in which they conduct their operations. Basic changes are needed in the way work is performed, managed, and accounted for.

A central focus of this volume is thus the internal day-to-day workings of management, and the actions that can be taken to improve the efficiency with which the work of an organization is performed. It is a book literally about remaking the way an organization works.

Nonprofits, like many professional service organizations, typically have depended entirely on increasing their funding as the principal means of offsetting increases in their costs; this volume indeed, in its later chapters, urges nonprofits to develop more innovative strategies for generating income. But something is lost when the focus is only on revenues. Reducing operating expenses through increased efficiency has been viewed as an exercise with very limited yield. Numerous reasons have been offered—even within my own prior book *Managing for Profit in the Nonprofit World*—why productivity could not be increased significantly in such organizations. Examples of a symphony orchestra or ballet were cited to illustrate the limited possibilities for achieving productivity improvement in professional service organizations. This view is challenged in the present work in the chapter "The Productivity Imperative."

At the same time, there is also a prevailing belief that the objectives of nonprofit organizations cannot be stated with sufficient specificity to measure then and then compare them to actual results, an essential element in the process of improving the efficiency of any organization. But this is an unduly defeatist view. The combination of American business' achievements in increasing productivity by better management of its resources and my own professional experience subsequent to writing *Managing for Profit in the Nonprofit World* convinces me that the productivity of nonprofit enterprises can be addressed and improved by management, and that exempt organizations can build a better record of defining the objectives they intend to accomplish and then account for their performance.

The Restructuring of American Business: Pointing the Way

In part, the case for change in the management systems of nonprofits is based on the changes that have been successfully effected in many American business operations. Many traditional American manufacturing companies have been at the forefront of transforming the way business organizations operate, doubtless because in the 1970s and 1980s these companies' very survival was challenged by foreign competitors. The steps taken by such companies to become more competitive are relevant to nonprofit organizations and have been summarized effectively in a pathbreaking study, *Made in America,* which made public the results of a commission convened in 1986 by the Massachusetts Institute of Technology.[6]

The commission focused on a major national issue—the decline in U.S. industrial performance in the 1970s and 1980s. More than two years later, the group of MIT faculty members from a range of disciplines constituting the commission published the report identifying similarities in the "best-practice firms"—firms that had responded successfully to the opportunities and constraints of the new internationally competitive economic environment. The commission found six "key similarities" among these firms: (1) a focus on simultaneous improvement in costs, quality, and delivery, (2) closer links to customers, (3) closer relationships with suppliers, (4) the effective use of technology for strategic advantage, (5) less hierarchical and less compartmentalized organizations with greater flexibility, and (6) human resources policies that promoted continuous learning, teamwork, participation, and flexibility. The commission concluded: "The six responses are mutually reinforcing. Indeed, they form a single, integrated strategy."[7]

These "six key similarities," the commission concluded, were also applicable to professional service organizations including, quite specifically, not-for-profit organizations. As the commission observed, "We believe our own production as an educational institution is hampered by many of the weaknesses that we have discovered in American industry." The commission then offered these specific examples:

> We are subject to short-term pressures in setting goals and in measuring the success of students, faculty members, and programs; we do not use as much creative energy as we might in measuring the quality of our product (students); we do not have adequate resources and mechanisms in place to manage educational change effectively; and we could do more to cultivate closer relationships with our "clients" who hire our students and our "suppliers," the secondary schools that provide them.

As the MIT commission's report indicates, the steps taken to transform American business show what gains could be achieved by restructuring the management practices of nonprofits. They also provide guidelines for effecting change in the nonprofit sector.

Lessons in Restructuring from Personal Experience

The professional endeavors I engaged in after writing *Managing for Profit in the Nonprofit World* further reinforced my sense that restructuring the management of nonprofits is a critical and feasible priority.

The first of these experiences was the time I spent right after the book's publication as executive vice president of the Prudential Realty Group, the real estate investment arm of the Prudential Life Insurance Company of America, which, during my tenure, had some $40 billion in real estate assets under management. The second was my role as the first Chancellor for Resource Planning and Development at Tulane University in New Orleans, Louisiana. I was responsible for developing a new long-range strategic plan for the university and for organizing the fundraising apparatus to raise increased funds as well as developing new sources of revenue by finding commercial firms to develop and market the university's scientific discoveries.

At both Prudential and Tulane, I played an important role in downsizing the organizations. From this work, I learned that a more productive and efficient use of existing personnel can be achieved, and unnecessary buildup of staff avoided, by analyzing regularly—not just in times of financial crisis—the "value added" of each activity performed by employees. Moreover, however intense the pressure to cut expenses, any expenditure reduction process has to be driven by a strategic view of what the institution is to be when all the surgery is finished, just as any expansion should reflect a plan for growth. My experience with these downsizing exercises also led me to wonder why so many American organizations, business and nonprofit alike, have become overstaffed in the first place, and how to deal with the hardship to workers who are laid off without being at fault. These issues are dealt with in Chapters 6 ("Downsizing: Activity-Based Cost Reduction") and 13 ("Developing Your Human Resources").

At Prudential, I also observed the benefits of a management system that establishes at the outset of each year concrete objectives, as well as specific timetables and actions for accomplishing them, and then reviews them periodically during the year. This experience provided the foundation for Chapters 8 ("Performance Management") and 9 ("Depicting Performance and Financial Condition"), which examine means of monitoring the progress of projects against preestablished, measurable objectives and of evaluating the cost-effectiveness of programs. The task of defining measurable objectives may not be easy for many nonprofits, but it can be done.

Prudential and Tulane are, of course, very different large organizations with obviously different goals, but both are suffused with intricate relationships that have developed among various operating and staff units over a long period of time. My experience at both institutions came at a time when they faced the need to make significant changes that cut against the grain of their time-honored ways of doing business. At Prudential, I saw the value of fostering change, of linking compensation to the accomplishment of carefully defined quantifiable objectives. This practice was reinforced by unambiguous leadership with a clear goal. The financial incentives gave employees a material stake in transforming the organization, and the clarity of leadership left no doubt as to what had to be done. Paradoxically, not offering for-profit level compensation does not preclude a nonprofit organization from establishing a highly disciplined and effective management team. Decisive, transparent leadership, coupled with rigorous attention to professionalism and reasonable compensation, can produce quality management in a nonprofit organization where pride in the humanitarian value of one's work can be a prime motivator.

Resistance to Restructuring

Restructuring an exempt organization to achieve productive, efficient management is, however, extremely difficult to achieve where powerful forces within the organization do not perceive how they will benefit from change and where, so to speak, the wolf—although clearly visible to any objective observer—is not yet actually at the door. Such resistance can be found equally in business and nonprofit organizations. (James Champy, the co-author of *Reengineering the Corporation,*[8] was so frustrated by middle management's opposition to his program of changes that he was provoked to write a second book, *Reengineering Management.*[9]) It may be that only an overwhelming economic threat to the very survival of an entrenched organization can break down internal resistance to change.

At Tulane, I was exposed to the difficulties that many universities encounter in trying to bring about change. At a university, the group that generally holds the reins of power—the tenured faculty—has a strong, vested stake in the status quo and little real incentive to accept change that could alter the content and scope of the academic program in ways it does not favor.

The rigidity of departmental faculties, organized in an era when a different kind of academic output was in order, does not yield easily to new realities. The result is that many universities are engaged in far more programs than they can afford and at the same time are falling behind the knowledge curve in new fields. This experience provided the basis for Chapter 4 "Carving Out a Strategic Niche."

The burden of dealing with such internal resistance to change has fallen almost entirely on university presidents, while at the same time the demands on presidents to raise money have increased almost geometrically. Small wonder that turnover in this post has become so high in recent years. Thought has to be given to apportioning university leadership between internal governance and external affairs such as fundraising and relationships with influential outsiders. (This is the model MIT has followed for years.)

The Board's Role in Fostering Change

It is time for university boards, and indeed all nonprofit boards, to reexamine the process by which they govern, just as boards of for-profit public corporations have begun to do. Given that there are no shareholders to intervene, trustees of nonprofits are the sole body that can monitor management and serve as an external catalyst for change. Chapter 14, "The Foundations of Effective Governance," takes a fresh look at the role the board of a nonprofit should play, drawing on an article I co-authored in 1994 with Burton G. Malkiel, Chemical Bank Chairman, professor of economics at Princeton University, and director of several financial and nonfinancial corporations, entitled "The Twenty-First Century Boardroom: Who Will Be in Charge?"[10]

In thinking about the future of nonprofits, it is now evident that exempt organizations will be functioning in a sharply changed political environment as well as a radically different working environment. These changes provide a context within which to consider how best to restructure the management of nonprofits.

Promoting Change in a Changed America

The significant changes taking place in America today are likely to shape the future role of nonprofit organizations. The growing criticism of—indeed outright cynicism about—government, especially at the national level, is likely to lead to severe constraints on government social, educational, and cultural programs. Without buying into the seeming antigovernment fervor of a substantial segment of American voters, one can agree that it is time for a whole range of fresh ideas and approaches to the problems that exist in the United States.

In this environment, many people are looking to nonprofit organizations to assume an expanded role in promoting social, educational, and scientific progress, complementing businesses and a restructured government in sustaining the well-being of our society.

The question naturally arises as to whether nonprofit status confers a special potential to effect change. The chapter "The Role of Nonprofits in a Changing America" offers a positive view of the potential of organizations whose purpose is to achieve social, educational, and scientific objectives and whose animating force is regard for beneficiaries of its programs—in short, humanitarian or altruistic organizations. Such organizations not only are especially suited to be innovators in their fields of interest, they also provide a rich opportunity for citizens to express their own personal sense of idealism and community, whether on a professional or a volunteer basis. Such activity is as essential to the health of American society as a globally competitive business sector and an effective, humane government.

A Radically Different Work Environment

The book also touches on the radical changes taking place in the nature of work in America. One can no longer expect to spend one's career with a single organization or even within a single industry. White- and blue-collar workers alike must prepare themselves to work, in the course of their lifetime, with multiple employers, often in a variety of businesses each requiring new skills, or to form their own business. This way of working requires a versatility of skills and a degree of self-motivation that was not demanded of earlier generations. But if these changes in work life impose new burdens on workers, they also pose challenges for organizations wishing to attract and retain the best talent. Although this complex subject is explored in Chapter 13, "Managing Your Human Resources," we are only beginning to understand the changes that will be the foundations of twenty-first century work, and the topic very much needs further exploration.

General Concepts Applicable to All Nonprofits

While this book draws heavily on my own experience in a variety of nonprofit organizations, it would be incorrect if the observations in the text were perceived to be limited to the institutional examples I cite. Extensive discussions over the years with my peers in the nonprofit world and with clients, as well as the inquiries I undertook in the preparation of the book, make me confident that the processes and systems discussed in the text have application across a wide range of nonprofit institutions in different fields of endeavor, and to both large and small organizations.

Fundamentally, most nonprofits are struggling with the same generic problems of improving their efficiency and their quality of performance, and finding the money to pay their bills. Thus they may find that the remedies they seek have more in common than one might think.

I have spent a good part of my career working for nonprofit organizations—the Ford Foundation, Children's Television Workshop, and Princeton and

Tulane universities. I have also pursued an active business career and served as a director of two public companies. My years in the nonprofit sector provided the lift that comes from being engaged in activities in which one is deeply interested, so that "work" is transformed into "discovery" and "learning." However, the years in the nonprofit sector would have been much less productive without the exposure I gained in business to modern management practices and the pursuit of concrete, measurable objectives. In fact, moving back and forth between the two sectors has enabled me to see just how the management practices of well-run businesses can be effectively applied to exempt organizations.

I also saw that our best businesses, while motivated by profit, are often driven by a sense of purpose that is as intense as a nonprofit organization's sense of mission. I observed this phenomenon first-hand when, as a director of Jack Bogle's Vanguard Group of mutual funds, I watched him build the group in two decades from a fledgling enterprise with $1.4 billion in assets, 350,000 shareholders, and nine investment portfolios, to the world's second-largest fund complex with over $150 billion in assets, five million individual and institutional shareholders, and 88 portfolios (as of the summer of 1995).

Vanguard was first established in 1975, when the mutual fund and investment counseling business of Wellington Management was divided into two separate enterprises. At first, Vanguard's mission was only to provide administrative services to the mutual funds Wellington managed. Then, two years later, Bogle presented his vision of a mutual fund complex fully independent of Wellington or any fund manager, and free to choose the best firm to serve as investment manager for each fund—a revolutionary concept in an industry where investment management firms typically create and control mutual funds. He also proposed breaking away from using brokers to distribute the funds (a system that results in the imposition of a sales charge on the consumer when he or she invests money in a fund) and instead marketing directly to investors, without a front-end sales fee ("no-load" funds, in the parlance of the industry). Bogle's marketing strategy proved to be the right move at the right time as consumers became more educated about mutual funds.

Pivotal to Bogle's strategy was his concept of being the low-cost provider of mutual fund services. He pounded home this vision every day within the organization. Virtually every decision had to meet the challenge of whether it was consistent with the objective of being the low-cost provider. Jack, a passionate advocate of his view, reiterated his philosophy constantly in a stream of communications to the public, the press, the industry, and the Securities and Exchange Commission, which regulates mutual funds. His constant emphasis on being the low-cost provider is now linked inextricably with Vanguard, giving its name a distinct identity in a crowded marketplace.

I also saw, in working in the business and nonprofit sectors, that excellent management existed in each and that outstanding leaders of the two types of enterprises had a great deal in common. This book is thus largely a product of the sum of my experiences in both nonprofit and business organizations.

Acknowledgements

While the book draws heavily on my own experience, it has also benefitted from the insights and observations of a number of people who have been leaders of nonprofit organizations: Frederick Bohen, executive vice president of Rockefeller University; William G. Bowen, president of the Andrew W. Mellon Foundation and director of a number of American corporations; David V. B. Britt and Emily Swenson, president and executive vice president, respectively, of Children's Television Workshop; Marcia Bromberg, former CEO of Tulane University; Myles Cane, investor, attorney, foundation trustee, and chairman of the board of Skidmore College; Sara Engelhardt, president of the Foundation Center; Paul Grogan, president of LISC, Inc.; F. Sheldon Hackney, chairman of the National Endowment for the Humanities and former president of the University of Pennsylvania; Todd Haimes, executive director of Roundabout Theater; Carl Halvarson, president of Cupp International; Frances Hesselbein, former head of Girl Scouts of America and executive director of the Peter F. Drucker Foundation; Louis Katz, vice president and treasurer of George Washington University; Ann Kearn, vice president of Heidrick & Struggles; Eamon Kelly, president of Tulane University; Burton G. Malkiel, Chemical Bank Chairman, professor of economics at Princeton University, and a director of a series of public companies; Peter Malkin of Wein, Malkin and Bettex, a member of the board of overseers of Harvard University, and a member of the board of trustees of Lincoln Center; Patricia A. Mulvaney of Price Waterhouse; John Regazzi, president of Engineering Information, Inc.; John Rosenwald, vice chairman of Bear Stearns, Inc., chairman of the board of Dartmouth College, and a board member of a number of other charitable organizations; and Stephen D. Solender, executive vice president of UJA-Federation of New York. I am grateful for their insights. I also want to express my appreciation for the wise counsel, over a number of years, of Stonebridge Associates.

I am also grateful to Talvi Laev for working so diligently and intelligently to copyedit the manuscript; it is a better book for her work. I am particularly appreciative of the support and encouragement of Rick Schoff, vice president for publications at the Foundation Center. Without his enthusiasm for this project and his readiness to be of assistance at every turn, the book would not have gotten done.

Finally, to Joanne: you have given a lift to my life, challenging all passivity with a diverse and rich menu of activity and a bright spirit.

NOTES

1. *The Chronicle of Higher Education,* July 14, 1995, p. B3.
2. The Commonwealth Fund 1994 Annual Report, p. 6.
3. Ibid, p. 4.
4. Peter Drucker, "The Age of Social Transformation," *Atlantic Monthly,* November, 1994, p. 74.
5. See Paul Firstenberg, *Managing for Profit in the Nonprofit World* (New York: The Foundation Center, 1986), pp. 13-21, 162-169.
6. Michael L. Dertouzos, Richard K. Lester, and Robert M. Solow, *Made in America: Regaining the Productive Edge* (Cambridge, MA: MIT Press, 1989), preface.
7. Ibid., p. 118.
8. Michael Hammer and James Champy, *Reengineering the Corporation* (New York: HarperCollins, 1993).
9. James Champy, *Reengineering Management* (New York: HarperCollins, 1995).
10. Paul Firstenberg and Burton Malkiel, "The Twenty-First-Century Boardroom: Who Will Be in Charge?" *Sloan Management Review,* 36:1, Fall 1994, p. 27. See also, William G. Bowen, *Inside the Boardroom* (New York: Wiley, 1994).

PART I

Post-Government America

CHAPTER 1

The Role of Nonprofits in a Changing America

This is a book about the essential techniques for managing tax-exempt nonprofit organizations dedicated to humanitarian, educational, social, and scientific goals. Because these organizations are driven by their sense of mission, the role they play in American life is a defining factor in shaping their cultures. Therefore, before exploring the management of such enterprises, I want to establish the larger context in which tax-exempt nonprofits operate in America, the uniquely American heritage from which they spring, and the role these institutions are likely to play in a changing America.

A Changing America

As I look back at the American landscape of the last 50 years, since World War II ended on the deck of the battleship *Missouri*, anchored in Tokyo Bay, it is clear that our country has undergone a profound change. This change is evident in almost every aspect of our political, economic, and social environment, in the velocity and random violence of modern life, and in our continuing involvement in the world's conflicts even since the end of the cold war.

The first part of the postwar era—the 1950s—was an uncomplicated time in which to grow up; the ground rules were simple and unequivocal, and we grew up largely innocent about ourselves and unaware of the psychological and emotional forces that shape who we are and how we act and react.

Since then, for example, a revolution has occurred in mores and sex roles. The human arrangements we were conditioned to accept as immutable—premarital virginity, lifetime marriages, and clearly defined, traditional male and female roles—have given way to an ever-widening latitude for individual choice and the legal and social struggle to formulate new boundaries of behavior.

I came of age when many subscribed to a vision that the world would yield to the force of intellect and the dynamics of an energetic spirit. Public service, we were repeatedly told in college, was the highest calling; our icons were not the CEOs of large corporations or Wall Street financiers; they were men like Averell Harriman, Chip Bohlen, George Kennan, Dean Acheson, and John McCloy who devoted their careers, or the most brilliant parts thereof, to the country's affairs. We believed that the Marshall Plan, NATO, the Berlin airlift, the space program, civil rights legislation, Medicare, food stamps, and later the Clean Air and Water Acts demonstrated the capacity of the national government to act with singular effectiveness.

Most of the national agenda initially formulated in the 1950s and 1960s has in fact been realized. But no one anticipated then that the inevitable shortcomings of some government programs would one day be used as an argument to cut all of the government's activities to the bone. Of course, all the national hopes raised in this era were not fulfilled, at least in part because in the 1960s our reach exceeded our grasp. We had not yet come to terms with the diversity and complexity of the world. We saw the challenges and did not accept that there were any limits to our capacity to meet them. (As Kennedy said in his inaugural, we were ready to "pay any price, bear any burden, meet any hardship . . . "). We were supremely confident of our talents and thought our nation—and ourselves—invincible.

We did not acknowledge that the ideas and policies framed then to tame the economy, promote social justice at home, and contain communism abroad were only imperfect instruments and one day would no longer work. The liberal policy momentum that flowed though the veins of government from FDR through Lyndon Johnson diminished as the country moved into the 1970s and 1980s, overtaken by events it had not anticipated, and unable to create new ideas to fit new realities.

In addition, over the last two decades, a series of underlying structural changes has set in: for example, the speed of many human transactions has vastly accelerated. And these changes in *speed* were accompanied by changes in *magnitude*. As George Shultz, former secretary of state and the treasury, has observed: "Scientific, economic and political matters are global in dimension and enormous in extent. They are outstripping the traditional means by which governments dealt with them."[1]

In the twentieth century, the sources of America's power have been its wealth of natural resources and its ability to produce a greater quantity of goods than any other nation. For half a century or more, the scale of production was the critical variable in determining market success (e.g., that of General Motors). In the new global economy, quality of production rather than quantity defines economic leadership—a theme I will return to in Chapter 5, "Systems Redesign," and that can be found in the work of Edward Deming.

With the emphasis on *speed* and *quality* to offset global competition, *knowledge* has become a crucial asset—not only its discovery and its rapid transformation into information, but also the education required to deploy it to one's advantage. Microsoft is the model of the new corporation embodying these values. It has become a leading force among all the giant corporations in the technology business because of its mastery of the design, application, and selling of software.

Many of our institutions—public and private, domestic and international— have been severely strained in accommodating the economic and social changes that have taken place since World War II. To cite just one example of this change: "Financial markets are no longer places," to quote again from George Shultz, "but electronic networks."[2] The concept of fixed exchange rates as one foundation of international economic stability, as envisioned in the Bretton Woods Treaty of 1944, has been overtaken by the enormous volume of currencies that the private market can move anywhere in the world at the flick of a switch. Money now moves electronically at such speed and in such volumes—reaching a trillion dollars a day—that even the combined power of the world's strongest central banks cannot control the flow by intervening in the currency markets. Fixed exchange rates have become anachronisms, and rates are now determined daily by the global markets' perception of the relative values of national currencies. The market has thus displaced government as the arbiter of exchange values, with a profound impact on international as well as domestic economic policies. As a result, our government and other governments are often caught between the conflicting demands of two distinct markets—the global money market and domestic political constituencies.

The visible straining of our political, economic, and judicial institutions to cope with a new world has undoubtedly been a prime factor in changing our perception of government's efficacy and the role it ought to play in our lives. This, in turn, has led to one of the greatest changes we have experienced in the latter half of this century. For decades, starting with FDR's New Deal, we perceived government, especially at the federal level, as the source of the remedial actions and policies required to keep our society economically and socially healthy and to execute our post-World War II assumption of world leadership in foreign affairs. In the mid-1990s, we appear to be in the midst of a counter-revolution designed to minimize radically the federal role.

The Antigovernment Fervor

For decades, the American public supported the concept of a national government that built a national social safety net (in the form of Social Security, unemployment insurance, and welfare); regulated the securities markets and the banking and airline industries; enforced antitrust laws; funded health care for the elderly; provided Head Start programs for the young, financial assistance for college students, and research monies for universities; created programs aimed at reducing the structural poverty that could not be eliminated by a growing economy; enforced health and safety standards at places of work; promoted opportunities for minorities; and established the cultural forces of the Endowments for the Arts and Humanities and public broadcasting. But that perception of the beneficent role of government disappeared by the 1980s. Frustration with leadership by Washington has mounted steadily since Lyndon Johnson's massive intervention in Vietnam. Optimism resurfaced briefly during the initial years of Ronald Reagan's presidency, but the steady decline resumed in his second term and continues to this day.[3]

Today, the activist and progressive government created by FDR in the 1930s, and which for so long shaped the character of American government, seems to be intellectually adrift and suffering from policy arteriosclerosis. The solution our present political process offers is to shrink the size of government, not only at the federal level but also at the state and local levels. We will see if such a remedy breathes fresh vitality into the Republic.

Distrust of government stems largely from two sources: pervasive fear of crime (and a consequent sense of personal insecurity), as well as a sense of economic insecurity. Personal and economic security are among the most basic guarantees that people today expect from government, and a government that does not deliver in these areas inevitably loses the public's trust. Although today's pervasive sense of economic insecurity is sometimes lost in the enthusiasm over macroeconomic figures, the underlying economic realities that shape people's physical lives are not comforting. At the end of 1993, real median income was only slightly higher than it had been a decade earlier, and in fact it has been declining in the 1990s, after peaking in the late 1980s.[4] At the same time, white-collar professionals who once believed that as long as they performed satisfactorily they would keep their jobs have been forced into the unemployment line by wave after wave of corporate downsizing. More disquieting to workers, the downsizing has continued even as corporations have returned to profitability, with the number of layoffs in 1994 equalling that at the height of the 1991 recession. Meanwhile, blue-collar workers find their opportunities shrinking as plants move overseas and work becomes more automated. As a result, blue-collar industrial workers, who constituted 40 percent of the work force in 1950, represented less than 20 percent of workers at the end of 1990. This percentage will diminish further by the year 2000.

In part, as Kevin Phillips argues, the perception that the national government lacks the capacity to respond to national needs may be fostered by the armies of well-financed lobbies that neutralize any effort to institute change that might adversely affect the interests they represent.[5] Many observers, in fact, believe that genuine reform will not be attainable until campaign financing reform is achieved and the power of special interests thus diminished.

It may also be that our traditional modes of policy innovation simply can no longer deal—at least at the federal level—with the complexities of modern society and the speed and scope of the changes that have taken place. It may also be, as James McGregor Burns has suggested, that the deeper problem is not simply that liberals, whose ideas dominated the political landscape for so long are emotionally wed to the programs they had put through; rather it is, in Burns's view, that they are "still living off the intellectual capital of the first 50 years of the century."[6]

Where does this leave the future of government? No institution, including government, is immune from the need to renew itself in a new era. Government plainly needs an infusion of new ideas and approaches. But if government's means of dealing with our society lag behind the changes that have taken place in America, that fact by itself does not necessarily dictate a radical downsizing of government functions. Scaling back or even dismantling government programs does not mean that those who do not earn enough to live above the poverty line without governmental assistance—those for whom there are no jobs, those who lack the training and education to get work, the children of unwed teenagers, the sick who cannot afford the burgeoning cost of decent healthcare, and those who cannot afford legal help—will disappear when the programs that served them are dismantled. Similarly, if we cut back the monies spent to improve the quality of education and to fund basic research, we cannot assume that our knowledge base will continue to grow at the same rate as before. The issue is thus not just whether we can reduce the size of government and balance the budget, but whether we can devise more effective means of dealing with the nation's social, racial, health care, environmental, and economic difficulties.

Various social programs may represent good policy undermined by overexpansion, poor management, or failure to adapt to changing circumstances; or they may represent once-good policy that has become outmoded, overtaken by changed conditions. In either event, simply demolishing a program does not deal with the ills it attempted to address; the holes in the American social fabric still need to be repaired.

Frances Hesselbein, formerly head of Girl Scouts of America and now president of the Peter F. Drucker Foundation, sums up the situation as follows:

"Beating up on the government is the least productive thing we can do," she said to me in an interview for this book. She then added pointedly: "We still have to build a cohesive society. As government relinquishes leadership, new leadership must bring people together and create alliances."[7] Hesselbein's attitude seems to be the better part of wisdom.

Where Will the New Ideas Come From?

Finding sources of effective new ideas is one of the primary challenges of this era. One of the driving forces behind the fervor to scale back the size of government is a profound skepticism that the new ideas for governing America can best be developed in the public sector. The question is, then, where do we turn for such new ideas and a political framework for their implementation?

Today's government at all levels is constrained in its ability to innovate by the following factors:

- ◆ The power of lobbyists for interests with a stake in any change in the existing scheme, coupled with the increased dependence of candidates for elective office on wealthy contributors and political action committees established by wealthy interests (largely to get around the limitation on individual contributions to candidates);

- ◆ The overlapping jurisdictions and consequent turf wars within government, whose basic organizational structure is inherited from an earlier time (since change in government is dealt with not by eliminating no longer useful agencies but by overlaying new bureaucracies on top of existing ones);

- ◆ Civil service requirements that tend to protect mediocre government servants from discipline, reinforced by the unionization of government workers and low pay scales (all of which discourages the hiring of lively, risk-taking public servants); and

- ◆ Conflicts between administrations and partisan, politically divided legislatures, along with erosion in party discipline, and the multiple political constituencies that have to be satisfied.

All these factors mitigate against effective innovation by government.

The limitations on government's and the major political parties' capacity to engineer the policy changes required by a new America make it tempting to look to the tax-exempt charitable sector—universities, research institutes, foundations, and other exempt organizations—as an increasingly important source of new ideas. The continual growth of the charitable sector, its diverse achievements, its role as an outlet for individuals' sense of altruism and civic responsibility, and the very form of such exempt organizations are all factors encouraging the belief that the sector can play an increasingly important role as an agent of change.

The Growth of Tax-Exempt Nonprofit Organizations

Organizations formed for charitable purposes have been a growth sector over the past three decades, although their growth rate has fluctuated during this period. As of 1993, the Internal Revenue Service recognized 575,690 organizations exempt under Section 501(c)(3) of the Internal Revenue Code from paying income tax. These organizations, commonly referred as "charitable organizations," can be distinguished in terms of tax law from other organizations exempt from income tax (which include many other types of entities) because 501(c)(3) organizations alone are entitled to receive tax-deductible contributions.[8] These figures do not include the estimated 350,000 religious organizations not required to file with the IRS the documents 501(c)(3) organizations must supply.

Charitable organizations are divided by the code into two categories: grant-making foundations and public charities.[9] In the quarter-century between 1965 and 1990, the number of foundations increased at an average annual rate of 2.5 percent, while the number of public charities increased at a rate of 6.5 percent. By way of comparison, the number of business incorporations increased during this period at an average rate of 5 percent per year. If one looks only at the formation of "large" grantmaking foundations—those with assets of at least $1 million or that made annual appropriations of at least $100,000 over the three decades from 1960 to 1989 and remained active in 1990—there were 5,008 new entrants during this period.[10] During these three decades, with the increase in the base of existing charities, the *rate of growth,* not surprisingly, slowed. Still, the total population of public charities had doubled by 1975 and tripled again by 1991. It has been forecast that, even with the slower growth rates of the late 1980s, the number of public charities can be expected to double again by the year 2005.[11]

The Accomplishments of the Nonprofit Sector

The sector has a remarkable set of diverse achievements to its credit:

◆ Development of the polio vaccine funded by the March of Dimes;
◆ Transference to developing countries of high-yielding seeds by the Rockefeller Foundation;
◆ The civil rights movement in the South, which was given significant support by many foundations;

◆ The growth of regional theaters and off-Broadway nonprofit theater (at least 40 percent of theatrical productions in the United States are mounted by nonprofit companies, accounting for 51 percent of employment in the field);[12]

◆ The nation's ballet companies, symphonies, and museums. Some 95 percent of the country's orchestras, chamber music companies, and operas are non-profits, and they provide 97 percent of employment in the field. More than 70 percent of the country's museums and art galleries are nonprofit entities, and they account for 95 percent of employment in the field;[13]

◆ The Public Broadcasting System and National Public Radio, which have provided programming alternative to that offered by commercial broad-casters;

◆ The scientific and medical discoveries at the nation's universities, from the fundamentals of smashing the atom and modern-day genetic engineering to the pioneering work of economists in modern finance, which has produced many of the new investment strategies and products employed by private investment firms and investment banks;

◆ The emergency relief provided to devastated communities by the American Red Cross, its management of half of the nation's blood supply, and its pio-neering work in developing a blood donor program;

◆ The relief brought to starving people around the world by organizations like Save the Children and Oxfam;

◆ Alcoholics Anonymous's remarkable program for assisting alcoholics;

◆ The international student exchanges mounted by numerous organizations;

◆ The environmental initiatives and programs undertaken by organizations like the Sierra Club, the Wildlife Society, and the Nature Conservancy;

◆ The regeneration of the South Bronx neighborhood in New York City by a community development organization after government had neglected the area; and

◆ The social welfare assistance provided by more than 60,000 nonprofit so-cial service agencies to a wide range of citizens, including the elderly, people with AIDS, troubled youths, and unemployed workers needing job training.

This list, which could be expanded endlessly, shows that America's nonprofit sector has played a vital, irreplaceable role in advancing the quality of life in this country and providing assistance to developing nations around the world. It also covers the full political spectrum, mirroring the diverse interests and attitudes of the nation, from the American Civil Liberties Union to the National Right to Life Committee.

An Outlet for Individuals' Sense of Altruism and Civic Responsibility

In addition to its specific accomplishments, the nonprofit sector provides a unique opportunity for citizens to engage in activities designed to aid or enrich the lives of their fellow citizens. The "third" sector thus provides an outlet for two of the basic impulses that help civilize a society: altruism and an individual sense of civic responsibility.

Nonprofit organizations give people the chance to take an *active* role in shaping their communities, rather than being *passive* participants in a society dominated by massive, impersonal institutions. As Peter Drucker has written:

> America's third-sector institutions are rapidly becoming creators of new bonds of community. . . . Increasingly, they create a sphere of . . . meaningful citizenship. . . . Now that the size and complexity of government make direct participation all but impossible, it is the human change institution of the third sector that is offering to volunteers a sphere of personal achievement in which the individual exercises influence, discharges responsibility, and makes decisions. . . . This may be the most important contribution of the third sector so far.[14]

The association of citizens to bring about change is part of a centuries-old American tradition of civic responsibility that has no real parallel in any other society. As Alexis de Tocqueville observed in 1840: "Americans of all ages, all conditions constantly form associations." Seeing this phenomenon as the underpinning of American democracy, he noted that these associations came in all sizes and shapes, "religious, moral, serious, futile, general or restricted, enormous or diminutive. . . . Wherever at the head of some new undertaking you see the government in France or a man of rank in England, in the United States you will be sure to find an association."[15]

Some observers now argue that the level of participation in associations is declining across the board, from PTAs to the Boy Scouts and the Red Cross, and attribute this development to the restlessness of new mobile elites.[16] One can appreciate the reasons why volunteerism might be declining in this age of working women,[17] dramatically increased numbers of single-parent households (as half of first marriages fracture), and the movement of people from the places where they grew up to new areas in search of better employment opportunities and a better quality of life.[18]

Still, despite these factors, an astonishingly large number of Americans continue to engage in volunteer work; in 1993, some 89.2 million adult Americans, nearly half of the population over 21, undertook some sort of volunteer activity, for 4.2 hours a week on average, according to Independent Sector, a Washington-based organization that promotes volunteer work.[19]

Organizational Structure and Purpose Lend Themselves to Innovation

The organizational structure and purposes of charitable institutions enhance their capacity to act as agents of human change. The critical foundations of such institutions are

- ◆ Freedom from the profit motive or the obligation to maximize the return to owners; and
- ◆ The sense of an idealistic mission that is the driving force of such entities.

These two factors enable charitable organizations to pursue endeavors that could not be financially justified by a for-profit enterprise and, equally important, to attract people who are disposed to challenging the status quo. Indeed, it is the idea of personal participation in bettering even some tiny corner of life that motivates many of the people who work, either professionally or as volunteers, for such organizations.

A nonprofit organization also enjoys relative freedom in its choice of mission. All kinds of people can pursue any idea or program they are motivated to undertake. Even a handful can promote a new idea; they need not seek a larger consensus, provided their concept finds enough appeal in the nonprofit marketplace to generate the support needed to pay the bills. Unlike government, an exempt organization need not establish that its goal or program is supported by some large constituency or powerful interest group.

At the same time, a nonprofit organization's dedication to a defined mission enables it to bring a sharper focus to its activities than is possible for today's large-scale government agencies, which embrace multiple programs that may or may not be related to one other.

At the same time, pragmatic considerations may influence the decision to form a nonprofit rather than a for-profit organization. Some exempt institutions produce a service that generates revenue but have chosen the nonprofit form, not only because their founders have a passion for their mission, but also because access to capital is more readily available to nonprofits than to for-profit businesses. Children's Television Workshop is an institution that conceivably could have been organized as a for-profit enterprise. Although the founders believed that nonprofit status was consistent with their aims, it is also true that in the late 1960s it was much easier to raise enough capital to develop an educational television show such as *Sesame Street* through a combination of foundation and government grants than if the founders had approached a commercial network.[20]

Perhaps the most powerful statement of the potential of nonprofits as change agents has been made by John Gardner in his introduction to the volume *America's Voluntary Spirit: A Book of Readings*. Gardner served as secretary of

Health, Education, and Welfare under President Johnson and later founded Common Cause, the watchdog group monitoring political spending and other areas of potential political abuse, and Independent Sector, which is designed to encourage the growth of nonprofit volunteer organizations. The following excerpts are from the introduction to his book.

> Every institution in the independent sector is not innovative, but the sector provides a hospitable environment for innovation. Ideas for doing things in a different, and possibly better, way, spring up constantly. If they do not fill a need, they quickly fall by the wayside. What remains are the few ideas and innovations that have long-term value.[21]

> Government bureaucracies are simply not constructed to permit the emergence of countless new ideas, and [they are] even less suited to the winnowing out of bad ideas. An idea that is controversial, unpopular, or "strange" has little chance in either the commercial or the political marketplace. In the nonprofit sector, someone with a new idea or program may well find the few followers necessary to help nurse it to maturity. Virtually every significant social idea of the past century in this country has been nurtured in the nonprofit sector.[22]

> The sector is the natural home of nonmajoritarian impulses, movements, and values. It comfortably harbors innovators, maverick movements, groups which feel that they must fight for their place in the sun, and critics of both liberal and conservative persuasions.[23]

Gardner, by the way, is not alone in believing that "virtually every significant social idea of the past century has been nurtured in the nonprofit sector." In the same volume, philanthropist John D. Rockefeller III and scholar and author Waldemar A. Nielsen make the same assertion. Nielsen, pointing to the last 40 years, cites such "transforming forces for change" as the civil rights movement, the women's movement, consumerism, and the antiwar movement during the Vietnam period as originating in the third sector.

Gardner's reference to the nonprofit sector as "the natural home of nonmajoritarian impulses" points to an essential thread that runs through the structure of American democracy. For the most part, the country is governed by the principle of majority rule. But the architects of our nation recognized the tyranny a majority can exercise over a minority and, for this reason, created a number of institutional counterweights to majoritarian governance. (One example is the review of the constitutionality of legislation by the federal courts, in which the federal judiciary can overturn even the most popular legislative measure, sometimes with wisdom, sometimes without.) Thus, the nonprofit sector, consistent with the American guardianship of nonmajoritarian interests, provides the opportunity for a counterforce to a prevailing wind.

One Vulnerability: Dependence on Government Funding in a Flat Private Giving Environment

For all these reasons, public policy should favor the nurturing and expansion of the nonprofit sector. However, the scaling back of government spending, which is occurring at all levels of government, poses a major resource problem for many exempt organizations. Government funding is critical to many exempt organization, from the research grants and student loans so important to universities and their students, to health and human services organizations, many of which receive 30 percent of their budget from government support.[24] In the current climate, as government expenditures are reduced, many exempt organizations will be forced to scale back their activities, even as the political rhetoric that accompanies the reduction in government spending suggests that charities step into the resulting gap to help nation's poor and maintain educational and cultural institutions.

Where will exempt organizations find the additional resources to offset the government cutbacks, not to mention expand their programs? Private contributions to tax-exempt organizations in 1994 totaled $129.88 billion, but they lagged behind inflation in the services sector in the previous four years; and the net gain in 1994 was all of about 0.5 percent! (See Table 1.1.) In short, nonprofits are entering an era in which more exempt organizations will likely be chasing the same, relatively static pool of private contributors. Inevitably, some nonprofits will not fare well, particularly social welfare, housing, and cultural programs; and consolidation or contraction of a number of such entities is very likely.

The experience of the 1980s would seem to bear this out. Research by Lester Salamon—cited in Bowen[25]—points to the development of an extensive public-private partnership in such fields as social welfare, with private entities largely dependent on government funding often developing at precisely the times of greatest governmental activity. Bowen, taking note of this research, observes that, "paradoxical as it may seem to some, it is likely that part of the reduction in the rate at which private nonprofits were formed in the 1980s was due to efforts in Washington to reduce the federal role in funding social services."[26]

At the very least, as a consequence of government funding cutbacks, a good many institutions will have to operate with less money or change their way of doing business in order to tap new sources of funding. The resulting cultural change within an organization may be quite dramatic. As the head of a large charity said to me in a conversation, "We have been able to leverage many times our funding of social agencies with government money. Now we are going to have to raise larger amounts of private money, and this means every part of our organization has to become customer-oriented. This will call for a radically different outlook on the part of many of our people."

Of course, government assistance has always come with a price tag in the form of the government rule book and its seeming mountain of often obtuse regulations. For example, there are 7,000 regulations for federal student aid programs; the Institute for Higher Education Policy found that in one typical year the Department of Education issued 171 letters to all institutions of higher education to clarify its regulations. The least that can be said about government money is that in its own way it is quite expensive.

A Second Vulnerability: Limited High-Quality Management

The nonprofit sector as a whole is in urgent need of developing strategies to improve its management and to increase its accountability for the actual results it achieves. As John Gardner observed in a 1979 speech:

> I have read statements on the independent or nonprofit institutions of this country which leave the impression that they are virtually faultless. We know better. Some nonprofit institutions are far gone in decay. Some are so badly managed as to make a mockery of every good intention they might have had. There is fraud, mediocrity, and silliness. In short, the independent sector has no sovereign remedy against human and institutional failure.[27]

Unless a realistic look is taken at the managerial competence of nonprofit organizations, the institutions and individuals funding exempt organizations, as well as the larger public, are going to have reservations about supporting such institutions. This, in turn, will decrease the ability of such organizations to expand their base of private support, even as government funding diminishes. The development of high-quality management, which can establish visible and measurable objectives and then meet them, is thus an urgent priority for the sector. In the coming Darwinian era of scarce public funding and fierce competition for private support, the organizations that fare well will have demonstrable records of effective programs delivered cost-efficiently.

Embracing Accountability

Recently, disturbing cracks have appeared in the wall of integrity that must surround the tax-exempt nonprofit sector. After all, such organizations depend on the willingness of public officials at the federal, state, and local levels not only to exempt them from taxation but also to grant charitable deductions to individuals and corporations contributing to such organizations. Exempt organizations

Table 1.1.　Giving by Source 1964–1994 (in billions of inflation-adjusted dollars)

	Total	% Change	Corpor- ations	% Change	Founda- tions	% Change	Bequests	% Change	Indivi- duals	% Change
1964	$72.46	1.90%	$3.35	7.31%	$4.42	-0.48%	$5.07	6.38%	$59.62	1.43%
1965	76.68	5.82%	3.67	9.62%	5.91	33.54%	5.33	5.20%	61.77	3.61%
1966	80.01	4.34%	3.95	7.52%	6.34	7.33%	6.64	24.61%	63.08	2.12%
1967	83.52	4.39%	3.99	0.99%	6.87	8.37%	6.87	3.41%	65.8	4.31%
1968	88.31	5.73%	3.89	-2.61%	7.53	9.56%	7.53	9.56%	69.38	5.44%
1969	92.91	5.21%	3.8	-2.23%	8.13	8.03%	9.03	20.03%	71.95	3.71%
1970	89.97	-3.16%	3.51	-7.47%	8.12	-0.07%	9.11	0.82%	69.23	-3.78%
1971	94.54	5.07%	3.37	-4.01%	7.87	-3.14%	12.11	32.93%	71.19	2.83%
1972	94.36	-0.18%	3.67	8.92%	7.73	-1.79%	8.11	-32.97%	74.85	5.14%
1973	94.38	0.02%	3.69	0.49%	7.39	-4.34%	7.39	-8.89%	75.9	1.41%
1974	92.14	-2.37%	3.57	-3.33%	7.25	-1.94%	7.11	-3.80%	74.21	-2.23%
1975	90.37	-1.92%	3.43	-4.03%	5.23	-27.80%	7.07	-0.54%	74.64	0.58%
1976	93.75	3.73%	3.64	6.26%	5.61	7.18%	6.79	-4.00%	77.71	4.11%
1977	95.7	2.08%	3.85	5.66%	5.46	-2.74%	5.78	-14.83%	80.61	3.74%
1978	97.14	1.51%	4.01	4.22%	5.48	0.46%	6.57	13.56%	81.08	0.58%
1979	100.51	3.47%	4.45	10.89%	5.24	-4.39%	5.22	-20.56%	85.61	5.58%
1980	102.83	2.31%	4.6	3.49%	5.95	13.56%	6.06	16.10%	86.22	0.72%
1981	106.4	3.47%	5.13	11.57%	5.91	-0.76%	6.89	13.70%	88.48	2.61%
1982	105.26	-1.08%	5.67	10.45%	5.62	-4.85%	9.27	34.53%	84.7	-4.27%
1983	105.28	0.02%	6.12	7.93%	6	6.69%	6.46	-30.26%	86.7	2.36%
1984	108.83	3.37%	6.84	11.85%	6.25	4.25%	6.39	-1.07%	89.34	3.04%
1985	109.88	0.97%	7.24	5.78%	7.36	17.77%	7.17	12.09%	88.12	-1.37%
1986	119.55	8.80%	7.3	0.79%	7.74	5.14%	8.12	13.38%	96.39	9.39%
1987	123.13	2.99%	7.49	2.64%	8.02	3.63%	8.98	10.47%	98.64	2.34%
1988	127.72	3.73%	7.3	-2.51%	7.98	-0.48%	8.53	-5.00%	103.92	5.34%
1989	132	3.35%	7.11	-2.62%	8.08	1.21%	8.6	0.81%	108.22	4.14%
1990	130.77	-0.93%	6.86	-3.52%	8.45	4.61%	8.93	3.87%	106.53	-1.56%
1991	130.94	0.13%	6.68	-2.59%	8.6	1.72%	8.66	-2.98%	107	0.44%
1992	128.9	-1.56%	6.33	-5.30%	9.23	7.36%	8.71	0.49%	104.64	-2.21%
1993	129.16	0.20%	6.24	1.41%	9.82	6.45%	8.8	1.14%	104.29	-0.33%
1994	129.88	0.56%	6.11	-2.04%	9.91	0.87%	8.77	-0.39%	105.09	0.77%

Source: *Giving USA 1995.* Copyright © 1995 by the AAFRC Trust for Philanthropy.

also depend heavily on both public and private support that rests on a foundation of trust and goodwill. But in April of 1995 *The Wall Street Journal* disclosed that colleges and universities had been distorting the data they submitted to various publications that rank such institutions.[28] That same month, the longtime president of the national United Way was convicted of stealing $600,000 of the organization's funds to support a flamboyant lifestyle wholly inconsistent with his position, even as his board sat in ignorance of this diversion of funds.

Another scandal hit the front pages in 1995—the New Era Foundation scam, in which contributors to the Foundation were promised double their money back from anonymous donors who in fact did not exist. The scam continued until its architect ran out of new contributors whose funds could be used to pay off old contributors. Very prestigious institutions are involved as contributors seeking to double their money, and once more questions will be raised about this grossly inadequate oversight of a nonprofit's activities—not to mention the oversight of the organizations that put their money in the hands of the New Era Foundation.

It is not scandal per se, however, which is of concern; there can be abuse in any form of institution. The issue is whether these breakdowns point to a general lack of adequate management control in a significant number of nonprofit organizations. The goal of this book is to encourage all nonprofit institutions to address with candor the quality of their management and to make improvements. *The object is to stimulate nonprofit managers into sculpting, from established best practices, their own set of management practices and analytical systems in order to enhance the effectiveness and efficiency with which their organization performs its mission.* Pursuit of a worthy cause is not the only obligation of a charitable organization; it is equally important to manage performance and willingly to accept accountability for the results achieved. The adoption of management practices that bolster the effective and efficient delivery of programs should not be seen as a diversion but as a means of enhancing the organization's performance of its mission. Prompt and accurate reporting of charitable organizations' performance and financial condition is indispensable to the public's perception of the integrity of the sector.

NOTES

1. George Shultz, "National Success and International Stability," in Anderson and Bark, eds., *Thinking about America: The United States in the 1990s* (Hoover Institution, Stanford University, 1988).

2. Ibid.

3. Kevin Phillips, *Arrogant Capital* (Boston: Little Brown, 1994), pp. 6–8.

4. The Bureau of Labor Statistics Employment Cost Index shows the wages and benefits of 90 million private-sector employees averaging $17.10 an hour in March 1995, 2.8 percent lower after inflation than in 1990 and 5.5 percent lower than when the index began in 1987. In general, most studies show that gains by employees following the end of the 1991 recession lagged very much behind those following earlier recessions.

5. Phillips, *Arrogant Capital,* p. 196.

6. James McGregor Burns, *The Crosswinds of Freedom* (New York: Knopf, 1989), p. 630.

7. Frances Hesselbein, interview with the author, April 1995.

8. *Giving USA* (AAFRC Trust for Philanthropy, 1994), p. 29.

9. For an explanation of the characteristics of foundations and public charities, see Paul Firstenberg, *Managing for Profit in the Nonprofit World* (New York: The Foundation Center, 1986), pp. 13–21, 167–169.

10. The growth in foundations during this period was quite uneven, with a sharp fall-off after passage of the Tax Reform Act of 1969 and then a regeneration of growth in the 1980s. See William G. Bowen,Thomas I. Nygren, Sarah E. Turner, and Elizabeth A. Duffy, *The Charitable Nonprofits* (San Francisco, Jossey-Bass, 1994), pp. 41–45.

11. William G. Bowen,Thomas I. Nygren, Sarah E. Turner, and Elizabeth A. Duffy, *The Charitable Nonprofits* (San Francisco: Jossey-Bass, 1994), pp. 4–5.

12. Lester M. Salamon, *America's Nonprofit Sector: A Primer* (New York: Foundation Center, 1992), p. 93.

13. Ibid. p. 93.

14. Peter Drucker, *The New Realities* (New York: Harper & Row, 1989), pp. 204–205.

15. Alexis de Tocqueville, *Democracy in America* (New York: Knopf, 1945), pp. 114–118.

16. See Putnam, "Bowling Alone: America's Declining Social Capital," *Journal of Democracy,* January 1995.

17. In 1960, 19 percent of married women with children under age six had jobs outside the home; by 1993, 60 percent did.

18. The fastest-growing areas in America in the 1980s were all cities that began the decade with fewer than 200,000 inhabitants.

19. Independent Sector, *Giving and Volunteering in the United States,* Washington, D.C.: Independent Sector, 1994.

20. Programming for children is more or less an orphan in the scheme of network television; by definition, it appeals to a very small audience compared to the 18- to 49-year-olds whom television advertisers prize so highly in their search to reach the largest number of potential consumers. As a result, the commercial networks allocate only Saturday-morning cartoons to serving the country's young children. Thus, at the development stage, it did not seem possible that the series would appeal to commercial broacasters, and indeed the networks have declined to broadcast it.

21. John Gardner, in *America's Voluntary Spirit: A Book of Readings* (New York: Foundation Center, 1983), p. xiv.

22. Ibid. p. xiv.

23. Ibid. p. xiv.

24. The following figures relating to Princeton University give an idea of the importance of federal support to universities: (1) approximately 7 percent of Princeton's $24 million scholarship budget is funded by federal grants; about another $2.5 million on students and 131 of 1,741 graduate students are financed with federal fellowships. Federal financing enables students to borrow at low interest rates; for example, students do not pay interest while attending school. If this benefit were eliminated, the amount students would have to repay would increase by 20 to 50 percent. (2) Federal agencies provide $62.3 million for the support of 75 percent of all sponsored research at the university, excluding a fusion research laboratory that is entirely funded by the Department of Energy at close to $100 million a year. Universities benefit in two ways from federally sponsored research; first, in being able to undertake research that would otherwise not be possible, and, second, the payment of a percentage of the research grant as reimbursement of the university's "indirect costs" related to the project. This indirect cost reimbursement formula allows universities to recover part of the costs of their facilities, such as libraries, and administrative expenses that federal auditors agree are utilized by the project. At least a portion of such costs would be incurred in any event, so the indirect cost reimbursement is a financial benefit to the university. See Harold Shapiro, "Federal Funds Support Student Aid, Research," *Alumni Weekly,* July 5, 1995, p. 57.

25. Bowen, et al., *The Charitable Nonprofits,* p. 47.

27. Ibid., p. 47.

28. John Gardner, in *America's Voluntary Spirit,* p. 372.

29. *The Wall Street Journal,* April 5, 1995, p. A1.

PART 2

Remaking the Organization

CHAPTER 2

The Productivity Imperative

Theorem: An enterprise that cannot reduce its unit labor costs through capital investment in new technology can still be made more productive by restructuring the way it organizes its work.

The single greatest challenge facing managers today is to raise the productivity of "knowledge" and "service" workers—that is the view of Peter Drucker, the dean of the country's management gurus.[1] Knowledge and service workers include research scientists, cardiac surgeons, lawyers, computer programmers, and architects, as well as hotel clerks, restaurant dishwashers, and the teenagers who work in fast-food restaurants.

Productivity in manufacturing, farming, mining, construction, and transportation has increased steadily as capital investment in plant and equipment has yielded a reduction in unit labor costs. The reduction in such costs enables the producer to absorb at least part of the cost of wage increases and is the key to noninflationary growth. The continuous increase in productivity in the world's advanced economies over the last century accounts for the rise in the standard of living and the quality of life in these countries. It has provided vast increases in disposable incomes and purchasing power. It has enabled people to enjoy an extraordinary increase in leisure time and has paid for increased education and a vast expansion of health care.

Today, contrary to popular opinion, productivity in the production and transportation of tangible goods and products continues to increase in America at a healthy rate. Increases in farming productivity in the United States are at record levels; manufacturing rose nearly 4 percent during the 1980s in absolute terms, an increase larger than the corresponding increases in Japan and Germany.[2]

But a larger and larger proportion of our economic activity is performed by workers who produce an intellectual product or render a service, and productivity in such fields has been flat. People engaged in the production of tangible goods and products and their transportation now account for no more than a fifth of the work force of our advanced economy. Thirty years ago such workers were in the majority. Today, the bulk of employment is in the knowledge and service fields.[3] Raising the productivity of knowledge workers is therefore pivotal to the future health of the American economy. Equally critical is raising the productivity of service workers; indeed, since large numbers of people lack the ability to qualify as other than service workers, increasing their productivity is essential to enabling them to enjoy a rising standard of living.

Most of the activity of nonprofits falls into the knowledge and service fields. Thus, exempt organizations face the inherent dilemma of such industries—how to achieve increases in productivity. Without such increases, costs will rise in direct proportion to increases in wages, driving up the price of their services (e.g., tuition) and, in turn, exerting pressure to limit future wage increases. The challenge in raising the productivity of such workers is rooted in the fact that capital cannot be substituted for their labor.

The nature of the productivity challenge facing knowledge and service organizations was illuminated by Bill Bowen and Will Baumol in their pioneering study *Performing Arts: The Economic Dilemma,* published in the mid-1960s.[4] They advanced the concept that the more rapid rise in the costs of the arts than in the economy generally stems from the relatively static productivity that is characteristic of the industry. Two years later, Bowen published an analysis of the economics of private higher education, *The Economics of Major Private Universities,* which found that the same was true of higher education.[5] Bowen and Baumol's thesis is that productivity, measured in the industrial sector by output per worker hour, is primarily a function of the investment of capital in new technology and the economies of large-scale production. This technology-driven increase in productivity simply is not available to anywhere near the same extent in education, the arts, or other professional service enterprises in which labor costs are the major expense item and the labor is so unique in character that it cannot be performed by machines. Such organizations can be said to have a "unique" labor component.

In essence, education, the performing arts, and other enterprises in which a "unique form of labor" is a major cost element, are wage driven. The ballerina, the pianist, or the teacher reviewing a student dissertation cannot be replaced by a machine whose efficiency is increased each year by technological innovation. To attract and hold a talented staff, wages must be increased more or less in line with the rise in the general wage level in the economy. These wage increases will translate fully into higher unit costs that must be passed on to the purchaser of the service, or must otherwise be funded by the organization increasing its revenue. "The faster the general pace of technological advance," Bowen and Baumol observed, "the greater will be the upward pressure on costs in any industry that does not enjoy increased productivity."[6]

In 1985, in *Managing for Profit in the Nonprofit World,* after referring to the work of Bowen and Baumol, I concluded:

> The blunt fact of life is that unless an organization's real (after-inflation) revenues are in fact expanding, it will be faced with having to curtail its programs. The dilemma of static productivity is thus one of the central vulnerabilities of almost all not-for-profit organizations and a compelling imperative for them to change their goals and mode of operation.[7]

This is true, as far as it goes, but in retrospect it is only half the story. The challenge for nonprofits providing a service is broader than what I described 10 years ago. Yes, revenue expansion is still extremely critical, but nonprofits also need to determine whether they can in fact perform their missions more efficiently. The lesson of the restructuring of American business over the last decade is that an enterprise can restrain increases in its costs by developing new, more efficient work processes and cost-saving practices even where it is not able to achieve productivity gains through capital investment in labor. Costs will, of course, increase over time. But, by permanently streamlining the way work is done, restructuring operations can keep the level of costs below what it would otherwise have been and do so without diminishing the level of output or work quality. The benefit of such cost containment will be reaped continuously over time because increases will start from a lower base than if the restructuring had not taken place.

Let me illustrate by a hypothetical example. Assume that an organization carries on its books 150 full-time employees at an average cost per person, including benefits, of $25,000. That's a total base payroll of $3,750,000. For our purposes, we'll say that these payroll costs represent 50 percent of the organization's operating expenses (although in the case of many service entities the percentage is even higher). The organization now reduces its permanent payroll by 10 percent (or 15 people), at $25,000 per person, without reducing its output or impairing the quality of its service. Say that as much as half of the $25,000 per employee is paid out in severance and other costs associated with the staff reduction. That adds up to potential net savings of $187,500 in the year the staff is reduced. But all the reductions will not be accomplished on day one or even during the first year. Thus, let's assume that the actual realized savings in the first year will be half, or $93,750. In the second and subsequent years following the reduction, the organization's baseline salary and benefit costs will be reduced by the full $375,000 a year.

At the same time, assume that salaries continue to rise at the rate of 3 percent a year in line with inflation. If no restructuring had taken place, the organization's costs would have risen by $112,500 in the first year of 3 percent pay increases (assuming the increases are granted at the start of the year). With the restructuring, the increase in payroll costs will be $101,250, or $11,250 less than if the changes had not been made (assuming all the staff reductions are made at the start of the year).

Moreover, because cost increases apply to a lower base, the differential between the costs with restructuring and what they otherwise would have been will widen in each subsequent year. In the second year, for example, costs would have risen by $115,875 if the original payroll had not been restructured; with restructuring, costs increase by $104,287, or $11,588 less than without restructuring. *Overall, the second-year payroll with restructuring is $397,838 less than if no restructuring had taken place.* The foregoing can be summarized in the following table.

TABLE 2.1. Effect of a 10 Percent Staff Reduction on Payroll Expenses over a Two-Year Period

Year 1

Without restructuring:

$3,750,000 [base payroll expense] + $112,500 [3 percent raise] = $3,862.500 [new payroll expense]

With restructuring:

$3,750,000 - $375,000 [salaries of eliminated workers] = $3,375,000 [base payroll expense]

$375,00 [eliminated base salaries] + $11,250 [raises of eliminated workers] = $386,250 gross savings

One-time cost of staff reduction: $187,500

Assuming half the potential savings is actually realized, net savings are:
$187,500 / 2 (= $93,750) + $11,250 / 2 (= $5,625) = $99,375

Year 2

Without restructuring:

$3,862,500 [base payroll expense] + $115,875 [3 percent raise] = $3,978,375 [new payroll expense]

TABLE 2.1. Effect of a 10 Percent Staff Reduction on Payroll Expenses over a Two-Year Period

With restructuring:

$3,476,250 [base payroll expense from Year 1, including 3% increase] + $104,287 [3 percent raise] = $3,580,537 [new payroll expense]

$3,978,375 [payroll without restructuring] - $3,580,537 = $397,838 net savings

---

Our hypothetical case makes an assumption the truth of which is borne out by experience: if the organization's work is restructured to eliminate tasks that do not add value and to create new, more efficient means of producing output, fewer workers can generate the same output. Restructuring will also likely involve rethinking the basic aims of the organization, both what it does and why. A genuine restructuring process thus requires more than trimming expenses to balance a budget; it fundamentally redesigns the way the organization does its work. Where a fundamental restructuring is achieved, the result is not just a reduction in the costs of delivering the same level of output, but a sharply improved quality of performance.

There are real-world examples of how restructuring can cut costs without impairing quality or curtailing the level of output. For instance, a large organization eliminated several millions of dollars in administrative costs in one year without decreasing the quality of service. Costs were cut by eliminating

- duplicative functions performed by different departments;
- tasks carried over from earlier times that no longer served a useful purpose;
- turf barriers to the introduction of improved practices;
- middle managers whose principal function was collecting information from one organizational layer and conveying it to a higher level without actually acting on the information themselves; and
- work practices that did not add value to the quality of administrative services.

The real art of restructuring lies in changing work patterns and habits by employing more efficient systems of operation. The restructuring process must be done in a way that strengthens the organization, not merely cuts its costs. Many cost-cutting programs in business have left companies in a weakened position because they simply slashed expenses, without addressing the issue of how to improve the performance of the company.[8]

Perhaps the best evidence of the power of restructuring to improve performance is the radical change that has taken place in the system of automobile manufacturing. The change was pioneered in Japan. The deep inroads Japanese auto manufacturers have made into the American market have forced U.S. auto-mobile manufacturers to deemphasize their classic commitment to mass produc-tion in favor of emulating what has been termed "lean production."

Mass production employs narrowly skilled professionals to design products made by unskilled or semiskilled workers operating expensive, single-purpose machines. Because the machinery is so expensive, mass production requires ex-tra supplies, extra workers, and extra space to assure smooth production. Be-cause changing over to a new product often costs a great deal, mass production retains standard designs in production for as long as possible. The result is that the consumer gets lower costs, but at the expense of variety.

By contrast, lean production, as practiced by Japanese automakers, employs teams of multiskilled workers at all levels of the organization and uses highly flexible, increasingly automated machines to produce volumes of products in enormous variety. Lean production uses less of everything compared with mass production—half the human effort in the factory, half the manufacturing space, half the investment in tools, half the engineering hours to develop a new product. Also, it requires keeping far less than half the needed inventory on site, which results in many fewer defects, and facilitates the production of a great variety of products.

"Lean production," in short, enables manufacturers to target specific prod-ucts for specific market segments, to increase the speed with which new products are brought to market, to reduce dramatically the number of defects embedded in a product, and to redesign products continually in order to improve their quality and to adapt rapidly to changes in the competitive environment.

In the 1980s, the impact of these differences in production methods was evi-denced by the substantially greater number of models Japanese producers put on the world market compared to U.S. automakers, and in the far shorter model life of Japanese cars compared to U.S. autos. For example, Japanese producers increased the number of models they sold on the world market from 47 in 1982, to 84 in 1990, while U.S. auto producers increased the number of their models from 36 to 53 in the same period. During this time, Japanese car models had an average life of four years while U.S. auto models had an average life of 10 years. Equally striking was the Japanese producers' shorter lead time in getting new models to the market—it was 46.2 months in the mid-1980s, compared to 60.4 months for U.S. producers.[9]

Why is a revolutionary change in a manufacturing process relevant to this book about nonprofits? Because the change in automobile production was brought about by revising the *objectives* of the manufacturing process and then reconfiguring the *process* to achieve those objectives. This revolution in manu-facturing is a striking example of how performance can be dramatically im-proved by restructuring the way in which an organization does its work.[10] This lesson should not be lost on nonprofits.

The chapters that follow address various methods for improving the performance of nonprofits. In the end, they boil down to this: carefully defining what needs to be done to accomplish an organization's aims most *efficiently* and *effectively,* and identifying what work can be eliminated without undermining the organization's ability to realize its goals. This approach to managing a nonprofit organization opens to scrutiny the "value added" of any and all of the inputs into the implementation of its mission.[11]

In the decade since *Managing for Profit in the Nonprofit World* was published, there have been significant changes in both the nature of information technology and its use by organizations. In the 1950s, 1960s, and 1970s, data processing was used primarily to process rapidly large batches of information, enabling more complex analyses to be made and reducing the clerical costs of managing data. Until the 1980s, the use of the technology did not permeate the whole organization. Information technology was still the province of management information systems units that functioned outside of the operating groups. This organizational separation reflected the fact that the utilization of information technology had not yet been integrated into the main operating lines of the business.

The introduction of the personal computer and user-friendly software at the start of the 1980s changed the role of technology within organizations. Today, information-processing technology is no longer the province of a central staff group; it is in the hands of everyone in an organization. Actually, technology is now being harnessed by operating personnel to gain strategic advantages. Offices where once there wasn't a computer in sight are now dotted with desktop and laptop computers. People sitting at their office workstations or even in their homes can access remote banks of information containing far more data than their local libraries ever did, communicate in real time with distant colleagues, and create new products without armies of assistants to perform supporting tasks. The result is a quantum leap not only in the speed at which business is conducted, but in the very nature of the way workers communicate with each other, as well as the way people of all ages—from pre-school children to adults—learn.[12]

This transformation of information technology opens up the possibility of achieving both significant cost savings and improvements in the quality of performance in the unique labor organizations that populate the nonprofit world. *In other words, today's technology can enhance both the efficiency and the effectiveness of nonprofit organizations.*

For example, until recently, the computer revolution tended to result in increased costs for universities, without producing cost savings equivalent to the costs of installing the computers. But we may be about to turn the corner. Right now, we can save dramatically on future increases in library costs—a major item in a university's budget. Computerized access to other libraries can now relieve individual libraries from continuing to build their own collections in every field and from the need to construct additional space to house the steadily increasing volume of books. Moreover, without the acquisition of additional equipment or systems, individual users in various disciplines can now access the information they want directly, bypassing the library altogether.[13]

It may also be possible to use expert systems to teach students, workers, and professional practitioners, capturing the unique knowledge of highly gifted experts and delivering it through interactive modes to all kinds of consumers. This is no longer a fanciful idea; as long ago as 1980, a team I organized began creating interactive learning systems for young children through computer programs. The learning that took place was very powerful because it was interactive, not passive, in character. The power of active learning will eventually transform all of our institutions engaged in instructing people—not just schools, but training programs as well as social reconstruction programs. If such learning is offered to a wide enough base of students, it can prove cost-effective and perhaps in some ways even more powerful than conventional teaching.

The necessary technology is now in place; the next step, for those engaged in education and instruction of all kinds, is to examine how to harness the gifts of that technology. Those of us who are engaged in providing services in which we deem the human element to be unique and irreplaceable, have not been aggressive enough in harnessing the new communication technologies' potential to provide a more effective product and to do so on a more cost-effective basis.

The challenge, in short, is to bring fresh thought to bear on how an organization carries out its work, taking advantage of new technologies wherever possible, but basically motivating people to work smarter and eliminating activities which do not add net value to the aims of the organization.

NOTES

1. Peter F. Drucker, *Managing for the Future* (New York: Truman Talley Books/Plume, 1992), p. 93.

2. Ibid., p. 95.

3. Ibid., p. 95.

4. William G. Bowen and William J. Baumol, *Performing Arts: The Economic Dilemma* (New York: Twentieth Century Fund, 1966).

5. William G. Bowen, *The Economics of Major Private Universities* (Carnegie Commission on Higher Education, 1968).

6. Bowen and Baumol, *Performing Arts,* p. 171. Even Bowen and Baumol are careful, however, not to overstate their thesis, allowing that increases in efficiency or in productivity per worker hour are not "completely precluded" (p. 165).

7. Paul Firstenberg, *Managing for Profit in the Nonprofit World* (New York: The Foundation Center, 1986), p. 25.

8. Don Tapscott and Art Caston, *Paradigm Shift* (New York: McGraw-Hill, 1993), p. 7.

9. James P. Womack, et al., *The Machine That Changed the World* (New York: HarperCollins, 1990), pp. 118, 119, 120.

10. For a full description of the challenge posed by the Japanese development of lean production, see Michael L. Dertouzos, Richard K. Lester, and Robert M. Solow, *Made in America* (1989) and James P. Womack, et al., *The Machine That Changed the World.*

11. See Chapters 6 ("Downsizing: Activity-Based Cost Reduction") and 13 ("Managing Your Human Resources").

12. Tapscott and Caston, *Paradigm Shift,* p. 7.

13. For instance, law professors and practicing attorneys today can sit at home and, through their computer terminals and telephone modems, access all cases and a good deal of other research material directly from commercial providers, without ever setting foot in a library. As Chapter 12, "Converting to a For-Profit Enterprise," describes, this kind of direct user access to remote data bases has already made it possible for engineers to get all the engineering and scientific data they require, while entirely bypassing the conventional library.

CHAPTER 3

Approaches to
Restructuring

Before delving into the details of restructuring, a brief overview of the process and guide to the subsequent chapters which deal with the topic may be useful.

Restructuring an organization is a multidimensional *process* for redefining the aims of an enterprise and changing, sometimes quite radically, how it operates to achieve those aims. At its most basic level, restructuring involves three primary subprocesses.

The first step involves a comprehensive strategic review that reevaluates the central purposes of the organization in order to sharpen the organization's focus and position it in a field in which it enjoys an edge over competitive forces. The organization's current and planned programs are then evaluated on the basis of two primary criteria: (1) their fit with the organization's central purposes, and (2) their managerial and financial feasibility (i.e., does the organization have the managerial and financial resources to undertake the program along with its other activities?). Programs that meet the criteria warrant priority support. Programs that do not satisfy both tests become candidates for elimination or at least sharp curtailment.

The second step requires looking beneath the strategic level of an organization and its departmental structure and analyzing the efficiency of day-to-day operations; *at issue is whether the work of the organization can be reorganized to produce output of the same or higher quality at a lower cost.*

The third step is the creation (or reinforcement) of a management system that establishes specific objectives and assigns to a specific person or unit within the organization the responsibility for achieving them within certain time frames. The management reporting system is shaped to enable management to track actual progress in achieving objectives (by comparing them with forecasts), as well as to identify specific variances between expected and actual results. Without timely and reliable data, management cannot effectively oversee actual performance or how it compares with projected performance.

These three processes form the foundation of a restructuring program; they are intended to relate to each other and together provide a means of remaking the strategic focus, the organization of work, and the internal controls of an enterprise.

The next six chapters elaborate on each of these principal elements and also describe the role a merger can play in reshaping an enterprise.

- Chapter 4, "Carving Out a Strategic Niche," shows how an organization can identify a niche in which it can achieve a leadership position.

- Chapter 5, "Systems Redesign," focuses on the redesign of the "systems" by which the work of the organization is carried out. The analysis of systems crosses departmental boundaries, focusing on all the factors that interact to create an organization's output.

- Chapter 6, "Downsizing: Activity-Based Cost Reduction," discusses how to streamline an organization by eliminating specific functions that add little or no value to the quality of the organization's performance or the control of its costs. This is a less macro, more micro approach than the redesign of systems; its focus is specific activities, and it can be targeted at the operations of a specific staff or department.

- Chapter 7, "The Merger Option," discusses the pros and cons of merging with another organization and shows that, in some cases, combining two enterprises can be done quickly and effectively and can produce measurable benefits.

- Chapter 8, "Performance Management," describes how to establish objectives, and action plans for achieving them, for each of the organization's principal operating units, as well as a system for tracking progress against forecasts.

- Chapter 9, "Depicting Performance and Financial Condition," discusses the creation of a reporting system that illuminates for management in a timely fashion not only the financial position of the organization but the critical variables that most affect that position. Such a system enables management to focus on the actions it can take to improve the organization's financial performance.

CHAPTER 4

Carving Out a
Strategic Niche

One of the most difficult challenges in today's world, where change occurs with unprecedented speed, is establishing, and then continually updating, the positioning of an organization so as to enjoy an advantage over its competitors. That is the function of *strategic planning*.

The word "plan" does not adequately convey the idea that strategic planning is not the production of a document but a *process*. Strategic planning is a living, breathing, continual effort to channel an organization's efforts in one or more directions in pursuit of a set of specific objectives and then to measure regularly the degree to which the organization is successful in meeting those objectives. Variances between objectives and results need to be explained, and either the organization's execution improved or its objectives revised.

One of the virtues, for nonprofits, of engaging in a strategic planning process is that it induces such organizations to look beyond the current year in order to identify possible future changes that could positively or negatively affect the organization. Too many nonprofits still confine their vision to the current year—which coincides with their major funding cycle—and do not look down the road.

One cautionary note: Although Peter Drucker and others were writing with great authority about the role of strategic planning in running a business in the

1970s,[1] the concept did not take hold in every major company right away. In fact, in 1985 I remember drafting for Prudential Realty Group, an enterprise with $40 billion in assets under management, its *second* business plan. The first plan, by the way, had been overkill, with each business unit within the group writing an inch-and-a-half-thick book describing its activities and plans. The result was that no one in senior management read them. I put together one plan that covered all units and ran only about 15 pages, and the chief investment officer of the company read and approved it. However, not until a year later, when we got a new CEO (who had, by the way, no background in real estate), was a plan put together that actually shaped the group's *behavior*. The new CEO's imperative was to translate the plan's objectives into individual objectives for each unit, regularly track how well the unit was accomplishing its charge, and understand any variances. Breaking down an organization's overall aims into assignments for each department and then tracking unit performance closes the planning loop.

Picking Your Shots

The opportunities to try to improve the human condition seem limitless. Unless a nonprofit organization carefully picks its shots, it may fail despite the best will in the world. Good intentions have to be matched with the financial and human resources required to produce results. Furthermore, the problem itself has to be amenable to correction. Unfortunately, not every ill can be overcome and not every wrong righted, even by the application of dedicated energy and skill.

McGeorge Bundy, former president of the Ford Foundation, made a set of similar observations. Among the factors accounting for a foundation's effectiveness, he cited "the quality of its staff in identifying a problem and the means of attacking it." He added, "And there must be something in the environment that makes people ready to respond . . . a ripeness or readiness for change. . . . Someone must be interested besides the foundation. . . ."[2]

The point is that a nonprofit institution has to choose its objectives carefully. It has to identify a problem or issue for which it can organize the requisite resources and talents to effect change, and there has to be a public receptivity to its efforts. This process of picking one's shots is the essence of strategic planning.

The emphasis in the planning process should be on the "strategic" aspects—that is, on the choices that will determine the nature and direction of the organization's development. The plan should not be simply a projection of current operations into the future.

A well-conceived strategic planning effort will encompass a number of integrated steps, including the following:

- ◆ Determination of mission
- ◆ Evaluation of the behavior of rivals
- ◆ Evaluation of the external environment
- ◆ Projections of multiyear expense and revenue trends
- ◆ Determination of specific goals (financial and programmatic)
- ◆ Positioning of the organization to give it an edge on its competition

Defining a Mission

At the heart of the strategic planning process is a clear definition of the specific mission of the organization. Simple and obvious as this task sounds, a good many nonprofit institutions have not defined their mission, at least not with meaningful specificity. Unless this kind of analysis is undertaken, organizational resources cannot be allocated or staff priorities set intelligently.

Strategic positioning or planning for an organization must begin with a vision of what the organization should be—i.e., its mission. Virtually every day, an organization is confronted with critical choices: what population to service, what services to offer, how to allocate its resources. An enterprise needs a conceptual framework for making these choices. This is the role of a nonprofit organization's mission concept. A mission concept should delineate the intended nature and direction of an organization—why it engages in certain activities and not others, and why it offers certain services and not others.

Without such an organizing principle, nonprofit institutions drift into areas in which they are not strong. Loss of direction and unintended change in the character of the organization are possible, if not probable, outcomes. The concept of "mission" is the driving force that enables an organization to decide what the scope of its services should be, and what populations it should serve.

Precision in defining an organization's mission can make a significant difference in the setting of an organization's direction. For instance, the mission of a television production organization may be defined as "employing television to educate children" or as "employing the mass visual communication media to educate children." Under the first definition, work with computers, video disks, and tapes would not be seen as part of the organization's mission. Under the second definition, these new technologies would be included.

A well-crafted mission statement serves as a central organizational compass. When drawn with enough precision, it enables management to sort out which activities it wishes to pursue and which it doesn't. For the most part, the statement will address the same kind of questions a profit-making business needs to ask itself in its strategic planning exercise. In the profit-making context, the questions are, "Why are we in the business we are in and not another? Why are we in the market we are in and not another?" The same questions apply to a nonprofit.

Identifying Unmet Needs and Comparative Advantage

In defining a not-for-profit mission, attention should first be focused on identifying the particular *unmet societal needs* the organization seeks to fill. This effort is an aspect of strategic planning unique to the not-for-profit world, and precision in defining the particular unmet needs should be coupled with an assessment of the institution's special capability to affect that need.

An organization's mission or aims cannot be defined in a vacuum. In framing an enterprise's mission, it is necessary to determine what the organization's edge—its comparative advantage—is in pursuing its proposed mission. "Comparative advantage" means what an organization does better than competitors, what it does uniquely well, its natural strengths. Determining a comparative advantage entails a realistic appraisal of an organization's strengths and weaknesses and how they compare to those of its competitors. Until an organization develops a clear view of what its strengths are in a highly competitive world, it cannot realistically define its mission.

For example, assume that an organization is concerned with mental health and is experienced in training community mental health professionals. Over time, the organization becomes interested in addressing the problem of chemical dependency. It finds, however, that there are already organizations in its area providing good services to people afflicted with such dependency. But the organization may have the capability to administer an aspect of the problem overlooked by other institutions and agencies: the training of medical professionals in the treatment of chemical dependency. Such a focus will enable the organization to concentrate its energies in area where it can establish a leadership position.

The point of analyzing comparative advantage is to prompt an organization to invest in its areas of strength and to cut back in areas in which it is competitively weaker. An enterprise needs to build on its principal areas of advantage. Over the long term, investing in carefully selected areas of strength is the key to sustaining superiority.

Other Questions to Consider

Other questions a nonprofit organization may ask itself when defining its mission include the following:

- ◆ *What is the cost-effectiveness of meeting the need?* Can society afford the cost of the perceived benefits? The cost-effectiveness of the *Sesame Street* television series is one of its appeals; for the roughly $10 million it costs to deliver 130 new shows each year, the series attracts nine million regular viewers under the age of six as well as millions of other viewers. Children who regularly watch the show gain skills. The size of the series' audience, relative to its production expense, means that the cost of these benefits, on a per viewer basis, is quite small.

◆ *What is the likelihood of drawing support for the programs in the mission?* Is there a market for the programs? More precisely, is there a demand for the service, *and* is there an effective constituency prepared to support, even fight for, the program?

◆ *Can the organization have an impact on the problem?* Can the organization raise (or earn) enough funds to launch effective programs in support of its proposed mission? Can people with the requisite talents to mount such programs be recruited at a cost the organization can afford?

◆ *Will the effort be likely to stimulate replications?* Is it a model others will emulate? One aim of exempt organizations is to be at the cutting edge, to blaze new trails for others to follow.

◆ *How does the mission contribute to the organization's reputation and image?* An organization that does not improve and does not modify or expand its program to keep abreast of the times, will gain a reputation as a staid entity and will be perceived as dull and lifeless rather than as an imaginative and lively place to work. Ultimately, the perception of an institution's liveliness will affect the quality of people who come to work for it and the level of support it gains.

Choosing a Mission Concept

The analytical framework we have outlined is useful in helping in the selection of a mission concept, but in the end, rational analysis by itself does not necessarily lead to a clear conclusion. For instance, in the case of a media programming organization, going through the preceding checklist does not compel a choice between a narrow television-based mission concept and a broadened communications-based concept. Ultimately, the choice is determined by to the personal values of those charged with determining the organization's mission. What do they believe is most important? What do they have the strongest convictions about? In the case of the media organization, do they care so intensely about television that it is of overriding importance to them, or is their interest centered on mass communication media?

Within the boundaries established by analysis, determining a mission is a statement of personal conviction and of personal commitment.

Tracking Rivals' Behavior

Competition is a fact of life for every nonprofit organization, although not all such organizations realize this. *All* exempt institutions compete at some level, whether for public financial support, or, if they are fully endowed, for the best talents, the best projects, and the most attention for their work. Very likely, an institution's plan of action will be affected by the behavior of its rivals. Accordingly, the identity of an organization's effective competitors must be delineated and the actions of such competitors monitored.

It can be a mistake to undertake too narrow an analysis of the competition a nonprofit organization faces. In some fields, the competition faced by a nonprofit may come from the commercial world. For instance, a public broadcasting station has a monopoly only on public television in its geographic broadcast area. It would be foolish to ignore the fierce and indeed often overwhelming competition it faces from commercial broadcast channels and cable systems. Public television must and does take into account in its programming the broadcast schedules of its commercial competitors. For instance, the PBS stations would be foolhardy to air a news documentary on Sunday evening in a time slot competitive with the CBS network news feature series, *60 Minutes,* one of television's most popular shows.

In surveying the competition, an organization should look for ways in which it can gain an edge on rivals, for areas in which it can deploy its strengths to play to its comparative advantage. A university, for example, may find that the colleges in its immediate area are really not its prime competitors for students, and that it can increase its appeal, relative to its real competitors, by offering joint programs with these neighboring institutions. Or a university may find that a major concern of students is getting into graduate professional schools. If it faces stiff competition for undergraduate students from institutions that do not have professional schools, it may advertise the fact that its own professional schools look with favor on applications from the university's undergraduates. Or a small community health services organization, in applying for a government grant in competition with larger organizations without a community affiliation, may tap the political power of its constituency to support its application.

The moral here is simple: do not try to overpower the competition if there is any chance that you can outmaneuver it.

Evaluating the External Environment

In addition to analyzing present competition, an organization also ought to look down the road to see how it will fare in its competitive universe in the future. In particular, it needs to keep an eye out for changes in the external environment in which it operates. It cannot expect to predict all future changes, but at least it can be alert to the possibilities of economic, social, or technological change that could either adversely affect the organization or open up new opportunities (e.g., in the case of educational institutions, the push for equality for women). An organization can also consider the possibility that other institutions will shift direction and compete more intensely for the organization's revenue sources and market (e.g., arts channels on cable television seek out the public broadcasting audience).

Making Realistic Multiyear Projections of Expense and Revenue Trends

Strategic planning also requires taking one's best shot at developing a multiyear forecast of expenses and revenues and the impact of economic trends on those projections. Failing to do so can have deadly consequences, as the experience of many universities over the last several decades illustrates.

Few universities had even heard of multiyear financial planning until the 1970s, when financial hard times pressed it upon them. Prior to that period, they tended to operate and react according to the opportunities of the moment, without examining longer-range trends. Reacting to demographic and government policies of the 1960s, many universities expanded thoughtlessly, adding buildings and programs for which, within relatively few years, insufficient financing in the form of tuition revenue and government grants was available. At the same time, they did not reinvest enough funds in their endowments to enable these funds to grow at the same pace as inflation-driven expenses. Moreover, in the 1960s, universities gave tenure to large numbers of faculty members on the assumption that growth would be continuous. As a result, there was too little room for new faculty in the 1970s, when the economic slowdown struck.

In short, a good number of universities drifted over time into serious financial difficulty from which they found it acutely painful to extricate themselves. That the future of higher education would be different from the present was foreseen by some. But many universities failed to look ahead, to make an effort to project future developments rather than assuming the present would continue into the future, and to assess the implications of potential new conditions. Had they engaged in such long-range planning, many of these universities might have avoided mortgaging their futures.

A number of nonprofit organizations find their current financial position so precarious that it is understandably hard for them to look beyond meeting next month's payroll to more long-range issues. But the plights of others stems—as in the case of universities—from a false expectation that past trends will continue into the future.

Of course, it is difficult to predict future trends with precision. It is, however, possible to develop an informed sense of what will happen. Look at William Bowen's study in the 1960s for the Carnegie Commission forecasting the impact of rising inflation on expenses in higher education,[3] or his recent book with Neil Rudenstine (now president of Harvard University) analyzing Ph.D. education.[4]

A nonprofit organization needs to appraise the future availability of support sources realistically in the same way that a business would project the trend of revenues. The point is to try to anticipate the larger trends, even if particular numerical projections do not forecast the future with exactness.

Setting Specific Goals

The result of the processes outlined above should be the development of specific goals for the organization to be accomplished in a given time frame. A "goal" differs from a "statement of mission," in that the latter sets out the basic purpose of the institution, whereas the former constitutes the specific aims the institution will pursue over a given length of time. These aims, when restated in an operational and measurable form, become the institution's objectives.

The following scenario illustrates the different meanings of these planning terms: A small private college in southern Wisconsin defines its continuing mission as the "applied liberal arts education business," with emphasis on career preparation through the liberal arts. Its goal in a given year may be to "increase enrollment," in which case the near-term objective will be "a 15 percent increase in the size of next fall's entering class compared to this year's."

Of course, one can become overly enamored of subtleties of planning language and the degree of precision it is possible to obtain in defining mission, goals, and objectives. However, rarely is the effort to do so wasteful, for it usually leads to new insights about the organization and its opportunities.

Establishing a Financial Bottom Line

One result of the planning process should be the adoption of specific financial as well as program goals. In essence, a nonprofit organization should have its own form of financial bottom line as an explicit institutional goal.

The adoption of a bottom line is an important way to express the connection between institutional financial viability and programmatic objectives. Further, it will serve as a source of constructive tension when pressure builds to increase expenditures.

The bottom line may simply call for budgets to be balanced each year, or it may contemplate a planned, manageable deficit, or it may establish as a goal that a certain amount of resources will not be expended currently but saved for future needs, with a view toward accumulating a certain amount of capital. The point is to have a specific financial objective for the institution and to plan how the institution will achieve this objective.

Establishing Performance Standards and Feedback Mechanisms

The argument is often made that the objectives of many nonprofit institutions are inherently too vague to measure. But such arguments assume that greater precision in stating the goals of a nonprofit organization is somehow impossible. The mere fact that a department is not a "profit center" in a financial sense does not mean that one cannot establish specific objectives and criteria for assessing whether these objectives have been achieved. The problem is one of definition.

The exercise of trying to set measurable goals for departments has an underlying value: to build a performance-oriented discipline within the organization. To establish such a discipline requires a process or structure that regularly informs people as to what is expected of them. Thus, the planning process should be conducted from the bottom up, with departmental objectives first drafted and discussed by various levels of working staff, until major organizational goals emerge for top management and the board to consider. Therefore, every department within an organization should be asked to establish specific objectives it will seek to accomplish within specific time periods. At year's end, both senior management and the board should evaluate the extent to which goals were achieved.

The overall aim of the process is to establish, as part of the institutional culture, the idea of managing for results, with individuals accountable for achieving agreed-on goals, using a given level of resources.

Competitive Positioning

When the planning cycle for a given year has been completed, one crucial result needs to emerge from the process: the organization must now be positioned to become a leader in a niche within the field it seeks to serve. The term of art for this process is *competitive positioning*.

Let's look at how the strategic planning process might work at "Ivy University," a hypothetical multidivision private university complete with law, business, engineering, and medical schools and a graduate school of government. First, however, some background information may be in order.

For decades, universities have designed their programs based on their own sense of the educational value of the program's components. Shaping a university to compete more effectively against specific competitors is rarely factored into decision-making. In reality, however, higher education is an extremely competitive industry: there are only so many students for all the openings in freshman classes; there are only so many dollars for all of a school's research and other funding needs.

What makes competitive positioning essential are the financial realities facing private universities. The opportunity for saving money through productivity gains is limited, because the operation is very labor-intensive. This fact, coupled with dramatic increases in the cost of technology required for teaching and research, means that university expenses rise faster than prices in the general economy, where productivity gains are more of a factor. An added pressure is the huge investment in financial aid that universities have made to ensure that they can admit talented students from a wide range of economic backgrounds, even as governments are cutting back research funding and scholarship dollars.

For more than two decades, most private universities have sought to contain these financial pressures, but not many have adapted in the fundamental ways that may be necessary for survival. They have cut expenses at the margin, boosted tuition, redoubled fundraising efforts, and kept their fingers crossed. That strategy led to a 300 percent tuition increase at private institutions between 1970 and 1987, an increase 70 percent higher than those at public institutions. During the 1980s, private university fees rose at almost twice the rate of inflation. In the 1990s, demographics promise a smaller pool of undergraduate applicants, calling into question the feasibility of continued steep increases in tuition. Nor can private universities expect to dominate the fundraising field as they once did, since they now face increasing competition from public universities and other nonprofit organizations.

The starting point for confronting these harsh economic realities has to be the way in which choices about spending are made. Universities generally make spending decisions without really examining the long- or short-term impact those decisions may have on the institution's competitive position. The ingrained reflex is to fund changes by increasing the operating budget, rather than by reallocating resources. The ever-expanding field of knowledge is used to defend ever-growing expenses, the implication being that the existing base is unchallengeable.

If economic reality dictates a fresh way of looking at resource decisions, how does one begin to move a university to do so? First, universities have to recognize that they usually gain at the expense of a rival. The average student, for example, is accepted by several universities. If the student enrolls at Ivy, the other schools may have to settle for another student who is not quite as desirable—or even for no student at all. This is also the case in attracting faculty and funding. But most private universities—unlike most successful businesses—are not accustomed to identifying and evaluating their competitive position.

The following scenario illustrates how knowing one's competitive position can affect decision-making within a university. Suppose a survey of undergraduate students who were accepted by Ivy University and by other competing universities showed that Ivy most often lost out in competition to a group of six private schools charging slightly lower tuition.

The presumption, without investigation, would be that this obvious difference between Ivy and its major competitors explains the recruiting advantage enjoyed by Ivy's rivals. But what if market research shows that tuition rates are not the most powerful factor influencing students' choices? Suppose, in fact, that Ivy is perceived—*relative to its competitors*—as an institution at which tenured faculty members spend far more time on research than on teaching, and which makes extensive use of graduate students to staff undergraduate courses? Lowering tuition, then, may not offset Ivy's competitive disadvantage in attracting students; rather, Ivy might be better off maintaining its tuition level and by investing more resources in undergraduate teaching. Clearly, Ivy's strategy can be intelligently formulated only on the basis of a realistic assessment of its competitive position.

To assess its competitive position, an organization must talk to its customers. As an administrator at Ivy, you would need to find out how students, faculty members, funding agencies, and grant givers perceive the university. Compare the university with its peers. Seek outside opinions about the quality of its departments and the employability of its graduates. In short, do what universities so infrequently do: ask about the expectations of various customers and how those expectations can be met or exceeded.

Then, identify the university's most frequent competitors for students, faculty, grants, and gifts. Find out the strengths and weaknesses of the competition, and explore the university's opportunities to exploit others' weaknesses. A university should, in fact, spend as much time studying its competitors as it does reviewing itself. Because the universe of competitors will vary among programs and departments, each academic department or school within the university should also examine its own set of competitors.

As the competitive realities become clear, a university must define the areas in which it wants to be strongest. Can it afford to be the equal of its competitors in all fields? Or should it build strength in a manageable number of areas in which it can enjoy a competitive advantage? Many private universities succumb to the danger of trying to be the best in every field—and end up with mediocrity across the board. In an era of limited resources, investing in a smaller number of areas, and truly excelling in them, is the more practical and more attainable goal.

Success requires not only a sharpened vision of what the university stands for and its place in the market, but also a willingness to make tough budget choices. Putting enough dollars in those academic activities that offer the best prospect of strengthening the institution competitively will very likely mean diverting resources from other long-established programs that are considered of significant educational value.

For example, imagine that Ivy's School of Government, staffed with faculty of modest attainments, offers a graduate program identical in almost every respect to those of the schools with which it competes. But it is often the second or third choice of its applicants. As long as the applicant pool for schools of government is significantly larger than the number of spaces in the competitive universe of schools, Ivy's School of Government will do acceptably well. But if career preferences shift, or there is a severe economic recession, enrollment will drop sharply as competitors attract a larger percentage of the diminished pool of applicants.

Suppose, however, that Ivy's School of Government targets its efforts on a market niche that has been overlooked by its principal competitors—for instance, the training of midlevel officials to help them advance further in their careers. To exploit this opportunity, the school reallocates resources from its master's programs to provide faculty and a curriculum suited to midcareer development. By so doing, Ivy's School of Government has transformed itself into a leader in midcareer development, rather than an also-ran in the race for graduate students. Moreover, the presence of midcareerists at the school constitutes a unique attraction for applicants to its master's programs. In short, by positioning itself adroitly, the School of Government is now more competitive in the higher education market.

In order to become more competitive, Ivy needs to take the following three steps:

1. Ivy must identify a competitive universe for each academic unit—that is, a reasonable number of peers with whom the unit competes for faculty and students.

2. It must rank each of its own academic units according to that unit's competitive position within that universe. A large element of subjective or qualitative judgment is involved, but objective factors can also be examined, including the number of undergraduate majors per faculty member, the amount of research dollars brought in by each faculty member, success in recruiting students against competitive institutions, per-capita instructional costs, success in placement of Ph.D.'s trained in the program, and the results of student evaluations of the unit's courses.

3. Ivy must tailor a plan to channel resources to those units with the highest competitive ranking or the greatest potential to gain on their competitors. Within limits, those units should be assigned the resources they require before funds are allocated to other units. The cardinal principle of a competitively focused strategy is *selectivity*.

Ultimately, this process will reshape the university by moving funds from the least competitive departments to the most competitive ones. Over time, such an approach will change a university's base budget so that it reflects the current competitive environment rather than past practice. Redirecting resources to their most effective use will reduce the constant pressure to find new sources of money for funding new initiatives.

The point of competitive positioning is to challenge the prevailing allocation of resources, developed over time through institutional inertia, and to reexamine periodically the entire academic program to make sure it is designed to strengthen the institution competitively and to maximize the effectiveness with which that institution's scarce resources are deployed.

The proposed competitive positioning approach will not—nor is it intended to—completely change the private university as we know it. Slavishly following a plan developed by considering *only* competitive positioning is as risky as ignoring the competition altogether. The allocation of resources must not only strengthen the university's competitive position, it must also produce a coherent academic program. For this reason, the resource allocation plan should be compared with priorities determined through more traditional academic procedures. Then the final budget becomes an amalgam that reflects a balance between traditional academic concerns and competitive considerations.

Establishing a strategy to strengthen an institution's competitive position is just the first step. An equally essential part of the process is setting up measures of success. In fact, the "scorecard" associated with a budget that is allocated on the basis of competitive resource planning may be the single most important element in bringing about institutional change. Specific, quantifiable goals are indispensable elements in molding institutional behavior.

To track results, Ivy must establish two kinds of criteria:

◆ *Task criteria*—those that measure whether the school (or unit) did what it said it would do. Did Ivy hire more faculty members in the medical school who could teach, do research, and treat patients?

◆ *Impact criteria*—those that measure whether actions have the impact Ivy projected. Did the additional faculty members teach as expected and in fact increase research and clinic net revenues as planned?

These criteria provide a basis for evaluating whether the institution is achieving its objectives. In turn, institutional objectives must be translated into a day-to-day operating reality that combines clear objectives with associated rewards for individual administrators. Those running the university's principal units must know just what is expected of them and how their efforts will be judged. They should be asked to develop a personal set of specific objectives and be measured on how well they achieve them.

Other incentives have to be devised to encourage all members of the academic enterprise to achieve agreed-on objectives. If the goal is to increase sponsored research, a more successful investigator should receive greater rewards for his or her work, perhaps in the form of sabbaticals or more desirable research space. An outstanding teacher might get a merit-based salary increase or a leave of absence to develop new course material. The point is simple: if the goal is to change behavior, then individual assignments, compensation, and perquisites must be linked to specific performance.

Introducing the realities of competition, then, is the key to strengthening an organization and to positioning it in front of the curve of change facing all nonprofit institutions in the next decade.

NOTES

1. Peter Drucker, *Management* (New York: Harper & Row, 1973).

2. McGeorge Bundy, interview with author.

3. See William G. Bowen, *The Economics of Major Private Universities* (Carnegie Commission on Higher Education, 1966).

4. William B. Bowen and Neil L. Rudenstine, *In Pursuit of the Ph.D.* (Princeton, NJ: Princeton University Press, 1992).

CHAPTER 5

Systems Redesign

In the last decade, fierce competition from international firms, radically chang-
ing technology, and the introduction of new products by upstart competitors
have forced many U.S. businesses to fundamentally restructure their busi-
nesses. While this restructuring has often involved substantial reductions in per-
sonnel, it has also called into question why the business has operated as it has
and whether its methods have to be radically altered if it is to achieve its objec-
tives. The nonprofit sector has not yet, for the most part, gone through such a
restructuring. In the near future, however, the ability of exempt organizations
to effectively perform their missions will be jeopardized unless they fundamen-
tally change the way in which they operate. At issue is whether such organiza-
tions are able to identify with specificity their objectives and then to deliver cor-
responding results; in essence, the nonprofit organization is going to have to
become accountable for its performance. This chapter, taking its key from Chap-
ter 2, "The Productivity Imperative," focuses on ways in which an organization
can reexamine and, if necessary, significantly modify the fundamentals of why
and how it operates.

The new chief budget officer of a private university, working in the world of
higher education for the first time, was struggling to develop a balanced budget
and turned to the admissions office for help. "After all," he reasoned, "we have
a large pool of applicants and accept only about a quarter of those who apply.

Surely, with a student body of 6,000, we could increase slightly the number of students who have not applied for financial aid without having to add faculty or facilities; admitting just 25 more paying students at $18,000 per student in tuition would bring in an additional $450,000 in badly needed additional revenue without really adding to our cost structure." When he talked to the head of admissions, he learned that the university had in reality *two* applicant pools—one consisting of students applying for financial aid, and one consisting of students prepared to pay the full price. The former was quite deep. The latter—the pool of students who could afford full tuition—was, to his surprise, extremely shallow. In fact, he was told that the university had as a practical matter admitted virtually all the qualified students who were not seeking financial aid. There was only a handful of additional students in this pool whom the school could admit without disregarding its minimum admissions standards. "In other words, you're telling me," the chief budget officer said to the head of admissions, "that we are encountering price resistance to our full sticker price and that we have to severely discount our price—that is, grant financial aid—to attract enough qualified students." The head of admissions confirmed that this was the case.

When the budget officer went back to his office and began to review the school's recent history, he found that the university had one of the fastest-rising tuitions in the country and that, at the same time, its financial aid budget was the fastest-growing item in the overall budget. In short, to attract the kinds of students it wanted, the university had to offer a severely discounted admission price to more and more students, and to make up for the loss in revenue by driving up the price paid by students who did not request financial aid. However, the school's pricing was at the point where the school had virtually run out of qualified applicants willing to pay the full price. Further analysis showed that, of students admitted by both the university and its two geographically closest competitors—whose tuition was several thousand dollars lower than the university's—the large majority among those not seeking financial aid chose a competitor.

The budget officer concluded that the university, already heavily dependent on tuition revenue, was facing a major crisis requiring an examination of the entire cost structure of the school. Since far and away the largest cost item in a college or university budget is labor (i.e., faculty and other staff), people and programs would need to be eliminated if the university was to avert the impending financial crisis. However, the officer found no support among senior administrators for such a broad review. The timing was bad, because the faculty and administration were already at odds over another issue; and to force a confrontation with faculty members, who would surely resist any reductions in the academic program, could lead to such an uproar that the president would be forced to resign. Instead, the president promised to approach the university's major financial supporters and see if a small group of donors could be tapped to close the budget gap for the year. Fundamental change would have to wait until a politically more propitious time.

This aversion to confronting fundamental structural problems is, unfortunately, all too common in the not-for-profit sector.

Changing the fundamental way in which an organization behaves requires three essential factors: (1) strong leadership that is unswervingly committed, for as long as it takes, to bringing about change, (2) the ability of such leadership to persuade the disparate parts of the organization that a genuine restructuring is essential, and (3) a fundamental rethinking of what the organization ought to be trying to achieve (i.e., its objectives), given available resources and the best means or "systems" for accomplishing such aims.

The term *systems* is important because it means examining the basic interactions between the various parts of an organization that lead to the delivery to the customer of a service or product. Envisioning an organization's performance in systems terms means digging beneath the organizational chart and learning what actually transpires, across organizational boundaries, when resources are acquired and then converted into a "product" that is delivered to a customer.

In recent years, a variety of techniques have been developed for effecting changes in business systems. These techniques have been called by various names, including "total quality management" (TQM), "reengineering," and "restructuring," but their basic objective is the same: to remake the way an organization does its work.

One of the founders of the systems approach was W. Edwards Deming. He spent the 1950s and 1960s teaching his principles to the Japanese; not until much later did American industry come to appreciate the value of his ideas.

In Deming's words, "a system is a network of independent components that work together to accomplish the aim of the system . . . without an aim there is no system." Deming maintained that any system must have results. Those results, the cost of achieving them, and the intended customers, he contended, shape the aim of the system. Deming added, "It is important that the aim never be defined in terms of activity or methods. It must always relate directly to how life is better for everyone . . . the aim is a value judgement."[1]

Management's role, according to Deming, is both to determine the aim of the system and to manage the system to accomplish that aim.

Deming believed that a business must look at the system as a whole, including not only its own processes but also those of suppliers and customers. Customers' needs and reactions had to be continually taken into account so that the system would continually improve.

At the heart of Deming's focus on systems is his concept that customers and suppliers are part of an organization's system and that their ideas can be tapped to improve not only the product but the system as well. In this respect, Deming was well ahead of his time. It was 30 years after he began teaching his ideas in Japan that Thomas J. Peters and Robert H. Waterman, Jr., in their 1982 best seller *In Search of Excellence,*[2] caused a stir in American business by urging business to stay close to its customers.

Deming sought to direct business thinking away from methods for producing quantity (see the discussion of mass and lean production in Chapter 2 of this book, "The Productivity Imperative"). Instead, Deming argued, the focus should be on continuously improving the organization's systems to produce the highest level of customer satisfaction, to which process he applied the term "quality management."

Deming's philosophy also makes a critical linkage between a focus on systems and the creation of a "constancy of purpose" for an organization—that is, a long-term aim that is widely understood within the organization. To develop such a purpose, he maintained, one had to answer the question "What are we doing, and why are we doing it?"

Although Deming's work was about for-profit business, his thinking has clear and direct application to nonprofit organizations. Following are three examples of how such an approach can make a difference in the operation of a nonprofit organization.

◆ An organization finds that recipients of its grants are not applying the funds as it expected. The organization's first instinct will be to tighten controls over the disbursement of funds to grantees, requiring grantees to apply for each drawdown under the grant with more detailed documentation as to how the funds will spent. This stringent oversight may be necessary, but a systems approach would examine the entire process, from the initial approval of a program at the highest decision-making level of the grantmaking organization to the writing of checks or electronic transfer of funds. The process would cut across organizational lines, from the body that approves the grants, to the program units that formulate the grants, to the accounting office that makes the disbursements, to those who post audit disbursements. Grantees would be interviewed in order to gain their perspective, in the very important step of bringing the customer into the process.

   This systems approach may well reveal that the root of the problem lies not in the disbursement controls but in the vagueness of the program concept approved at the top of the organization. When definition of a grant program's specific objectives is left to lower levels of an organization, there is a risk that the expectations of those who approve the grants will not be met, because objectives are not defined precisely enough.

◆ An organization that raises funds from a well-defined constituency and then transfers money to a wide range of social service agencies experiences frequent conflicts between the program objectives of the agencies and those of the funding organization. The organization wants to align the programs of the agencies more closely with its own aims. Its first instinct is to review the degree to which the fundraising organization oversees the work of the agencies, and to reduce the scope of the decision-making discretion currently granted the agencies. A systems approach would step back from this narrow focus and inquire why the agencies had been chosen to carry out the fundraising organization's program objectives, and why the agencies had turned to the organization for funding (the "why question"). A parallel inquiry would be made into the process by which the various organizations established their objectives and communicated them to one other.

It may be that what is missing is a joint strategic planning exercise in which agencies and the funding organization determine what their common objectives should be and identify these with enough specificity so that agency performance can be measured against these objectives. In the absence of such an agreement, tighter control over the agencies' actions will require the funding organization to divert time and resources from its other priorities and will effectively put it into the social service business. Yet this is precisely what the organization sought to avoid by funding the agencies in the first place.

◆ A university wants to expand significantly the amount of contributions it raises from its alumni. Its fundraising trails that of competitive universities both in amount raised and in the percentage of alumni giving. A systems approach would examine how the university's competitors conduct their fundraising efforts ("benchmarking"), and it would also examine how the university creates a sense of loyalty among its students while they attend the school and after they leave. It is critical to address how the alumni's commitment to the university can be strengthened as well as how to ask for their money more effectively.

Reengineering is a term coined by two management consultants, Michael Hammer and James Champy, who modestly call their approach a "manifesto for business revolution."[3] The concept sold a tremendous number of books, brought their firm a lot of consulting business, and has already enabled both to churn out a second book on why reengineering does not work in certain companies.

However, even allowing for their entrepreneurial interests, Hammer and Champy are driving home the same valid and important message as Deming: that genuine organizational change requires looking "across and beyond functional departments to processes (systems)." "Almost always," they assert, "this process of change was accompanied by an equally radical change in the shape and character of those parts of the organization that were involved in performing it."

In language that echoes Deming's, Hammer and Champy write:

> We discovered that the most impressive companies we examined . . . were asking themselves a different question from that asked by other organizations; they weren't asking, "How can we do what we do faster?" or "How can we do what we do better?"

or "How can we do what we do at a lower cost?" Instead, they were asking, "Why do we do what we do at all?"[4]

Then the two authors offer this definition of reengineering: "the fundamental rethinking and radical redesign of business processes to achieve dramatic improvements in critical, contemporary measures of performance, such as cost, quality, service, and speed."[5]

The four key words in this definition are "fundamental," "radical," "dramatic," and "processes." Combined, they mean that it is necessary to address what a company must do, not what it does, in order to make substantial (as opposed to incremental or marginal) changes in the systems by which it generates products and delivers them to its consumers.

Like Deming's work, Hammer and Champy's approach can be readily applied to a nonprofit organization. The authors, indeed, specifically assert that reengineering is applicable to nonprofit and other nonbusiness organizations: "Reengineering is concerned," they write, "with the redesign of work . . . and is relevant for any organization in which work takes place. . . ."

In a subsequent book, *The Reengineering Revolution*, Michael Hammer elaborates on his view that reengineering is applicable to nonprofit organizations, stating:

> One of the great misconceptions about reengineering is that it applies only to businesses, and large businesses at that. . . . Reengineering is not primarily about profit and loss, the stock price, or any of the other appurtenances of modern capitalism. It is about work. Reengineering is concerned with the design of work so that it can be performed in a far superior way. Therefore, reengineering is relevant for any organization in which work takes place: large or small, manufacturing or service, profit or nonprofit, private or public sector.[6]

To further reinforce his point, Hammer quotes from a study of the Stanford University School of Medicine which concluded the following:

> Even though its model is flat and decentralized, we found that the school has the unmistakable feel of the hierarchical setup described by Hammer and others. These hierarchies, the webs of responsibilities and accountabilities, are duplicated in dozens of departments. Each department's organizational chart is a mini-hierarchy, overseen by central hierarchies in a multitude of functional areas: personnel, finance, sponsored projects, and the like. Furthermore, the smaller hierarchies are often mirror-images of the larger ones. The problems arise from the labyrinthine route a project or a piece of paper takes to reach its final destination. Routine items lumber from one approval or review to another, oftentimes doubling back for small clarifications. When an item

needing special attention comes across someone's desk, it becomes petrified as it sinks under a morass of piecemeal work.[7]

As Hammer notes, the critique sounds like those made of many business corporations. Hammer does, however, offer some qualifications of his view that mission-driven organizations can be reengineered, observing that there are "two dilemmas" inherent in virtually every restructuring of nonprofit organizations. The first, he notes, is how to determine success; and, in the case of nonprofits, defining "success" in the absence of a profit measure can prove to be more difficult than in a profit-making organization. (However, see Chapter 8 of this book, "Performance Management," for how nonprofits can quantify their aims.) The second problem facing mission-driven organizations, in Hammer's view, is "identifying their customers." In the case of a nonprofit, identifying the customer may not be as simple as in the case of a business. Hammer maintains that this is why the first mission-driven organizations to reengineer have in general had well-defined customers and performance measures expressible in financial terms.

As an example of the power of reengineering a mission-driven organization, Hammer describes the experience of the Jet Propulsion Laboratory (JPL), which is a nonprofit undertaking operated by the California Institute of Technology in Pasadena. The JPL designs and operates—develops and flies—unmanned planetary exploration spacecraft. NASA, the primary funder of the lab, directed the JPL to increase the number of its missions without increasing overall expenditures. The cost per JPL mission had to be significantly reduced. To accomplish this, the JPL embarked on the redesign of its entire operation.

Throughout its history, the JPL's primary focus had been on spacecraft design. This emphasis on spacecraft design overshadowed the rest of JPL's activities. Spacecraft design has major implications for operations, the process by which a spacecraft is managed from launch to mission completion. Every decision about spacecraft design has a major impact on operations design.

JPL's old systems did not take into account this interconnection. The designs—first of the overall mission, then of the spacecraft, finally of the operations—were developed almost as if they had nothing to do with one another. It was only at the end that costly consequences of the spacecraft design for operations were noticed, but then it was usually too late to make significant changes. As a consequence, operations costs kept rising—from less than 10 percent to more than 40 percent of total mission cost—as the spacecraft became more sophisticated.

JPL's senior management had to resolve a basic question at the beginning of their reengineering effort: "What business are we in? What's our real purpose?"

The JPL had operated as if its mission were to build spacecraft. JPL's leadership now recognized, however, that the organization's real mission was to visit planets, take photographs, and collect data to send back home. Its mission, as Hammer observes, was missions.

JPL's reengineering caused its three major processes—mission design, space-craft design, and operations design—to be conducted concurrently rather than sequentially. Previously, its work could be seen as a string of 25 to 30 functional activities divided into those three processes. Now the three processes effectively operate as one, with all work being performed by seven skilled groups that apply their talents across the entire spectrum of mission, spacecraft, and operations design. The seven groups, all housed at a new facility called the Project Design Center, specially constructed to facilitate teamwork, are integrated by a coordinating mission team. So far, the results of the reorganization look good, according to Hammer.

The JPL example should not be read as implying that the aim of reengineering is expense reduction. That misrepresents the purpose of reengineering. Reengineering—or more broadly, restructuring—is not simply an excuse to cut the payroll, although that may be a byproduct. The success of any such effort must be a long-term improvement in both the effectiveness and the efficiency of an organization.

Reengineering's fundamental assumption—that a company is best viewed as a set of horizontal processes for serving customers—is as powerful a basis for revenue building as it is for cost cutting. It is wrong to view reengineering as essentially an expense reduction methodology. Any successful form of restructuring of the work of an organization will enhance the enterprise's capability for growth.

Despite the ardent advocates of TQM and reengineering, accomplishing a transforming change of an established organization is very hard to do. Neither the business nor the nonprofit sector is overflowing with examples of clear successes. Harvard Business School professor John Kotter has observed more than 100 companies trying to remake themselves over the past decade. He concludes that a few such efforts have been "very successful," a few have been "utter failures," and "most fall somewhere in between, with a distinct tilt toward the lower end of the scale." "The most general lesson to be learned from the more successful cases," he adds, "is that the change process goes through a series of phases that, in total, usually require a considerable length of time."[8]

Kotter then lists eight specific factors that he believes account for the failure of companies to succeed at remaking themselves:

1. Not establishing a great enough sense of urgency,
2. Not creating a powerful enough guiding coalition,
3. Lacking a vision,
4. Undercommunicating the vision by a factor of 10,
5. Not removing obstacles to the new vision,

6. Not systematically planning for and creating short-term wins,

7. Declaring victory too soon, and

8. Not anchoring changes in the corporation's culture.

Kotter is not alone in emphasizing how much sustained hard effort is required to transform the work habits and attitudes of an organization. Hammer and Champy confessed to *The Wall Street Journal*[9] that they had seriously underestimated the extent to which the process they conceived for redesigning a business would be subverted by managers who were opposed to change. In fact, both wrote books about it.

The essence of Hammer's explanation for why reengineering did not take hold in so many companies is the opposition of middle managers—what he terms "the death zone of reengineering." These are the people who are faring well under the status quo and have the most to lose from change. He adds that resistance to change "is not limited to the lower levels of the organizational hierarchy." Rather, he observes,

> The higher people rise in the organization, the more they have to lose; the greater their investment in the current structure, the greater the risk of not finding an equivalent position in the new order. Consequently, without relentless pressure from the top, middle management will invariably smother a reengineering effort.[10]

Certainly, the resistance to change on the part of those who are profiting from the status quo comes as no surprise, but in my experience this kind of resistance can occur at any level of the organization, even among the most senior executives.

At a university some years ago, the provost (chief academic officer) strongly opposed the idea that the president and his chief planner draft a new strategic approach to the university's future, dealing with both academic and nonacademic aspects of the university. He fought their ideas every step of the way, even conducting his own independent strategic planning process outside of the one authorized by the president and before the latter could get a process underway. For the provost, the issue was jurisdiction. He saw himself as in complete charge of the academic side of the university, with the right to operate autonomously.

In the end, the president held firm, and a plan embodying change for the entire university was put forth. At the same time, the president deftly secured a presidency for the provost at another university, thus removing him as an obstacle to change.

In remaking an organization, there is, in the end, no magic black box, no formula of equations, no computer program that will spew out answers; what is required is fresh thought by a wide range of employees (or cross-functional teams) in the organization who approach the task with a clean piece of paper, so to speak, and as a stimulating challenge, not a process to be resisted or subverted. Building that kind of approach within an organization is no easy task for the CEO. But where it is achieved, genuine change can happen.

To envision the potential of systems redesign, consider how the plan of undergraduate education is devised at a typical college or university. Normally, every once in a while, a faculty committee reviews the fields of study to which undergraduates should be exposed and how many hours of study in the undergraduate's major field should be required. Often this review will be limited to the courses offered within the current departmental structure, and to a modest debate over the extent to which course choices should be prescribed, as opposed to allowing students to choose their courses freely. Courses will invariably be seen as 14 (or 10) weeks in duration, with an examination at the end. Generally, there will be another modest debate over whether all courses must be graded or whether some may be taken on a pass-fail basis. From time to time, the faculty will approve a new course offering, but the labor involved in convincing instructors to let experimental ideas be tried can be severe enough to deter a good many such ideas from being put forward. Rarely will faculty members address the fundamental question "Why do we do what we do?"

But what if a school took a different tack and asked what skills and knowledge students should acquire in their undergraduate years, and how best to organize the teaching program to serve that purpose? In other words, what if a school looked at the undergraduate education program as a system?

Suppose that at a midsize college of arts and sciences the answer developed to the basic question "Why do we do what we do?" is this: the principal objective of the educational experience we offer undergraduates is to inculcate in students a lifelong love of learning, and, to this end, enable them to develop the skills to learn continuously on their own. Given this aim, modes of instruction may be as important as curriculum content.

This goal might lead, in turn, to new methods of instruction aimed at increasing students' ability to instruct themselves, to acquire new skills and knowledge on their own after formal schooling ends, and to tap the cultural and educational resources offered by communities. In addition, students might be taught how to access informally the knowledge of people with experience or expertise in a given area.

Under this mission, there would be less emphasis on students sitting through standard 14-week curriculums and passing typical exams in the traditional disciplines and more focus on self-teaching, independent work, interactive computer-assisted instruction, and interdisciplinary learning.

As the focus in higher education shifts to devising new modes of instruction, emphasis can be directed toward how to harness, in teaching students, the potential of computer-driven communications technology. For centuries, teachers have stood at the front of a classroom or lecture hall, talking to students, sometimes lecturing, sometimes engaging in an exchange. Now there is the possibility of a revolutionary change in the way students learn, from creating engineering designs in three dimensions on computer screens, to accessing, on their own, information through the Internet, to problem solving through interaction with the computer. Deriving maximal benefit from the new media, however, will require constant experimentation, including devising new tests of student performance appropriate to computer-assisted instruction. But the most critical step will be educating and training faculty in how to exploit the new technology. If there is to be a revolution in teaching, it will have to begin by making teachers the architects of change.

In other words, an examination both of the system by which an undergraduate learns and how well the resulting education conforms to the school's aims can lead to the emergence of new modes of instruction, new fields of knowledge that cross present disciplinary boundaries, and new educational experiences. Some of the costs of change could be offset by eliminating courses or programs that do not meet current learning requirements. Focusing on the system of undergraduate education can thus open the door to significant change.

I have been writing primarily about enhancing the effectiveness of programming. However, nonprofit organizations need to examine not just programming, but the entire functioning of the organization, including the factors that drive up their cost structures. The object is to improve the performance of the entire organization. By reorganizing the flow of work (as discussed in this chapter) or downsizing functions (as described in Chapter 6), it is possible to improve quality and reduce costs in service enterprises, *without undermining the ability to deliver a quality product.*

One of the questions I am often asked is, What does it take to bring about fundamental change in a nonprofit organization which, unlike a business, is not under pressure to raise its earnings and share price, and whose existence is not directly challenged by a competitor? Without such pressures, exempt organizations tend to be more comfortable with the status quo than with embracing change, often until it is too late and they find they can no longer survive.[11]

Resistance to remaking an exempt organization can be overcome only by forceful, determined leadership at the top—and not just the president. The board of trustees must be steadfast in demanding change. The board cannot be put off by objections that it is interfering in the programming of an organization. Nowhere is such resistance stronger than in the case of higher education, and nowhere is informed board leadership more urgently required.

Faculty members will quickly assert that the board has no right to interfere with the academic side of the university, because that constitutes an infringement on academic freedom. True, the board does not have the right to tell faculty how to teach or what the content of courses should be. But it does have a right—indeed, a duty—to inquire into whether a coherent set of objectives exists for the academic program, and how the faculty determines whether those objectives are being met. The board also has the right and duty to examine how the school's academic program stacks up competitively, whether the resources are available to support the academic program being offered, and whether there are more cost-effective ways to deliver the educational program without undermining its quality. These are management issues of the highest order, and trustees, responsible for the overall, long-term welfare of the university, have the duty to look into such basic policy issues.[12]

This fundamental examination by the board need not be adversarial; if the dialogue is properly organized, it can and should be constructive and informative to both the staff of the organization and the board, with each learning from the other. It is at the very least a process that can begin to provide the accountability by nonprofit organizations that is essential to their credibility vis-à-vis funding sources, governments, and the public at large.

This chapter has focused on opportunities for restructuring the work of nonprofits. The key concept in this form of restructuring is the *system*. Chapter 6 approaches the restructuring process in a different way, analyzing each *function* performed by employees to evaluate how cost-effectively it contributes to effecting the organization's specific objectives.

NOTES

1. Quoted in Lloyd Dobyns and Clare Crawford-Mason, *Thinking about Quality* (New York: Times Books, 1994), p. 34.

2. Thomas J. Peters and Robert H. Waterman, Jr., *In Search of Excellence* (New York: Harper & Row, 1982).

3. Michael Hammer and James Champy, *Reengineering the Corporation* (New York: HarperBusiness, 1993).

4. Ibid., p. 4.

5. Ibid., p. 32.

6. Michael Hammer, *The Reengineering Revolution* (New York: HarperBusiness, 1995), p. 274.

7. Ibid., p. 276

8. John P. Kotter, "Leading Change: Why Transformation Efforts Fail," *Harvard Business Review,* March–April 1995, p. 59.

9. *Wall Street Journal*, January 17, 1995, p. B-1.

10. Three Vanderbilt University economists studied the pace at which institutions of higher education adopted a set of 30 specific "innovations" that had been put into practice at one or more other colleges or universities. They found, in a survey of 200 institutions, that the average time between adoption of an innovation by the first institution and its adoption elsewhere was more than 25 years in the case of half the institutions surveyed. John J. Siegfried, Malcolm Getz, and Kathryn H. Anderson, "The Snail's Pace of Innovation in Higher Education," *Chronicle of Higher Education* (May 19, 1995).

11. Regina E. Herzlinger of the Harvard Business School and Denise Nitterhouse of DePaul University refer to the balancing of current expenditures with preserving resources to maintain the continuity of an organization as "intergenerational equity." Regina E. Herzlinger and Denise Nitterhouse, *Financial Accounting and Managerial Control for Nonprofit Organizations* (Cincinnati: South-Western Publishing Co., 1994), p. 139.

12. Ibid., p. 140.

CHAPTER 6

Downsizing: Activity-Based Cost Reduction

Organizations are learning that they cannot simply reduce expenditures randomly or arbitrarily when the budget is in deficit. First, the costs of an organization's individual activities must be compared with their value to the organization's aims. This approach to reducing expenditures is termed "activity-based cost reduction"; it applies equally to businesses and nonprofit organizations and is the focus of this chapter.

However, even activity-based cost reduction must be conducted in the context of a long-term strategy to promote the improved performance of the organization. This requires not simply changing the budgets of individual departments on the basis of activity-based cost reduction, but an examination of processes for delivering products and services that cut across departmental boundaries.

At one time or another, most organizations confront a potential gap between revenues and expenses and are forced to cut back their expenditures in order to restore financial equilibrium. The causes of such a situation can be quite varied. Frequently, senior management, lulled by good times or inertia, allows more and more additions to the budget. Soon, the buildup of expenditures starts to exceed the normal rate of increase in revenues. The inevitable crunch will be worsened if, at the same time, revenue growth slows, sometimes for reasons beyond the organization's control (e.g., because a funding source reduces its support, or because a downturn in the economy adversely affects the flow of contributions). On occasion, some unforeseen adversity (e.g., severe storm damage to a university's campus buildings) strikes either the expenditure or the revenue side of the budget. Even endowed institutions such as foundations may encounter a period during which the securities markets take a nosedive and the total return from investments falls significantly.

Few institutions are wealthy enough to ride out such periods by allowing their capital to absorb operating losses. Since it is often hard to predict how long a period of adversity or disequilibrium may last, the prudent course is either to find new sources of revenue or to scale back expenditures lest the organization find itself in a deep financial hole from which it cannot easily dig itself out.

Unfortunately, organizations often look for cost-cutting measures only after experiencing (in the case of a business) a sharp fall-off in profits, or (in the case of a nonprofit) a looming budget deficit. Such hasty measures are born of an urge to slash expenses and shore up the bottom line or balance the budget as quickly as possible. This can be a costly mistake, for how one goes about curtailing expenditure growth will have a powerful effect on the future character and strength of the enterprise.

Cutting costs in a time of contraction demands as much strategic thinking and careful implementation as the building of new programs in a time of expansion. Examining the "value added" of each activity in an organization, relative to the costs of implementing the activity, is a method of systematically establishing the positive or negative value of each activity in an organization.

The test of an activity's value is whether the organization would be hurt in its ability to carry out its mission effectively—especially relative to other organizations in the same field—and whether its long-term financial strength would be undermined if an activity or function were eliminated. If the answer is no, the decision to eliminate the function is easy. If the function does contribute significantly to the programmatic or financial strength of the organization, then one needs to determine whether its value is worth its cost. For instance, if the budget is in the red, can one eliminate or reduce in size the department that evaluates whether programs achieve their aims? Is it possible to cut back the staff that supports volunteers or creates programs for alumni without hurting the organization's fundraising?

As a rule, the tasks with the least value added should be the first to be scaled back or eliminated. The idea is to anchor a cost-reduction program in the curtailment of the lowest-value-added work, and then to cut staff to reflect the reduced work load, rather than first eliminating people and leaving the surviving staff members to figure out how to get the work done. The evaluation of the value added of activities is a process that I have applied in both a complex for-profit business and a nonprofit institution, and it works equally well in both environments.

Traditional accounting systems break down expenses by category: salaries, fringe benefits, supplies, and fixed costs. In contrast, activity-based accounting views an organization as groups of individuals performing a wide variety of specific activities. Under this system, costs are allocated to what the entity pays for the different tasks its employees perform to produce the product. This process can also be used to identify opportunities for outsourcing functions, or to pinpoint functions that can be redesigned for increased productivity.

In the case of service organizations, where personnel costs make up the bulk of expenditures, activity-based cost reduction is likely to be a much more productive approach than simply slashing the costs of various units. Any extensive cost-containment program within such organizations invariably means reducing staff size. Cutting people from a payroll is very different from curtailing capital outlays, reducing inventories, or slashing advertising and promotion budgets.

The turmoil associated with layoffs harms the survivors of the enterprise as well as the people who lose their jobs. Managers will resist such staff cuts if they perceive that the reductions will undermine their ability to get the job done. Unless specific tasks are eliminated first, cutting personnel will leave a unit facing the same work load with a smaller staff, an unappealing prospect for any manager.

Activity-Based Cost Reduction At Work

Let's start with a hypothetical example to illustrate how activity-based cost reduction can work. Assume an organization whose mission is to raise funds from the community and from government sources on behalf of a variety of social agencies that would not be effective at raising funds if they sought support independently. In our assumed case, the umbrella agency is anticipating a substantial reduction in government funds and has decided to reduce its administrative expenses before cutting funding to its affiliated agencies. Rather than simply announcing an across-the-board cut in the expenses of all departments, it begins to examine the functions performed by its staff. It has a half-dozen program officers and an equal number of assistant program officers. The organization asks each program officer and assistant program officer to describe his or her activities.

The assistant program officers supply the information shown in Table 6.1.

Table 6.1. Activities of Assistant Program Officers in Hypothetical Organization

Task	End Product	Intended Use	% of Total Time Devoted to Task	Cost of Task	Value Added
Compare grantee's actual use of funds with budget categories approved by agency	Disbursement compliance report	Review by program officers and auditors	75%	75% of salary and benefits = $50,000; plus out-of-pocket expenses ($10,000) = Total cost $60,000	Program officers do not make use of reports

The conclusion that can be drawn from this information is that the preparation of grantee disbursement compliance reports is an activity whose scope could be reduced considerably. Instead of each assistant program officer preparing a regular report on all grantees in his or her portfolio, reports could be prepared on grantees selected at random, and the compliance function could continue to be overseen by the auditing staff. By reducing the scope of this function, the agency will be able to eliminate half of the assistant program officers and will save $150,000 in salaries and benefits, plus an estimated $30,000 in out-of-pocket expenses associated with the disbursement compliance report. In addition, the staff reduction will permit the elimination of one secretarial position and will save on space costs. The ultimate savings, on the order of $200,000, will not impair the effectiveness of the agency's program.

A detailed examination of the program officers' activities shows that they spend much of their time reading applications for assistance and writing recommendations for funding approval by the agency board of directors. In fact, the bulk of the agency's funding consists of repeat grants to prior recipients. Few new agencies are funded. Analysis reveals that use of a standard form application and standard form funding request for agencies who have been previously funded would save a substantial amount of time—enough to free up the equivalent of three-quarters of a program officer's time. As a result, one program officer is assigned to work part-time with the agency's shorthanded post-grant evaluation staff.

The reader is likely to protest that real life is not as simple and straightforward as the hypothetical example makes it seem, and that is true; but hopefully it points up a process of analysis that can be applied to a real world set of facts.

Three Principles of Cost Reduction

Any cost-reduction program must address how the organization is going to maintain the quality of its products or services once expenditures and staff are reduced. Often, top managers simply give up on identifying specific reductions and dictate that each of their subordinates reduce expenditures—meaning any form of expenditure—by a certain percentage or dollar amount. This "blunt instrument" approach fails to meet three principles that should be inherent in any sound cost-reduction program:

1. The cost-reduction program should serve as a method of restructuring and strengthening the enterprise competitively; at a minimum, it should avoid damaging the organization strategically over the long term.
2. The savings identified should be realizable and sustainable over time.
3. The savings should be sufficient to achieve its financial objective, so that everyone is not soon forced to try to cut expenses even further.

Cost reductions need to be made in accordance with a plan for reshaping the enterprise to make it more competitive. Otherwise, cutting expenditures may produce a temporarily balanced budget at the expense of long-term ability to deliver quality services. A long-term perspective is thus as important in reducing expenditures as it is in making outlays for new endeavors. Both are resource investment decisions.

Before scaling back the budget of an organization that is on shaky ground, one needs to give careful thought to the feasibility of reassembling the scarcest resource—talented people who work well together. It may prove wise to underwrite a part of the organization during the down cycle, even at the expense of short-term budget deficits, especially if the employees involved are versatile and, given time and training, may be able to adapt their talents to new work within the organization.

In activity-based cost-reduction analysis, here is what each unit or department is asked to do:

◆ Identify objectives in order to establish a set of priorities against which to evaluate its activities, staffing levels, and expenditures.

◆ Break down its staffing and expenditures according to the specific tasks performed by the unit, and then evaluate the importance of such tasks to achievement of the unit's short-term goals. This comparison of the cost of a task to its value is what determines the task's "value added."

◆ Consider the potential impact of various possible levels of resource availability on the nature and amount of work the unit can perform. This involves detailing what tasks would be curtailed or eliminated if expenditures were reduced by various amounts (e.g., 5 percent, 10 percent) and the consequences of such cuts.

The activity-focused formulation asks management to prioritize its cost reductions in the same manner as it would rank potential areas of expansion—by relating the work currently being performed in an enterprise to the organization's primary objectives. The impact of proposed reductions on strategic priorities can then be assessed and actions taken that are consistent with these aims.

Activity-based cost reduction can lead to expenditure reductions in several ways. Functions that are identified as relatively "low added value" will ultimately translate into the elimination of positions and, generally, related cash and expenditure savings. For instance, when the aggregate of tasks performed by a specific position represents a relatively low overall level of value added, the position becomes a candidate for elimination if expenditures must be cut. The incumbent, if a valuable employee, may be transferred to another position if one is vacant; otherwise, the incumbent must be terminated. When a position is a mixture of low-value and high-value functions, it becomes a candidate for consolidation with another similarly rated position. When this happens, one of the two incumbent employees must be transferred to another post, or terminated.

One of the fruits of activity-based cost reduction is the identification of organizational redundancy—areas of duplicated effort that develop when management fails to define unit responsibilities clearly, or when one unit fails to perform competently, leading others to build their own duplicate systems to fill in the gap. This kind of redundancy is one of the principal sources of organizational fat.

Activity-based cost reduction can also help to identify excess layers of management. For example, in some organizations there is an additional layer of review between frontline executives and senior management. This layer of management collects and repackages information and then transmits it to a higher level. The value of this additional review (or "coordination," in organizational jargon) is questionable in many instances and bears close scrutiny in terms of value added.

Activity-based cost-reduction analysis can also help establish the appropriate range of executive "span of control." The conventional theory is that an executive can only adequately supervise five or six people reporting directly to him or her. Today this concept is being rethought as organizations consider whether staffing subordinate functions with more talented individuals, who are given clear responsibility and authority, will reduce the extent of executive oversight required of subordinates, thus enabling senior officers to exercise control over much larger numbers of staff members.

As Peter Drucker has observed, span of control should be thought of as "span of communication, with control turning out to be the ability to obtain information." This, in turn, means the number of people reporting to a single supervisor is limited only by the subordinates' willingness to take responsibility for their own communication and relationships. Activity-based cost-reduction analysis can help determine whether supervisors are exercising the broadest feasible range of oversight or whether an organization is plagued with too many executives exercising too narrow a span of oversight.

The efficiency of an organization's managerial structure should, of course, be evaluated whether or not the organization is facing the need to cut expenditures. Activity-based cost-reduction analysis serves to illuminate whether an organization is using its staff in the most efficient and effective manner. It also allows an assessment of whether resources are being assigned to the enterprise's highest priorities. Rigorous application of the process can, therefore, avoid the need for more painful cost-reduction programs forced by a suddenly ballooning deficit. Activity-based cost analysis is also an effective way to identify opportunities for outsourcing functions (those with the least added value) and to pinpoint functions that need to be redesigned for increased productivity.

A Managerial Safeguard

Activity-based cost-reduction analysis can also serve as a managerial safeguard against the development of unnecessary expenditures; it can help organizations avoid excessive buildup of staff in good times. At the same time, when cost reductions are needed in order to restore equilibrium, the analysis is the most effective way to pinpoint reductions in the areas of least priority to the organizations. The following specific examples show how activity-based cost-reduction analysis can identify work that can be eliminated without harming the enterprise.

A university established an extensive system for allocating maintenance and office repair costs to business units on the basis of the number of hours and level of skills actually used by particular business units. It kept extensive records of the types of personnel called on to provide service to each department, and of the frequency and length of the service calls. Then it charged each department's budget for the "actual" cost of the services utilized. This careful system for allocating costs does provide a detailed accounting to departments that object to their maintenance bills, but it does not improve the efficiency or quality of maintenance services and the entire system requires elaborate record keeping by clerical staff. By switching to a system of billing departments on the basis of a predetermined cost-allocation formula, the university can save several hundred thousand dollars a year without in any way affecting the quality of its maintenance.

Other examples of expenditures where the value to the enterprise does not justify the costs of the operation include the following:

- ◆ An internal auditing staff whose size and cost substantially exceed the savings the group is able to identify and whose control functions duplicate the work of the firm's outside auditors;
- ◆ A weekly financial report that requires the effort of several full-time staff members to prepare but that is rarely used by executives; and
- ◆ An item-by-item review of expense accounts by an expense control unit. Testing such reports against formulas requires fewer personnel to perform and is just as effective in keeping expenses within acceptable limits.

In some cases, looking for the value added of the individual tasks actually performed by staff will turn up situations in which personnel are engaged in activities that have outlived their original purpose or that are simply a waste of time. For instance, one organization maintained duplicate systems of financial reports, even though the older system was no longer of value. No one had told the central accounting office that their reports were no longer being utilized by management.

In another case, the central accounting office and operating units did not utilize the same methodology for measuring expenditures and revenues. Thus, they issued reports with conflicting results that, in turn, took additional management time (often at quite senior levels) to reconcile.

Paradoxically, in some cases, activity-based cost reduction may point out areas in which increased internal expenses may actually save the organization money. One entity maintained a very small legal staff, for example, because it felt it was easy to justify the legal fees incurred by outside counsel. In fact, much of the legal work done outside was of a recurring nature and could have been done by competent attorneys in-house at a lower net cost. By adding several attorneys to the in-house staff, the organization was able to save substantial legal fees.

Implementing Reductions

Reducing expenses through activity-based cost-reduction analysis and cutting expenditures through attrition each have their drawbacks. Identifying low-value-added positions as candidates for elimination enables an organization to reduce staff in a manner that is strategic, cutting back in lowest-priority areas. But it is likely to result in more discharges of incumbent personnel than if expenditures are reduced through attrition caused by voluntary departures or retirements. On the other hand, attrition produces openings on a random basis and without regard for strategic priorities. For this reason, attrition may prove to be a more expensive means of cutting staff.

In any case, in order to make significant reductions through attrition—in a manner that does not impair the enterprise—the organization must be able to redeploy personnel and funds to the highest-priority tasks. Whether it is a secretary or a senior executive who chooses to leave, that person may be performing an indispensable function. If that is the case, the organization is faced with one of two choices: It must (1) hire a replacement, in which case there is no savings (and, in fact, the recruitment procedure will cost the organization additional money); or (2) reassign an existing employee to take over the work of the ex-employee. This step demands tight management control at the senior level to overcome any resistance to such redeployment, especially if an employee is transferred across organizational lines. It also requires a flexible and adaptable work force. This, in turn, means designing a staff development system that trains and encourages people to become skilled in a broad range of the organization's operations.

While the process is going on, activity-based cost reduction creates uncertainty for personnel. This uncertainty may hurt morale and may encourage key people to seek jobs elsewhere. Setting a timetable for the changes and briefing key personnel about the timetable as well as their importance to the organization can mitigate some drawbacks.

Just as important, the cost-containment plan—and the reasons behind it—must be carefully explained to the executives charged with carrying it out; indeed, these executives should "own" the plan by participating in its formulation. Without their support, managerial resistance may undermine cost reductions.

In addition, a careful review of the organization's termination policy should precede the process. A sensitive termination plan not only is fair to those who are asked to leave, it also has a positive effect on those who continue working.

An alternate approach is to freeze current salaries. This strategy lowers the increase in base expenditures and slows the growth of costs. It is also a savings that is clearly capturable and has the appeal of equity. Unfortunately, its impact is hard to calculate. It often does not address the root cause of expense increases. It affects the morale of outstanding employees and those who need an increase to make ends meet. As tempting as a salary freeze may seem, it also has many drawbacks.

It is in the organization's self-interest to be considered thoughtful and fair if a downsizing is deemed necessary. A well-planned downsizing can be critical to the success of the organization and will certain minimize damage and pain to affected employees.

Perhaps most important, the process of expenditure containment must be continuous. Expenses eliminated from the budget during a period of financial stringency tend to creep back as soon as the budgetary heat is off and top management's attention is turned elsewhere. As a precaution, all functions should be reviewed on a rotating basis every three to five years to reassess their ongoing value added to the enterprise. As an organization evolves, certain functions may lose their relative importance, or the organization's financial situation may demand a more rigorous assessment of value added.

Ideally, of course, an organization should avoid hiring unnecessary personnel in the first place. Regrettably, most organizations loosen the reins when revenues are growing and start adding personnel without close scrutiny of the value they add to the enterprise, or consideration of whether the enterprise will be able to afford them in a downturn.

A policy of expanding staff only if the value added is clear can produce an organization that benefits from the cohesion of a stable staff, secure in its sense of the organization's commitment to it and, in turn, sincerely committed to the organization's progress.

Making Reductions Stick

The same activity-based cost-reduction process serves both for-profit and non-profit enterprises. In both forms of organization, there is generally little enthusiasm on the part of most managers for controlling or reducing expenses; cost cutting is not a process most managers find satisfying, even in a profit-making organization, where reducing expenses should increase profitability and presumably the baseline for managerial bonuses. I have found that managers reflexively regard cutting their staff as making them more vulnerable. Moreover, despite the fanfare attached to the initiation of the process by the CEO, if, once specific proposals for cuts have been made to him or her, no one comes around to see whether the proposed actions are taken or to tie the unit executive's incentive compensation to the accomplishment of the proffered savings, the whole process will come to naught. As revenues rise again, everyone forgets about eliminating activities that generate little or no added value.

Accordingly, regardless of the process adopted for cutting expenditures, certain principles must be followed if cost reduction is to be effective:

- ◆ The organization's top executive must establish a specific dollar level of reduction.
- ◆ A system must be established to monitor whether promised cost-saving actions are in fact taken.
- ◆ Because an organization will invariably capture fewer than all promised expense reductions, the target established for savings must be higher than necessary to achieve the desired financial goal.
- ◆ Organizational unit heads must be held accountable by the CEO for achieving the savings target established for their unit.
- ◆ Future proposals to add to expenditures must be separately flagged in the unit's budget submission and must be subject to the value-added test that was applied during the cost-reduction process. The object is to avoid "expense creep," whereby the expenditure level set during a period of financial stringency is unknowingly allowed to creep back to pre-reduction or even

higher levels. The idea is to put the executive spotlight on any proposed increases from the baseline of expenditures produced as a result of the cost-reduction program.

This discussion of activity-based cost reduction covers the basic ways in which an organization can be restructured and retain its independent status. The next chapter talks about mergers—converting the organization into a different entity.

CHAPTER 7

The Merger Option

Mergers and acquisitions—M&A, as they are often called—are commonly thought to be the exclusive province of businesses and investment banks.[1] In comparison with the pace of mergers and acquisitions in business, it is rare for two or more enterprises in the nonprofit world to be consolidated. However, nonprofit mergers have been pulled off successfully.

In the late 1960's, the all-girls preparatory school Rosemary Hall, located in Greenwich, Connecticut, and the all-boys prep school Choate, about an hour away in Wallingford, Connecticut, were threatened by the trend toward coeducation. Standing alone, each of the two schools might have failed in this new environment. But in 1971 the schools merged, and today, situated on a single campus in Wallingford, Choate–Rosemary Hall thrives with strong support from the alumni (including those who graduated prior to the merger), a deep, high-quality applicant pool, and a healthy endowment.

The Choate–Rosemary Hall merger overcame the formidable obstacles of physically separate campuses, separate faculties, separate administrations, and intense alumni loyalties to the separate institutions. The merger also had to overcome the fear of some male alumni that women were a threat to male values and bonding.

The Rosemary Hall campus in Greenwich was sold to another school, and a separate set of three dormitories was constructed for women above Choate's

73

existing dorms. In 1971, Rosemary Hall students moved onto the Choate campus, attending the same classes as the male students but retaining their own administration in addition to their separate dorms. This was very much an evolutionary approach to merging the institutions. But today, Choate–Rosemary Hall is clearly *one* school, physically and administratively integrated. Walking around the place and visiting with its students, faculty members, and administrators, one would never know that, once, two independent schools existed.

Putting together the two schools was no simple feat. This is hardly surprising when one recalls the controversy that attended efforts by universities such as Tulane and Columbia, years later, to merge already-affiliated women's collegs into the university, long after women students had attended the same classes as men. Graduates from earlier years objected vigorously to these mergers. But Choate and Rosemary did emerge as a single effective institution. This example of a successful merger of two nonprofits shows that a well-planned and well-implemented consolidation is a valid option for nonprofits. Nonprofit organizations might combine for one of the following reasons:

- ◆ To consolidate their fundraising programs and to gain efficiencies in administration, or to broaden their joint appeal beyond the reach of either individual enterprise. The goal would be to increase the net take from fundraising through cost reduction or increasing revenue.

- ◆ To bring together two organizations operating in the same market, where the market is not large enough to support both institutions (e.g., two hospitals serve the same community), or to avoid duplication of services (e.g., both hospitals build expensive oncology services).[2]

- ◆ To expand the resulting organization vertically in order to capture revenues in an allied market by broadening its customer base (e.g., a hospital acquires a nursing home or a health maintenance organization).

- ◆ To combine the publicly recognized reputation of one nonprofit with revenue-generating capabilities of a less well known organization (e.g., a television production company with a powerful brand name in the children's market but no computer product combines with a computer software company that has outstanding software programmers but little brand recognition).

- ◆ To enable a small organization that is struggling to raise enough funds to support its program, to merge with a larger, more financially stable organization. The two organizations have complementary programs, but the smaller entity operates in a market where the larger enterprise is not present. The larger organization wants a presence in this market, and its entry is eased by capitalizing on the smaller organization's contacts and relationships. In exchange, the larger organization can raise for the smaller entity's programs additional grant funds that the latter lacks the managerial depth to acquire.

◆ To expand an organization's field of service by acquiring the staff, programs, and funding relationships of an organization in an allied field with the expectation that the insight gained from participation in related activities will enhance the quality of performance of both entities. In effect, their merger will produce a synergy in the programming area (e.g., an organization dedicated to assisting troubled adolescent women combines with an organization serving troubled adolescent men).

Most of the models above represent instances where the act of combining has a potential direct financial benefit. In the last example, there is a reference to the need to achieve a "synergy" in order to gain benefits from a merger. The idea behind the concept of synergy is that the personnel of the merging organizations learn skills from one another and are able to perform in more effective ways than they did acting independently prior to the merger. Based on my personal experience and my studies of for-profit mergers, I am skeptical that such synergy can be achieved in most cases. For example, the Prudential Life Insurance Company is a full-service insurance company that also offers institutions and individuals an array of financial services. In the 1980s, it acquired an old-line Wall Street brokerage firm which, following the acquisition, was named Prudential Bache. One of the hoped-for benefits of the acquisition was that the insurance agents of Prudential and the brokers of Prudential Bache could cross-sell brokerage and insurance products. In fact, however, insurance agents and brokers are motivated by quite different factors, and their training and experience do not equip them to cross-sell each other's products. This and other synergies hoped for from the merger did not materialize.

The Prudential experience of not realizing hoped-for synergies in an acquisition is more common than most businesses that engage in mergers and acquisitions will admit. In addition, there is evidence in the for-profit world that the general expectation that mergers lead to greater profits for the merged enterprise has often not been realized.[3] Thus, prospective mergers require cautious, realistic evaluation and careful due diligence.

If a merger of two nonprofit organizations is to work, a number of things have to be done well:

◆ Both organizations must think through in advance the strategic, financial, and managerial costs and benefits and must have a clear idea of how the combined entity is going to perform more effectively and efficiently than the separate enterprises.

◆ The management structure of the combined enterprises must be resolved quickly, diligently, and decisively. Peoples' minds will not be on business while they are waiting to see what job they get or whether they will have a job at all in the combined enterprise. Power struggles, as factions and individuals contest for positions, are counterproductive.

◆ Both parties must have a good sense, before they merge, of the differences in their respective organizational cultures, whether the two staffs can co-exist, and, if so, how to blend them. Unless the cultures are blended, it is unlikely that the two organizations will operate effectively as one enterprise.

◆ The new senior management must move quickly to meld the two companies at every level, including operations, management, and culture. Unless the combining of the two organizations is done rapidly, not only will performance be undermined during the delay, but employees who feel their interests threatened by the merger may solidify practices that undermine the bringing about of an effective consolidation.

One of the frequent barriers to blending two management teams is figuring out the pecking order of officials in the new entity. Here, a small team of board members from both organizations may be helpful in resolving conflicts, or an outside management consulting firm can be brought in to provide advice. It is best to determine the composition of the board and the CEO of the new enterprise prior to the merger.

Since a nonprofit is not a stock company, it has no shares to exchange in a merger. (This also means that there can not be an unfriendly takeover of a nonprofit through the acquisition of publicly traded shares.) To effect a merger, the trustees of both organizations have to agree to it, and they have to obtain the approval of the state attorney general (the government office involved in general supervision of charities). It is also prudent to contact the IRS in order to ensure that there are no objections from a federal tax standpoint and that the merged organization, as a new legal entity, will receive the same 501(c)(3) tax status as the predecessor organizations did.

NOTES

1. A "merger" implies combining two equals, whereas an "acquisition" refers to a stronger organization's taking over a weaker enterprise. In most mergers and acquisitions, one party is dominant and calls the shots. Often an "acquisition" is announced as a "merger" in order to save face with customers, employees, and others.

2. The fact that merging organizations are nonprofits does not necessarily give them immunity from antitrust laws. Colleges and universities that shared information on prospective tuition rates and financial aid packages were held to run afoul of the antitrust laws' prohibition of price fixing, notwithstanding their status as 501(c)(3) organizations. However, two enterprises in the same market may merge where other, more powerful entities also exist, so that the merger does not produce market dominance.

3. "The Case against Mergers," *Business Week,* October 30, 1995, pp. 122–130.

CHAPTER 8

Performance Management

Performance is the ultimate test of an organization's value.
Frances Hesselbein Executive Director, Peter F. Drucker Foundation[1]

One of the most urgent issues facing charitable organizations is developing more effective managerial processes for ensuring that organizations maximize their effectiveness and efficiency. The typical brochure or report of a nonprofit organization is filled with descriptions of the programs the organization has implemented and its plans for the future. Little comment, however, is offered on how effective its programs have been. Furthermore, many funders of nonprofits fail to examine the level of management control over performance exercised by their grantees. This is not so much an oversight by nonprofit leaders as a perception on their part that there are few reliable means of measuring programs in objective terms. Nevertheless, assessing the results achieved—and at what cost they were achieved—is essential to the effective management of nonprofit enterprises.

The goal of this chapter is to persuade readers of three basic notions:

◆ *There are processes that can be adapted from the "best practices" of business as well as the work of nonprofits for improving the effectiveness and efficiency of an organization and its programs.*

◆ *Establishing verifiable performance objectives and accounting for the degree to which they are achieved is feasible and also essential to gaining public and financial support.*

◆ *Grantmaking organizations' review of grantees' management practices is both in the best interests of the grantees and a fiduciary obligation of the grantor.*

If the nonprofit sector is to enhance its credibility, documenting the quality of program performance must become a central focus of the sector in the years ahead. Appeals for greater contributions are likely to get a better reception if a nonprofit can demonstrate to potential contributors that their support will produce tangible results. With a vast number of organizations seeking tax-deductible contributions, a powerful means of distinguishing an organization is to demonstrate the effectiveness and efficiency with which it performs its mission.

The Absence of a Bottom Line

In developing a managerial system for maximizing the effectiveness and efficiency of a program or programs, nonprofits do not have the benefit of a profit measure to apply as a litmus test of how well their enterprise is run. In the case of a business, the level of profit earned and its relationship to capital invested or assets owned provide a ready means of quantifying how well managed the business is. More than a decade ago, Anthony and Herzlinger, two Harvard Business School professors, pointed up the dilemma created for nonprofits by the absence of profit yardstick:

> The absence of a satisfactory, single measure of performance that is comparable to the profit measure is the most serious management control problem in a nonprofit organization. (It is incorrect to say that the absence of the profit *motive* is the central problem; rather it is the absence of the profit *measure*.)[2]

The two professors do not mean to suggest that management control cannot be achieved in a nonprofit organization; in fact they argue quite the opposite. Their thesis is that, since nonprofits lack the criterion of profitability, they need an effective system of control even more than a business does. They spend most of their 591-page book explaining how to construct such a system. In a more recent book, Herzlinger, joined in 1994[3] by Denise Nitterhouse of DePaul University, focuses on the same topic and expresses the same viewpoint. For readers who want to delve into all the nuances of management control in a nonprofit organization, both of these volumes make excellent reading.

This text strives to demonstrate to managers and trustees of nonprofit organizations that they can control the quality and cost of their operations and ought to do so in their own interest. Here I present, in a modified form, a model of oversight from a process I worked with in business. But each nonprofit will want to design the precise system that serves it best in light of its financial and staff resources.

Performance Management Defined

The term *performance management* describes the set of processes for controlling the quality and cost with which programs are delivered. The essence of performance management has a number of elements:

◆ Identifying up front, in the *preprogramming phase,* in measurable form, the *objectives* an organization intends to achieve, or, where objectives cannot be quantified, identifying the specific *tasks* to be accomplished;

◆ Establishing a *budget* for achieving these objectives and tasks, and an *action plan* that enumerates the steps that have to be taken by each unit within the organization, including a timetable for accomplishing these steps;

◆ Tracking actual progress in implementing programs against the *action plan* and the *budget* adopted at the outset; and

◆ Comparing actual costs, timetable, and results with those set forth at the outset, and, whenever possible, with similar programs mounted by other organizations.

Why Performance Management?

Performance management provides a reasonably objective basis for assessing how well an organization is accomplishing the mission it has defined for itself. Equally important, it also provides a clear sense of direction to the staff as to exactly what is to be done, when.

When I joined Prudential's real estate investment group, it was largely an opportunistic, transaction-driven enterprise. When an attractive opportunity to acquire or develop a property came along, and the deal structure was appealing, the property was snatched up; similarly, if the group received a very attractive offer to buy a property, it was considered, especially if at the moment Prudential needed cash to pay an investor or to invest elsewhere. The strategy worked for years as Prudential was the first major insurance company to undertake large-scale investment in real estate and seek pension funds to co-invest with it, and for a time Prudential was the unchallenged leader in the field. However, as other aggressive players entered the field and the competition for good properties and clients intensified, Prudential began to lose its leadership position.

At that point, the organization was restructured to pursue a set of specific objectives for the group as a whole. In turn, the units in the organization—which heretofore had largely pursued their own agendas—each negotiated with management a set of measurable objectives and supporting action steps. This process, aside from setting a basis for bonuses, established a blueprint of the actions each unit was charged with undertaking and of what it was expected to accomplish, and when. In a complex organization with more than 1,000 people working in various locations across the country and with a wide range of skills and function, setting specific, measurable objectives and the requisite action steps provided a sense of coherent direction to the organization as a whole. The process was an effective tool in getting everybody to support a common set of purposes and to work in concert to achieve those ends. Under this new approach, "the deal" was no longer paramount; transactions had to fit within the strategies established for each investment fund so that strategy, not deals, became the organization's driving force. As one of my colleagues said, "When you get out of bed in the morning, you don't have any doubt about what you have to do during the day or where you are trying to get to."

The system also provided an effective means for Prudential's top management to track the progress of the organization through the year, and to focus on a unit that might be lagging behind in order to find out why it was lagging and what could be done to speed up progress.

Performance management is also helpful in allocating resources among competing programs. For example, when management is evaluating a request to divert staff members from one program to another, it can get a rough sense of the transfer's impact, positive or negative, on each unit's ability to achieve its measurable objectives. Performance management is not a precise science, but it does equip management with working tools other than pure intuition.

Performance management lies at the heart of the responsibility of officers and trustees of nonprofit organizations. As fiduciaries, they have an obligation to assess the effectiveness of their programs and their organization as a whole and to identify what works and what does not. This is an obligation that the public, the Internal Revenue Service, and federal and state legislatures (which grant tax exemptions to qualified nonprofits), as well as state attorneys general (who have the authority to supervise charities), are likely to become increasingly insistent on. Demands for more stringent oversight may be triggered by a high-profile scandal in which funds of an organization are flagrantly used for improper purposes, or by pressure put on legislatures by businesses that resent increasing competition from nonprofit organizations, or by an aggressive public official who senses the vulnerability of nonprofits. In any event, it would be a costly error in judgment to doubt that nonprofits will become subject to more outside scrutiny and that they will be on the defensive if they cannot document the effectiveness and efficiency of their efforts.

Credible performance management by nonprofits is also essential to rebutting the typical public impression, especially among business executives, that such enterprises are "soft" and poorly run and that money invested in them does not result in concrete accomplishments. One indication that donors are placing increased emphasis on demonstrable quality performance and results is the rise of restricted giving to higher education. While the dollar value of unrestricted gifts to higher education have remained flat over time, gifts that involve restrictions on their use have more than doubled in size. (See the survey for years 1975–1990 of 290 four-year institutions by the Council for Aid to Education.)[4]

Documenting the quality of program performance must become a central focus of the nonprofit sector in the years ahead if the sector is to enhance its credibility.

Measuring Performance

Of course, not every activity can be measured in quantitative terms. This is also true in business. The point is to measure in objective terms what can be quantified and to obtain qualitative information about other tasks. For instance, an organization may have the goal of improving the lives of young women who grow up in poverty. This goal is a compelling one but it does not lend itself to quantification. However, when the broad goal is broken down into specific objectives, as it must be to create concrete programs, those specific objectives can be quantified. For instance, one objective might be to reduce by a specified percentage the rate of pregnancy among teenage women who participate in the organization's program in a target community, relative to the rate of pregnancy among teenagers who do not join. The extent to which this specific objective is accomplished and the cost of doing so can be calculated and compared to the cost to society of dealing with teenagers who give birth. This comparative cost analysis can be factored into an overall evaluation of the program's effectiveness and efficiency. (Note, however, the caution in the next section about the difficulty of linking causes and effects.)

An organization's performance can also be compared with the performance of organizations that undertake similar tasks and are considered to employ the "best practices" in the field. In business, it is taken for granted that leadership over one's competitors in a given field is the name of the game. Leadership and the reputation that go with it are important in the nonprofit sector as well. The sector is engaged in competition—for funding, for talent, for community support. How an organization performs relative to its "competitors" is therefore relevant. The competition among colleges and universities has long been an acknowledged fact. *U.S. News & World Report*'s annual best colleges survey and *Business Week*'s annual survey of the "best" business schools have capitalized on this reality, and these magazines' rankings of schools have an impact on the market. Other types of nonprofits must deal with the same reality.

Moreover, competitive considerations aside, one of the most effective ways to improve performance is to understand how others who are thought to be outstanding performers accomplish their goals. By comparing the degree to which specific measurable objectives are achieved, and the costs associated with achieving them, one can assess the degree to which another organization is more successful and/or cost-efficient in achieving its objectives. Moreover, the most important aspect of the comparison is not the comparison of numbers; rather, it is the inquiry into what specific actions of the other organization account for its superior performance.

Identifying the Best Practices

How does one identify organizations with the best practices in certain areas? First of all, the term "best practices" is a bit of a hyperbole, and one shouldn't get trapped by it. What one is really after is an organization from which one can learn how to improve one or more of one's own group's systems. No one, even in the quantified world of business, can say with certainty which company is the best at a particular function. But some companies enjoy a reputation among knowledgeable people as being outstanding at one or more aspects of their business, and their bottom line will very likely show an enviable profitability. Therefore, one need not therefore get caught up in an elusive search for the "best" model as long as the focus is, as it should be, on improving a particular function or functions of one's organization. As Boxwell observes in his book on benchmarking, "The most important criterion in selecting targets is to choose those from which you will be able to learn, learn, learn."[5] For these reasons, I prefer to think in terms of "advanced management practices" rather than "best practices."

Spending some time on library or on-line research and holding discussions with staff members, board members, grantmakers, and people in the organization's field should easily uncover an organization or organizations from which a nonprofit can learn. This organization may be either a nonprofit or a for-profit enterprise.

For example, if you want to learn how incentive compensation tied to performance objectives operates in a nonprofit environment, visit the Local Initiatives Support Corporation, which employs such a system; if you want to see how in-staff training can be provided by a combination of business school faculty members and the organization's own executives, talk to the UJA-Federation of New York; if you want to understand how a needs analysis and cost-benefit analysis—or other forms of evaluation of a social program—can be done, visit Girls, Inc.; and if you are interested in how an organization adheres to its strategic niche over a period of years while growing its enterprise, talk to the management of Children's Television Workshop.

Many other nonprofit organizations have devoted resources and considerable effort to developing managerial practices worthy of replication. It would be an important contribution to the management of the nonprofit sector if an institution were chosen and funded to establish a data base of organizations with advanced management techniques that could be accessed by any exempt organization at a reasonable fee. In the business world, the availability of collections of such data is an asset that firms market. Price Waterhouse advertises that "best practices is one of the surest way[s] to improve overall performance" and that its "Knowledge View" data base, "in the hands of a skilled Price Waterhouse advisor," can enable firms to "see what and how other companies are doing better and more successfully." Big Six accounting and consulting rival Arthur Andersen advertises that "using [its] proprietary Global Best Practices knowledge base . . . will offer insights into how the world's finest companies have managed change."

The time, it would seem, is ripe for a clearinghouse of advanced management practices to be established for the benefit of the nonprofit world.

Factors that Can't Be Quantified Still Count

The structured form of performance management does not preclude other considerations from being taken into account. The level of local and national interest in the program is relevant, especially as it relates to the availability of funding. So is the value participants and the community attach to the program. Indeed, feedback from the target consumer is as critical in any assessment of a nonprofit organization's performance as it is to any evaluation of a business. Listening carefully to consumers may open up new, more effective ways of providing the service, or it may spot mistakes that if allowed to accumulate over time, will undermine the program (e.g., boys in the community won't date girls in the pregnancy prevention program, which, in turn, causes participation by the girls to decline). Analysis of customer feedback may also reveal whether participants' responses are distorted by the very fact of participation in the program (e.g., participants respond differently because they know they are being watched).

The Availability of Comparative Data and Analysis

Of course, one of the handicaps nonprofits often face in assessing performance is the absence in the sector of the equivalent of industry-wide performance data as well as widely applicable financial performance yardsticks. In business, at least in the case of companies whose stock is publicly traded, there is a wealth of information available about companies in any given line of business: reports that must be filed with various government agencies; analyses of companies and their industry by the thousands of Wall Street security analysts who follow American business; and reports in trade journals and general business magazines. But perhaps the most valuable information for evaluating one's own company comes not from published sources but from talking to people who know the business and the company's competitors—customers, bankers, attorneys, accountants, consultants, suppliers, distributors, sales reps, and former employees of competitors. While some of these sources operate under the restriction of confidentiality with respect to a particular client, they can provide useful information about industry practices. Indeed, it is increasingly common today for one company's researchers to call on another company—which may or may not be a competitor—that is known for its skill in a given area, in order to learn what accounts for that company's outstanding performance.[6]

Following are some sources of information about nonprofits and how they operate:

- Form 990, which the IRS requires every nonprofit to file annually, contains a wealth of financial, payroll, and program data and is open to public inspection. Despite its flaws, the form enables any nonprofit to learn a good deal about other organizations, including those with whom it sees itself in direct competition: for example, information about the funds raised for programs, the expenses incurred, the salaries of top officials, and the "outputs" or "products" of major programs. (See *The 123 of Evaluation: An Introduction to Three Basic Tools*, published by the National Charities Information Bureau.)[7] The IRS also maintains two data bases, the Exempt Organizations/Business Master File and the files maintained by the Statistics of Income Division of the IRS. (For some of the ways in which these two data bases can be utilized, as well as the flaws in Form 990, see *The Charitable Nonprofits*, by Bowen, Nygren, Turner, and Duffy.)[8]

- The amount of research published about nonprofits is steadily increasing, especially as university researchers take an interest in the field. Careful literature and on-line searches can uncover this information.

- Professionals who service nonprofits, such as lawyers, accountants, consultants, former employees, academic commentators, and trustees, can provide valuable insights.

- Recipients of services provided by one's own organization can be interviewed, and their answers compared with those of recipients of services provided by other similar organizations.

- Field visits can be conducted to other organizations renowned for their outstanding practices. The Massachusetts Institute of Technology study on industrial productivity, cited in an earlier chapter, noted that a "characteristic of all the best-practice American firms, large or small, is an emphasis on competitive benchmarking; comparing the performance of their products and work processes with those of the world leaders in order to achieve improvement and to measure progress."[9] Boxwell sees field comparisons as the key to benchmarking in business,[10] and Porter sees them as key to analyzing an industry and one's competitors.[11]

Limited Resources for Management Oversight

One obstacle to assessments of performance effectiveness and efficiency is the scarcity of resources that many exempt organizations face along with their need to husband their funds for the support of programs. The real world of many nonprofits involves such a struggle to find the money to run programs, even on a shoestring, that performance management may strike them as an out-of-this-world luxury. When I was teaching a course on nonprofit management at the Yale School of Management, the topic on a particular day was multiyear strategic planning. A student in the class who had worked for several years in a nonprofit stood up and with some exasperation explained that her organization did not know from week to week where the money for continued operation was going to come from, so planning for several years ahead was simply out of the question. Performance management may not be practical for struggling nonprofits, just as many formal business practices don't work in the case of fledgling, entrepreneurial entities. Still, limited resources may call for simpler, less expensive forms of oversight rather than for overlooking performance management altogether.

The Specific Elements of Performance Management

Below is an overview of the principal components of performance management and a discussion of how each part is interrelated with other components of the process. The terminology and detailed pattern of actions set forth here are not intended to imply that there is only one perfect formula. Indeed, each organization should adopt a process that suits its needs, taking into account the resources it has available for this purpose as well as the training and experience of those who will be involved in doing the work.

A system of performance management can be viewed as involving six steps:

1. *Identify goals and objectives.* As part of a planning process prior to the start of a program, identify the *goals* of the program and the specific *objectives* that will achieve those goals. *Goals* are an intended result of the project or program as a whole; they are broad and general.[12] *Objectives* are a specific *measurable* and *time-limited* result of an activity designed to bring about the goal or goals of the program. Staff members as well as selected outsiders should participate in the goal- and objective-setting process.

2. *Formulate action plans.* Assign the specific goals and objectives to the component units of the organization best suited to effect them. Then ask each unit to come up with an action plan consisting of (a) the specific steps required to achieve each assigned objective, including obstacles to be overcome and the extent to which the authorization, cooperation, or support of others is necessary, (b) identifying the person or persons responsible for accomplishing each task, and (c) a timetable for accomplishing the objectives and the sources of the funds required. The action plan should be submitted to senior management for review and discussion with staff members and should receive a final blessing from both groups before the program is implemented.

3. *Identify advanced management practices in the field.* In setting goals and objectives, and in designing an action plan to achieve them, examine, to the extent feasible, what other organizations have been able to accomplish with similar programs, and especially how they were able to accomplish what they did. As I noted earlier, in business, this practice is known as *benchmarking.*[13] This exercise is by no means limited to discovering what measurable results other organizations have achieved in similar programs, although that information is worth having in setting your own standards. The most important function of the exercise is to understand the managerial and operational practices that enable outstanding organizations to achieve the results they do.[14] The focus of comparison can be any aspect of your organization's activities that you believe can be improved, even a part of a program.[15] For example, one organization may be renowned for making effective use of volunteers; another organization may be skilled in setting performance objectives for its staff members; a third organization may have a model budgeting process, and a fourth an outstanding strategy for using its management information system to shape its program practices. There is no point in reinventing the wheel if one can simply emulate or even improve on an established practice of another organization.

4. *Identify necessary data.* Identify in advance the data that will have to be collected and collated to enable an evaluation of the extent to which program objectives are achieved as well as their overall impact, whether intended or unintended.

5. *Review progress.* Once the action plan gets underway, management and staff should periodically compare actual progress with the plan, including cost overruns and other problems, and decide on corrective action.

6. *Evaluate results.* When the program is complete, or the funds for it have been exhausted, undertake an evaluation of what has been accomplished, including (a) the degree to which the specific objectives of the program have been achieved, (b) the variances between the program as actually implemented and the action plan adopted at the start, with an analysis of reasons for the variation, (c) the actual outcomes of the organization's efforts, whether intended or unintended, and the extent to which the outcomes are consistent with the goals of the program, and (d) the cost of the program compared to the value of the benefits achieved. In item c, the specific outcomes achieved in your program should be compared with the outcomes achieved in other programs. The point of this comparison is not only to assess how effective your organization's performance may have been but—also quite important—to develop more insight into what objectives are attainable in a given field and the best means of attaining them.[16]

Critical to the success of this six-step process is *preprogram planning*. Many a laudable program goal has foundered in implementation because the *means* chosen will not work to accomplish the desired end. In many cases, insufficient work has been done prior to starting the program to investigate and analyze what steps will enable an organization to achieve its intended results.

An example of choosing the wrong means is the Ford Foundation's 1967 graduate education initiative. Ford's broad, if highly ambitious, goal was no less than to reform graduate education in the humanities and social sciences. To accomplish this, Ford selected the specific objective of establishing four years as the norm for completing a Ph.D. in these fields. That way, the humanities and social sciences could be as "efficient" in producing Ph.D.'s as the "hard" sciences. The means to this end was to provide the same level of financial support to students in the humanities and social sciences as students in the hard sciences received. It was thought that providing students with the wherewithal to remain continually enrolled as full-time students would reduce the number of years needed to acquire the doctorate. It did not. The Ford Foundation program, educators Bill Bowen and Neil Rudenstine observe, "did not succeed either in establishing a new norm for time to degree or [in] reforming graduate education." The Ford program, Bowen and Rudenstine conclude, "was by all accounts a failure in achieving its stated purpose."[17]

In fact, Bowen and Rudenstine point out, providing equivalent amounts of financial support to humanities and social science Ph.D. candidates did not make these disciplines as efficient as the sciences in turning out doctorates. The emphasis on time to degree was misplaced; instead, emphasis should have been placed on finding ways in which attrition, a more serious problem, could be reduced.

Of course, in any pioneering effort, there will be failures, either because the goals are not attainable by any available means, or because there is insufficient experience with the implementation techniques. This does not mean that careful preprogram planning cannot reduce the chance of error.

Another very important aspect of performance management is *postprogram assessment*. In their book on graduate education, Bowen and Rudenstine describe a series of national fellowship programs that have been undertaken in this country for which no postprogram assessment has been made. Their book highlights the importance, wherever feasible, of examining, as part of such assessments, the operation and results of other similar programs. Comparing the results of a range of efforts provides a fuller picture of what goals are attainable in a particular field and what means are the most effective for achieving those ends. Where such an undertaking is beyond the financial resources and personnel capabilities of a particular organization, then the entity that funds the program should consider it part of its funding responsibility to see that such an overall assessment is made at a suitable time by appropriate experts.

A Hypothetical Illustration of Performance Management

Let me amplify on how these elements operate by illustrating their application to a hypothetical organization dedicated to aiding young women who live in conditions of poverty.

The first step in establishing a process for managing performance is to create a set of attainable and measurable performance objectives for the organization as a whole and then to break down those overall objectives into more specific objectives for each component unit of the organization. Our nonprofit, in order to achieve its broad overall goal of aiding certain groups of young women, will identify specific behavioral goals that it seeks to achieve (e.g., a reduction in teenage pregnancy, increased attendance at school, completion of a high school education, reduction of criminal activity) and then zero in on its highest priorities. The first priority is a reduction in the rate of teenage pregnancy in a discrete number of targeted communities. Next, given its available resources, the organization must determine how large a reduction in pregnancy over what period of time among how large a group of young women in how many target communities is a reasonable specific performance objective.

There is a tendency in the nonprofit world, as well as in government, to attribute value to the size of an organization's program: the bigger the staff, the more participants, and/or the larger the geographical area covered, the better. This kind of outlook is in many ways a product of the fact that performance management is not widely practiced. If it were, the focus would be on the degree to which tangible results were delivered at an efficient cost or, in the economist's jargon, attention would be directed at the quality of outputs rather than the volume of inputs.

Assume that in our target community, prior to the implementation of the program, one-fifth of the women become pregnant in their teens. Our nonprofit can set out to reduce that percentage by a significant degree, in increasing increments each year over, say, a three-year period. It may take some trial and error to establish realistic, quantifiable targets, but the organization will make its best estimate after talking to experts and potential participants. One of the factors that may be taken into account in setting objectives is the experience of other organizations operating similar programs. For simplicity, we will skip the potential input from the experience of others. In the early years, senior management will assess whether a target is missed because the objective is unrealistically high, or because the staff does not execute the program well, or because there is a design flaw in the program.

Assume further that the organization's management sets as an objective reducing pregnancy among women under the age of 18, compared to pregnancy among women who do not participate in the program, by 25 percent. Since change will not happen overnight, a time frame has to be established for accomplishing the performance objective. A useful approach is to establish increasing targets over time—for example, 10 percent in year 1, 15 percent in year 2, 25 percent in year 3.

To achieve this measurable objective, a program has to detail the specific tasks to be performed by the organization's various units. This is each unit's action plan. For instance, the organization's department in charge of recruiting participants may be given the specific objective of recruiting for each program cycle a certain number of participants that takes into account the projected dropout rate of participants in the program.

Assuming the overall goal is to reduce pregnancy among teenage girls in the first year of the program by 10 percent compared to girls in the target community at large, the nonprofit's program department's effort can be broken down into four discrete functions: (1) recruitment of participants and counselors, (2) design of the program's content and its implementation, (3) administrative support, and (4) program assessment. Sub-objectives and action plans are then developed for each unit. The actual counseling of women will be conducted in three-month cycles.

A bottom-up process is employed in which each unit comes up with its own set of proposed objectives and action plans. These proposals are then reviewed with senior management to ensure that they are feasible, and that the objectives and plans of the various units form a cohesive overall program. Management also will make sure that no one is presenting overly low projections in order to increase the odds of achieving them.

The combination of objectives and action plans for Year 1 of the program may then look something like this:

RECRUITING UNIT

Objective: Recruit and train five counselors; to be completed by end of second month of program

Action plan:

- ◆ Write jobs specs and establish compensation
- ◆ Obtain management approval for above
- ◆ Contact local schools of social work
- ◆ Contact persons who previously worked for organization
- ◆ Advertise in social work journals
- ◆ Network among social work professionals
- ◆ Screen applicants
- ◆ Initiate training sessions with accepted applicants

In reality, an action plan would assign dates for completion to virtually all individual steps; for simplicity, I have established one completion date for all steps.

Objective: Recruit 25 participants for each three-month program cycle; recruitment to begin 60 days before start of a cycle and be completed by one week before the cycle commences

Action plan:

- ◆ Post notices in high school and community centers
- ◆ Visit homes and hospitals for unwed mothers
- ◆ Network among leaders of other community programs
- ◆ Interview high school teachers
- ◆ Interview welfare officials
- ◆ Hold informal meetings with prospects to explain program and encourage them to sign up for it
- ◆ Interview potential participants
- ◆ Introduce program officials and counselors
- ◆ Visit prospective participant's home environment, interview her teachers, and check police records

ADMINISTRATIVE UNIT

Objective: Prepare space for program; to be complete by the end of second month

Action plan:

◆ Identify suitable space for program sessions, both group and individual counseling sessions

◆ Make arrangements to secure space

◆ Obtain computer system for maintaining necessary data base

PROGRAMMING UNIT

Objective: Hold 24 group sessions (2 per week) and 150 individual counseling sessions (3 per participant) over each cycle

Action plan:

◆ Ensure that teaching materials for counselors and materials for participants are prepared by month 2 and reproduced in quantities necessary for distribution

◆ Hold training sessions for counselors in month 3

◆ Assign participants to groups to be led by different counselors in various session formats

◆ Conduct group and individual sessions

PROGRAM ASSESSMENT

Objective: Deliver program assessments; to be completed within 12 months after cycle ends

Action plan:

◆ Interview all participants who complete program after end of program and again at later intervals

◆ Develop comparison with similar programs in at least four other locations

◆ Draft assessment and review it with program counselors and outside experts in the field

The object of this exercise is to create a blueprint of what is to be accomplished, and how. Forcing staff members in each unit to think through their specific measurable objectives and the actions they must take to achieve those objectives reduces inefficiency once the program gets underway and gives each staff member a clear sense of direction. At the same time, the blueprint is not a straitjacket. If experience during implementation dictates change, then the action plan and even the objectives can be revised.

The degree to which an organization's specific objectives and action plan are being accomplished within the projected time frame should be reviewed regularly by management during the progress of the project and also once the program is completed. Even if unexpected benefits result from a program, management still needs to evaluate whether its staff can consistently achieve the objectives it targets at the outset, and, if not, why not. Does the problem lie in the forecasting process (and, if so, what can be done to improve this process)? Or are there problems in the implementation process that could be corrected with the help of closer oversight by management?

Naturally, experience may dictate modifying the unit performance objectives over time. Some may not prove ambitious enough (e.g., the dropout rate of participants proves higher than expected so the number of recruits has to be increased). Others may prove unrealistically high (e.g., the original target for the maximum number of dropouts). Changes are especially likely to be needed when external conditions change, or when a program is being tried for the first time.

Analyzing the Financial Cost of a Program Relative to Its Achievements

The process described here is analogous to the analysis of a for-profit enterprise's "bottom line." The object is to compare the costs of a program (both direct outlays and indirect administrative and overhead costs) to the total positive measurable outcomes of the program as expressed in quantifiable terms. The focus is not only on the degree to which the specific objectives established at the outset of the program are accomplished but on how other positive outcomes, which may not have been foreseen, are brought about. Not all program outcomes can be expressed in quantifiable terms. For example, in the case of our hypothetical program, young women who delay pregnancy may have the opportunity to choose from a wider range of career options. Self-awareness, pride, and knowledge about contraceptives may also enable participants to establish sounder relationships and make a more informed choice about when to bear children. These positive outcomes cannot be quantified but ought to be included in an evaluation of the cost-effectiveness of a teenage pregnancy prevention program.[18]

Still, a program's cost-effectiveness can be calculated, albeit perhaps not exactly. For instance, in the teenage pregnancy prevention program, the number of pregnancies delayed can be arrived at (1) by calculating the rate of pregnancy among nonparticipants, (2) subtracting from this result the rate of pregnancy among participants, and (3) multiplying the difference by the number of participants.

To see how this works out we don't have to rely on a hypothetical illustration; we can turn to an actual evaluation done for Girls, Inc. This "real life" evaluation found that 28 of 147 young women between the age of 12 and 20 classified as nonparticipants became pregnant within two years from the start of the program, while 33 of 290 women in the same age range who participated in the program also became pregnant. In other words, 19 percent of nonparticipants became pregnant, compared to 11.4 percent of participants, or a difference of 7.6 percent (22 women).

The value of this benefit can be quantified by estimating the savings to society, based on public investment in Aid to Families with Dependent Children, Medicaid, and food stamps. The Girls, Inc., evaluation consultant estimated the program's savings to society at $8,580 for each participant who did not become pregnant. When this figure is multiplied by 22, the total savings to society is $188,760. The cost of delaying pregnancies in 22 women can also be calculated; in the Girls, Inc. case, the evaluation consultant determined the costs to be about $33,640.[19]

The results of this cost-benefit analysis can now be compared with similar analyses of other programs of the same agency or with figures for other social programs of other agencies, involving goals such as reduction in substance abuse, reduction in recidivism among first-time juvenile offenders, completion of a high school degree, or job training. These quantified comparisons, adjusted for qualitative considerations, can inform a nonprofit's judgment of how effective and efficient a program is, compared to other programs the nonprofit operates and, where data are available, to other similar social programs aimed at the same target population(s).

Again, it would be beneficial if an organization were funded to collect systematically and categorize the results of program evaluations now being done by a wide number of organizations.

Cause and Effect

In all assessments, it is necessary to determine whether the linkage between cause and effect is strong enough to justify the conclusions reached. For instance, in our hypothetical case, there are a number of reasons why pregnancy rates could decline in the program group of young women, other than the content of the program itself. For starters, by joining the program, the participants have shown an interest in avoiding pregnancy (i.e., the group is self-selected). Influences at home or in other facets of the women's lives may influence their decisions to avoid pregnancy. Certainly, if pregnancy rates did not decline over the entire period, the program's effectiveness would be in doubt. Thus, assessments may be more valid in proving the negative than the positive.

The Role of Grantors in Ensuring Grantee Performance

A review of the quality of grantee performance by grantors is not only in the best interests of improving the management of grantees but also the fiduciary responsibility of grantmaking organizations. This view has always had its detractors, who argue that grantor oversight inevitably leads to unwarranted grantor intrusion into the running of grantee organizations.

The UJA-Federation of New York has established a model for striking the appropriate balance between permitting oversight by the grantor and allowing the grantee the appropriate degree of freedom in implementing a grant. The Federation provides some $60 million in annual funding to more than 130 social agencies in New York City. These agencies, in turn, leverage this funding by raising some $45 billion in funding from government and other sources. The Federation's relationship with these agencies has been carefully worked out over time and rests on several critical elements set forth in the UJA-Federation's June 17, 1993, strategic plan:

◆ Determining the most effective mode of service delivery is the responsibility of the agencies.

◆ The UJA-Federation will periodically determine whether the agencies meet established standards of financial management practice.

◆ All agencies are expected to assess their own performance periodically. "Those assessments should take into account the *best current practice in the relevant field,* the views of the community served, and especially the views of the recipients and users of services as to the quality, accessibility, and adequacy of the services." [Italics added.] The Federation will provide grant assistance to help agencies conduct such self-assessments.

◆ The intensity of assessments should vary with the scale and complexity of the agency's functions, but they must be performed.

◆ Outstanding performance will be rewarded with longer-term and/or larger funding; where performance does not fully measure up, the Federation will provide technical and managerial advice or other assistance that may be needed. But if "poor performance persists" and it is clear that another provider can provide more effective assistance, then funding will be shifted to the other provider.

Another constructive approach to grantor oversight is establishing explicit performance objectives for grantees. The Andrew W. Mellon Foundation, for instance, includes in its grant memoranda to its board detailed "expected outcomes" for each grant it makes. Some outcomes, of course, place more emphasis on quantifiable objectives where the grant program lends itself to such analysis. An expected outcome can be very explicit—spelling out, for example, how many contemporary works a performing arts group must revive in how many forthcoming seasons, and specifying that by the end of the grant period the group must have raised its membership dues sufficiently to be able to continue to revive contemporary works without further funding by the foundation. Other "outcomes—where quantification of objectives is difficult—focus on the tasks to be completed by the grantee.

NOTES

1. Frances Hesselbein, *The Nonprofit Times,* August 1955, p. 32.

2. Robert N. Anthony and Regina E. Herzlinger, *Management Control in Nonprofit Organizations* (Homewood, IL: Richard Irwin, 1980), p. 35.

3. Regina E. Herzlinger and Denise Nitterhouse, *Financial Accounting and Managerial Control for Nonprofit Organizations* (Cincinnati: Southwestern Publishing Co., 1994).

4. Council for Aid to Education, *Voluntary Support of Education 1992* (New York: Council for Aid to Education, 1993), p. 15.

5. Robert J. Boxwell, Jr., *Benchmarking for Competitive Advantage* (New York: McGraw Hill, 1994), p. 74.

6. See Robert J. Boxwell, Jr., *Benchmarking for Competitive Advantage* (New York: McGraw Hill, 1994), and Michael E. Porter, *Competitive Strategy: Techniques for Analyzing Industries and Competitors* (New York: Free Press, 1980), pp. 368-382.

7. National Charities Information Bureau, *The 123 of Evaluation: An Introduction to Three Basic Tools* (New York: NICB, 1989).

8. William G. Bowen, Thomas I. Nygren, Sarah E. Turner, Elizabeth A. Duffy, *The Charitable Nonprofits* (San Francisco: Jossey-Bass, 1994).

9. Michael L. Dertouzos, Richard K. Lester, and Robert M. Solow, *Made in America* (Cambridge: MIT Press, 1989), p. 119. The study emphasizes the need to scan globally to identify the best practices in a company's field.

10. Boxwell, *Benchmarking,* ch. 6.

11. Porter, *Competitive Strategy,* ch. 7.

12. This chapter does not deal with the competitive positioning of an organization to enable it to pursue programs in which it has the opportunity to be a leader because of a comparative advantage it enjoys relative to other organizations in the same field. This topic is covered in Chapter 4, "Carving Out Your Strategic Niche." For the purpose of the analysis of performance management, I assume the organization has found its appropriate niche.

13. Boxwell defines benchmarking as "two things: setting goals by using objective, external standards and learning from others—learning how much and, perhaps more important, learning how....Benchmarking is not a numbers-only exercise. Setting quantitative goals, often called metrics, through benchmarking is arguably the best way to set goals, but keep in mind that setting goals comparable to or beyond those of the best-in-class without understanding the underlying processes that enable the best-in-class to achieve their results can be useless or worse. Understanding how the companies you study achieve their results is usually more important and valuable than obtaining some precisely quantified metrics" (*Benchmarking,* p. 17).

14. Ibid., p. 35.

15. Boxwell describes the benchmarking process as determining (1) which value activities in an organization are the activities where improvement will allow the business to gain the most through benchmarking, and (2) the key factors, or drivers, of these value activities, and then identifying the companies with the foremost practices in those value activities. He adds: "These foremost practices may be found at competitors or companies from unrelated industries—any companies that perform the value activities well. For example, Xerox benchmarked L. L. Bean's warehousing and distribution system after determining that Bean's practices were the foremost practices in that particular activity" (ibid., pp. 20-21). The term "value activities" is defined in Porter as the "physically and technologically distinct activities a firm performs." Michael E. Porter, *Competitive Advantage: Creating and Sustaining Superior Performance* (New York: Free Press, 1985), p. 38.

16. There is a considerable body of literature on program evaluation techniques. See Council on Foundations, *Evaluations for Foundations* (San Francisco: Jossey-Bass, 1993), and Girls, Inc. *Assess for Success: Needs Assessment and Evaluation Guide* (New York: Girls, Inc., 1991).

17. William Bowen and Neil Rudenstine, *In Pursuit of the Ph.D.* (Princeton: Princeton University Press, 1992), p.211-214. Neil Rudenstine is currently the president of Harvard University. He previously served in various deanships and then as provost at Princeton. He and Bowen left Princeton together in 1988 to join the Andrew W. Mellon Foundation, Bowen as president and Rudenstine as executive vice-president.

18. Gerald L. Schmaedick, ed., *Cost-Effectiveness in the Nonprofit Sector: Methods and Examples from Leading Organizations* (Westport: Quorum Books, 1993), p. 36, and Council on Foundations, *Evaluation for Foundations* (San Francisco: Jossey-Bass, 1993), p. 278.

19. Brent C. Miller, Josefina J. Card, Roberta L. Paikoff, and James L. Peterson, *Preventing Adolescent Pregnancy* (Newbury Park, CA: Sage, 1992).

CHAPTER 9

Depicting Performance and Financial Condition

Chapter 8 established the fundamental elements of a system for managing the effectiveness and efficiency of a nonprofit's performance. To complement that system, management and the board must receive reports that detail how well the organization is performing its mission and the related issue of the condition of its finances. For this purpose, an enterprise must organize performance and financial data in a way that is useful to management and the board in their efforts to run the organization on a day-to-day-basis. The fund accounting system that the accounting profession uses to certify the financial condition of nonprofit organizations is not designed to serve as such a management tool, and each enterprise must create its own internal reporting system. The principal components of such an internal system are set forth in this chapter.

Statements depicting the performance and financial condition of nonprofits are prepared for a variety of audiences. The nature of that audience, and the message a nonprofit wants to convey to it, shapes the form and content of the documents. External audiences may include the media and the general public, current or prospective funders, lenders, and the Internal Revenue Service; the internal audience consists of the board and management.

Management Information versus Accounting

The information that management needs to run an enterprise is often different from that which the accounting profession needs in order to prepare the entity's financial statements. Management information must be organized in a way that highlights quickly and easily for executives the key variables that reveal how an enterprise is faring; how well it is meeting the objectives established for it at the outset of the period; and, if it is off track, what factors account for this. In addition, the information has to be available to management at certain crucial time intervals, if corrective action is to be possible. These managerial considerations generally dictate that an enterprise organize its financial information in a format that enables management to oversee the operations of the organization. This is particularly important for nonprofits because the system of fund accounting used to report to the public on the financial condition of an exempt organization does not readily lend itself to managing the enterprise.

Over the years, the accounting profession has worked to make fund accounting more useful in depicting the financial condition of an exempt organization. Fund accounting was conceived, however, to serve the basic purpose of demonstrating whether donated or restricted resources (resources that can be used only for specified purposes) were used in a manner consistent with the instructions of those who gave them. In order to satisfy grantors of resources to an exempt organization that such resources are being used for the specified purpose, nonprofit accounting entries are classified by funds. Each fund is, in essence, a separate compartment in which resources restricted for a specific purpose are stored. Funds are separated from one another because their resources are restricted to certain specified purposes, and transactions are treated as transfers between funds. (For example, the expenditure of income from the endowment is treated as a transfer from the endowment fund to the operating fund.)

The difficulty with relying on fund accounting as a management tool is that *the basic reporting unit is not the nonprofit entity itself, but rather the various funds established in connection with the entity.*[1] The result is that fund accounting does not treat a nonprofit as a living, breathing *operating enterprise* but as a composite of a series of separate funds (and funds within funds).

There is no denying that the underlying purpose of fund accounting is appropriate, *but management must still deal with the fact that nonprofit organizations do in fact have financial objectives and that the management information needs to disclose how well these are being met.* The performance and financial results of the exempt organization as an entity must also be elements of a nonprofit financial reporting system.

While recently the accounting profession has limited significantly the number of different types of funds and has made provision for depreciation accounting and cash statements, fund accounting still does not meet all the needs of the managers of an enterprise. A management information system responsive to those requirements has to be designed. The need for tailored management information applies to most for-profit enterprises as well, thus, this chapter's goal is to establish the different purposes that management information and accounting serve. An exempt organization can prepare an informative picture of its program accomplishments and financial condition by designing its own form of financial disclosure to augment the fund accounting statement.

Full Disclosure

The chief failing that I have observed in financial reporting by both for-profit and nonprofit enterprises is a tendency to bury unpleasant realities. Too often, organizations seem to take literally the cynical comment that financial statements are designed to obfuscate rather than to educate. An institution should not kid itself about its true financial condition, but many do. They resort to unjustified optimism about future revenues, understate the vulnerability of their accounts receivable, or underestimate the amount of plant maintenance required or other liabilities for which provision must be made (e.g., severance payments and earned but unused vacation leaves).

Hiding liabilities leaves an organization vulnerable, not only to errant judgments but also to the risk of a sudden, unmanageable jolt to its financial position when a day of reckoning arrives. The appropriate strategy is to make adequate provision for meeting *all foreseeable* obligations in a manner that minimizes their adverse impact. For example, actual outlays for plant maintenance may vary considerably from year to year, according to the nature of the repairs to be made. Instead of simply booking the actual expenditures each year as they occur, an organization can fund the cost of such maintenance over, say, a five-year period by an annual charge to the budget equal to the *average* yearly outlay.

Does a Nonprofit Need a Bottom Line?

Unlike a business, a nonprofit organization has no single aggregate numerical measure providing a baseline for demonstrating the financial performance of the entity. In business, the profit measure, or "bottom line," provides a baseline that, when related to other financial markers (e.g., net profit as a percentage of revenues, net profit as a return on assets or as a return on shareholders' equity, earnings per share, and the ratio of share price to earnings per share) illustrates the financial condition of the enterprise. It is these *relationships* between net profit and other financial markers that provide a gauge of a business's performance. Such ratios also permit comparisons with other businesses in the same or different lines of business. In a business, this form of quantification is appropriate because a business's mission is to maximize the financial return to its owners. The aggregation of the varied financial data in a number of earnings-based ratios also aids public investors in choosing among publicly traded securities, thus facilitating the operation of our capital markets.

In addition, a structure to oversee the financial reporting of corporations whose shares are publicly traded has been developed by a group that includes the Securities and Exchange Commission (SEC), institutional shareholders, mutual funds, underwriters of new capital, lenders, thousands of security analysts who follow companies and publish their findings, and trade and general business publications. The financial penalty for publishing misleading financial statements can be quite severe and can be imposed not only on managers but also on the independent auditors who certified the company's financial statements, as the Big Six firms who represented savings and loan associations found out to their chagrin.

But being responsive to the needs of the capital markets is not relevant to the function of nonprofits. Thus, the issue is not whether a nonprofit can calculate operating profit in the same fashion as a business does (it can), but the relevance of such a calculation. Whereas a business's single goal is to maximize the return to its shareholders, an exempt organization has a dual agenda: (1) maximizing the effectiveness and efficiency of its programs, and (2) achieving financial stability. Generating revenues in excess of expenditures—the driving goal of a for-profit enterprise—is not, as a rule, an exempt organization's object; rather, it typically seeks to utilize all its available resources to expand the impact or scope of its programs.

A few operating nonprofits, such as Children's Television Workshop, have from time to time set aside part of their revenues to build an operating reserve fund for future contingencies or to fund new initiatives.[2] Of course, organizations with an endowment do not generally spend all they earn in a year; part of the appreciation and income earned by the endowment fund is reinvested in order to maintain the real value of the fund in the future. But, even with these qualifications, earning a profit is not an objective of an exempt organization and thus is not a useful baseline measure for such organizations.

Equally pertinent, the audience for an exempt organization's financial statements is not public investors but senior management and the board and on occasion a lender or grantor. Accordingly, the aim in the case of a nonprofit is to *disaggregate* the financial data in order to reveal the variables that have the greatest impact on the organization's financial condition. It is unfortunate that most grantors do not undertake a due diligence review of the financial condition of organizations to which they make grants. Since the grants are nonrepayable, grantor organizations feel little motivation to conduct such an examination, and most do not have staff members qualified to perform such an examination. In my view, this is a serious shortcoming, for, if grantors regularly reviewed the financial condition and reporting of grantees, they would impose an important discipline on nonprofits.

Actually, some grantors do review grantee organizations' financial condition—namely, foundations that make "program-related investments." The Ford Foundation originated such investments and remains the most active in making them. A program-related investment (PRI) is just that: funds are advanced in the form of an equity or debt investment, or a guarantee of another's investment, in an organization important to the foundation's program objectives. The investment is made on more favorable terms than could be obtained from commercial sources. One of the Ford Foundation's objectives in launching a PRI program was to stretch foundation resources by recouping funds advanced under the program. In 1970, I served as the Ford Foundation's second head of PRI, taking over shortly after the program was launched. While the recoupment objective made sense, in my experience the greatest value of the program was that the foundation conducted a due diligence review of potential recipients and imposed conditions on their operation. In addition, PRI staff members often worked with recipients to strengthen their management and financial control systems. Continued monitoring kept the pressure on.

But some of my colleagues at Ford considered it inappropriate, even under a PRI, to impose conditions on the operations of a recipient. In their view, once a grantor selected an organization to fund, it should step back and let the organization act as it deemed best. I did not agree with this view then and do not agree with it now, although it prevails throughout much of the grantmaking world. Only if grantors carefully review the management and finances of organizations they fund, will there be widespread improvement in the management of nonprofits.

Multiple Factors Depict Organizational Performance and Finances

In order to depict fully the effectiveness of a nonprofit enterprise, one has to examine a number of critical factors that together provide a fair picture of the organization's productivity and its financial condition.

Examining only the operating statement is not sufficient. For example, the productivity of a nonprofit's programs may—unlike that of a for-profit business—generate no revenue, only expense. Thus, program productivity must be reported and analyzed separately from the operating revenues and expenses of a nonprofit organization.

In addition to the operating statement, one also has to examine a series of factors I group under the heading "capital condition." For example, many nonprofit organizations do not have a planned program of expenditures for major maintenance and often literally wait until the roof caves in before addressing the issue. Yale University, for example, is now conducting a major capital campaign to fund repairs of a good part of its physical plant, which it allowed to deteriorate over the years. In contrast, standard hotel accounting requires annual reserves to be set aside to provide for the periodic refurbishment of the hotel. Fund accounting does not, however, require the establishment of a reserve to provide for periodic maintenance of a nonprofit's plant.

For an organization with many buildings, especially if these house extensive science or medical laboratories, failure to take into account the cost of keeping the plant in good physical condition—and also up to the standards set by the Department of Labor's Occupational Safety and Health Act and federal requirements with respect to access by the handicapped—presents a serious financial burden. Any financial report that does not provide for the cost of maintaining an organization's physical plant will present a seriously misleading picture of the entity's financial condition.

It is also important to report on the organization's cash position separately from its statement of revenues and expenses. The latter is not the equivalent of cash. If a building program is underway, substantial outlays of cash may appear on the financial statement as capital expenditures that are not charged to the operating statement. Similarly, repayments of debt principal are not charged against the operating statement but are reflected in a reduction of indebtedness on the balance sheet. Cash actually available to pay current bills *must* be separately identified.

The treatment of gifts also requires care. Some gifts may be payable over a term of years; others may be used only for certain specified purposes (e.g., the hiring of a tenured faculty member to the classics department); still others may be restricted to being added to the university's endowment, so that they can be spent only in accordance with the formula adopted by the school for spending a percentage of the income and capital gains earned by its endowment. The total cash that the university can utilize to meet current needs may thus be only a fraction of the total amount of gifts received in any one year. That figure needs to be separated from the total of gifts received. For these and other reasons, the management information reporting for a nonprofit must cover a range of analyses.

A Reporting System for Management and the Board

The following six critical analyses form the core of an exempt organization's management information report:

1. Program evaluation
2. Annual operating results
3. Sources and uses of cash
4. Capital condition

5. Risk management issues
6. Management report

For each of these analyses, the data must be disaggregated until the factors that have the greatest impact on the organization are identified. In addition, the data should be viewed over a number of years in order to identify trends that may represent a change in the organization's condition.

A Balanced Budget Masks Precarious Financial Condition

The following hypothetical case illustrates the importance of disaggregating data and searching for *trend lines*.

Eastern University proudly announces that it has balanced its operating budget for five years in a row, reporting total revenues equal to total current expenditures, and that during that period it has expanded its educational plant, raised faculty salaries, and increased the size of its professional school faculties. But if one breaks down the data further, a very different picture emerges (see Table 9.2). An analysis of trends over this period reveals that Eastern has balanced its budget essentially by raising the cost of undergraduate tuition, room, and board. The percentage of Eastern's revenues accounted for by tuition, room, and board fees has increased over the five years from 45 percent of total revenues to more than half of the school's revenues. The increase in these fees—ranging from 12 to 14 percent a year—significantly outpaces inflation as measured by

Table 9.1.   Revenues at Eastern University over a Five-Year Period
(dollars in millions)

	1990	1991	1992	1993	1994
Revenues	$200.0	$216.0	$233.3	$252.0	$272.2
Tuition, Room, and Board Fees	90.0[a]	102.8	116.6	131.6	147.8
Grants and Gifts	80.0[b]	83.2	86.7	90.4	94.4
Auxiliary Revenue	10.0[c]	10.0	10.0	10.0	10.0
Distribution from Endowment	20.0[d]	20.0	20.0	20.0	20.0

a. Tuition, room, and board fees in 1990 represent 45 percent of total revenues and increase at a rate sufficient to fund 80 percent of the increase in expenses(revenues).

b. Grants from government and private sources and unrestricted gifts from private sources represent 40 percent of total revenue in 1990 and increase at a rate sufficient to cover 20 percent of the increase in expenditures (revenues).

c. Auxiliary revenues include principally gross revenues from athletic events and revenues from the university-owned store, royalties on technology licensed by the university, and miscellaneous other incidental revenue. The dollar volume of such revenues remains constant throughout the period, but declines as a percentage of total revenues.

d. Distribution from the total return of the endowment, in accordance with the spending policy approved by Eastern's board of trustees, represents 10 percent of total revenues and continues to provide a constant flow of dollars throughout the period, but it represents a declining percentage of total revenues as endowment returns decline.

Table 9.2.   Breakdown of Tuition, Room, and Board Fees in, Dollars, Percent Increase From Prior, Year Fees, and Fees as Percentage of Revenues (dollars in millions)

	1990	1991	1992	1993	1994
Increase in Dollars from Previous Year	N/A	$12.8	$13.6	$15.2	$16
Percent Increase from Previous Year		13.3%	13.4%	12.9%	12.3%
Fees as Percentage of Revenue	45%	47.6%	50%	52%	54%

the consumer price index, as well as the more relevant educational inflation index (more relevant because educational costs do increase faster than the price level in the economy as a whole).

At the same time, Eastern's fee increases are greater than those of its several principal competitors for undergraduates, as determined by identifying the schools at which a significant proportion of students who reject Eastern actually matriculate. An examination of the percentage of students who choose Eastern over these principal competitors reveals, over the five-year period, a significant decline in the percentage who attend Eastern. Consistent with this pattern, Eastern's admissions "yield"—the percentage of students admitted who chose to attend the admitting school—declines over the five years during which Eastern has a balanced budget. This situation forces Eastern to offer admission to more students in order to meet its revenue goals for tuition, room, and board. The result in Eastern's case is that it is forced to admit students whose qualifications are lower than those of the students it admitted when its yield was higher.

Equally disquieting, the pressure to maintain student quality forces the admissions office to offer admission to a very high percentage of those who do not apply for financial aid, making ability to pay a clear factor in admissions decisions, despite the university's official policy of admitting the most qualified students without regard to whether they need financial aid.

The ultimate negative outcome is that *U.S. News & World Report,* whose ranking of colleges and universities affects students' decisions regarding which schools to apply to, lowers its ranking of Eastern because of the decline in the school's yield and the lower median SAT scores of its student body. The result is a further fall-off in admissions applications, which further shrinks the pool of quality candidates.

The hypothetical case of Eastern University demonstrates the importance of disaggregating gross data to identify critical trends in the factors having the most impact on an exempt organization's financial condition. Eastern, which on the surface appeared to be a growing institution in good financial shape, is in fact in perilous condition, with its financial viability in jeopardy and the quality of its student body declining as it loses ground to its principal competitors.

Following is a more detailed exposition of each of the six analyses I have identified as forming the core of a nonprofit's financial report.

Program Evaluation

The health of a nonprofit institution cannot be measured only in terms of financial data. The vitality of its programs, the care with which these are targeted, and the depth of their impact are at the heart of the organization's strength. The program is the nonprofit's "product"; if the marketplace is not receptive to it, this rejection will soon be reflected in the organization's financial figures, just as the rejection of a commercial product will hurt the financial position of a business.

For each program, factors such as the following need to be evaluated:

Program outcomes versus original objectives   (i.e., the extent to which the measurable objectives established at the outset of the program have in fact been achieved). Remember our hypothetical organization dedicated to aiding young women who live in conditions of poverty. The objective in year 1 was to reduce pregnancy in women under age 18 who joined the program by 10 percent compared to pregnancy rates for their peers in the community at large. Assume that 20 of the 100 women who joined the program became pregnant in year 1 and 80 did not. That means the program's output was 80 women who did not become pregnant. If 25 women (who did not participate in the program but served as a control group) out of 100 became pregnant, then the program can be said to have reduced the level of pregnancy by 20 percent in Year 1 (25 divided by 5)—well above target.

Program cost versus budget.   While our hypothetical organization's output exceeded the targeted objective for year 1, how did the expenditures for the program compare with the budget established at the outset? Did the cost per output, or the cost of deferring pregnancy in 20 cases, fall within the budget? What was the ratio of inputs of costs to outputs? Did the organization achieve the projected efficiency?

Key factors accounting for variances in outcomes and costs, versus the original plan.   Were the variances the result of inaccurate forecasts or of better execution than one could have expected at the outset? Were they the result of factors within the organization's control or of uncontrollable factors? Is there a causal connection between the organization's programs and the objectives achieved, or do factors unrelated to the organization's efforts provide an equally, if not more, likely explanation of the results?

Annual Operating Results

In the case of a nonprofit, the purpose of an operating statement is to determine, on an accrual basis, whether the organization is operating at financial equilibrium. Equilibrium means that the organization does not have to draw on its capital to make up for a deficit, or lacking capital, to cut expenditures or borrow funds. Accrual accounting provides an important perspective because revenues are those earned during the year, whether or not the amounts were received in cash, and expenses are the resources used or consumed during the year (not the resources acquired, as is the standard accounting practice in most nonprofits).

The differences between cash-basis and accrual-basis accounting is principally one of *timing*. Accrual accounting looks at an entity from the perspective of the relationship between revenues and expenditures based on activities during the year. If equilibrium is not achieved on this basis, an inability to pay the bills will eventually occur, even if at a given moment the organization has on hand plenty of cash or its equivalent generated in past years (or has cash allocated to restricted accounts as in the example above). On the other hand, if activity that produces revenues on an accrual basis is not converted into cash—because fees for services are not paid in full, or because donors default on grant pledges, or because the institution has been spending large amounts of cash for capital construction (which is not included in the operating statement)—the organization can be in a cash bind even though it has a balanced operating statement. In short, both the operating and cash flow statements require examination.

The organization's operating statement of revenues and expenses should be broken down by principal types of revenues (e.g., grants, earned income, fundraising for current operations) and expenses (e.g., management and staff salaries and benefits, office rent, travel, program materials). Some organizations may also find it useful to trace particular revenues and expenses to specific operating and administrative units. For instance, did the expenses of administrative offices exceed the expenditures of the division that ran the programs? If so, why? Did one program unit incur more of a certain form of expense than another unit? If so, why? The aim is not only to examine whether revenues and expenses, as shown on the operating statement, balanced out, but also to identify the variables that most influenced operating results. In addition, it is advisable to pinpoint where expenses can be curtailed without undermining the program, and to review all sources of revenue to see if they can be counted on to increase or at least continue at the same level in the future.

Just how detailed a breakdown of revenues and expenses is useful will depend on the nature of an organization's activities and purposes. Some organizations may find it convenient to follow the expense breakdown called for in part 2 of IRS Form 990. Part 1 of the form's breakout of revenue sources may also be a convenient format as long as one is aware that the IRS form does not distinguish between current revenues and capital contributions, and as long as one takes care not to repeat that error in one's own operating statement.

Sources and Uses of Cash

As noted above, the operating statement is not the same as cash. Cash flow from operations should generally be positive; otherwise the organization will have trouble meeting its operating expenses. Detailing the sources and uses of cash separately is thus critical in determining the liquidity of an organization or, more simply put, its ability to pay its bills. Steven A. Ross and Randolph W. Westerfield, in their leading textbook on corporate finance, maintain that, although there is no official accounting statement for businesses called cash flow, "the most important thing that can be extracted from financial statements is the actual cash flow.[3]

Cash may be generated by programs, fundraising, earned-income activities, the sale of fixed assets, or the incurring of short- or long-term debt. When one is specifying the sources of cash available to a nonprofit, cash that is restricted as to its purpose should be excluded whenever the restriction precludes the use of the cash to meet expenditures in the current year. For instance, gifts to an organization's endowment would be excluded. However, many so-called restrictions are very broad, and each restriction should be carefully examined to determine whether the funds can be used for some current purpose, even a purpose that the organization had intended to finance from general unrestricted funds. Then the restricted fund can be applied to this purpose and the general funds used for another purpose.

Cash outlays may be made for operating expenses or capital expenditures. Thus, cash may be advanced to pay salaries and utility bills as well as to buy computer equipment or repair a building or pay the interest on principal due on a debt. Cash available to the organization contingent on the payment of a penalty (e.g., income from a certificate of deposit if it is cashed in before its maturity date) should be identified along with the amount of the penalty that would have to be paid.

An important issue for the board of trustees to decide is the investment policies that are to govern cash, including how much money should actually be maintained in the form of cash and how much should be held in short-term securities, readily convertible into cash (keeping in mind that the latter earn a return while cash does not).

Sound cash management also requires setting policies relating to the speed with which payables are retired and to how efficient the institution is going to be in collecting cash due. These policies can involve sensitive matters and can have an important financial impact. For example, should a school require all tuition for the year to be paid in full a month before the first day of the term? Should a nonprofit pay its bills exactly when they are due, even if in practice it could drag its feet without incurring a penalty? (It is not uncommon for major corporations to pay their vendors 30 or 60 days late.) At the least, it does not make sense to pay bills before they are due, when there is no discount provided for early payment (as I have found some organizations do to generate goodwill, especially among local vendors).

To appreciate fully the cash position of an organization, one needs to break down cash inflows and outflows into a *month-by-month cash inflow and outflow budget* and then compare actual results with the budget forecast. This breakdown will show whether an organization is temporarily pinched for cash or even in a deficit position because of the timing of inflows and outflows. Depending on the nature of the problem, management may be able to solve it by taking steps to accelerate certain cash payments or defer certain outlays, or it may have to borrow short-term working capital for a brief period. At the same time, analysis of the month-by-month breakdown may show that a cash shortfall is not a temporary problem but that long-term erosion in the organization's cash position is taking place and that more radical reform is required.

In addition, a *detailed aging analysis of accounts receivable* is useful, since it identifies amounts owed to an organization that should ordinarily be paid in cash during the accounting year. If for some reason these accounts are not paid and converted to cash in a timely fashion, the organization's cash inflow will be less than budgeted. For this reason, an organization should prepare, as a supplement to its cash flow statement, a breakdown of accounts receivable that are past due by various number of days—30, 60, 90, and 120. Management then needs to evaluate the likelihood of being paid for the receivables that are well past due (e.g., 90 days or more) and, when the prospects are dim indeed, write off the amounts in question.

Capital Condition

For our purpose, the capital of a nonprofit consists of its long-term resources, namely:

- funds set aside for investment;
- long-term debt;
- physical assets; and
- reserves against future liabilities.

A primary responsibility of the board is to determine the investment policies that should govern the investment of funds to be held for the long-term welfare of the organization (i.e., an endowment), particularly the targeted return to be sought and the level of risk to be accepted in pursuit of such a return.[4] In setting investment policy, the board must also establish a "spending policy" that determines what portion of the current appreciation, dividends, and interest should be spent on the current needs of the organization and what portion should be reinvested for the future well-being of the institution. The ideal formula will call for reinvestment at least equal to the anticipated level of inflation, so that the real value of the investment fund is maintained. Restrictions imposed by donors on gifts to the endowment need to be examined to see whether they differ from the spending policy set by the board.

Another important policy issue is how much debt it is reasonable for an institution to assume. A university setting provides a good illustration of some of the questions that can arise. It may be tempting, when the faculty is pressing for a new building or the president wants a visible testimonial to his administration's activity, to borrow a good percentage of the money required for construction, rather than wait until all the money is in hand. But if a university accumulates debt in this manner, at some point the level of principal and interest payments due may force the university to slash its educational expenditures in order to meet debt service. The total cash flow from tuition and gifts and other sources may be more than enough to cover the debt service—but only if educational programs are cut. Should debt be incurred only where it can be invested to generate sufficient income to service the debt (e.g., enlarging the capacity of the law school so it can accept more applicants), or should debt be used to fund non-income-producing activities (e.g., to refurbish a classroom or replace worn-out roofs) in the hope that future fundraising will service the debt? In the latter case, what percentage of university revenues should be exposed to debt service requirements if new funds to pay the debt are not found? This judgment determines the degree to which the debt will threaten the university's current programs if future revenues do not rise.

The cost of maintaining physical assets in good condition should be planned for and funds set aside over time for this purpose. Most nonprofits do not follow the business practice of depreciating an asset over its useful life, but even this accounting approach may or may not accurately reflect how frequently repairs of physical assets are required. The trustees should create a plan that predicts future major maintenance requirements and provides for a portion of such future requirements to be funded on a current basis. The institution's own history, or that of comparable organizations, coupled with a physical inspection by qualified consulting engineers, should provide ample guidance for drawing up such a plan.

If the organization's financial condition permits it, a funded reserve against future contingencies should be established. Such a reserve can cushion unanticipated expensive damage to the plant (e.g., by a storm) or an unanticipated short-term adverse change in the organization's operating or cash position. Such a reserve can also be used to fund initial work on the development of a new program. This kind of exploration funding is very difficult, if not impossible, to raise, and having even a relatively small amount of money available for such exploration can enable an organization to renew itself continually over time.

Risk Management Issues

Another decision the board must make is to determine what types of insurance, and how much of each, to carry against specified risks. The risks to which an organization is exposed will vary with the nature of its activities and can range from liability incurred by an employee for wrongfully inflicting harm on another party (e.g., medical malpractice) to the damage a storm can cause to buildings. The type and amount of coverage, and how large a deductible (the amount the insured will pay) an organization decides to live with, will affect the size of the insurance premiums it has to pay. Before the issue is decided, bids should be obtained from a series of insurance companies.

Management Report

The chief financial officer of an exempt organization should author, with the chief executive officer, an annual report offering their evaluation of the program performance and financial condition of the organization. Such a report generally centers on the types of analyses outlined in the preceding discussion, with the ultimate objective of informing the board about how well the organization is performing, where it may be vulnerable, and where improvements are possible. The board should insist that the report be candid and realistic. Moreover, the board should be required to adopt a formal resolution accepting the report (as is, or with modifications made by the board) or rejecting it. The report and the board's resolution regarding it should be part of the minutes of the meeting. The object is to create a process that requires the board to make a detailed examination of the exempt organization's program performance and financial condition.

The Role of the Board Audit Committee

The board of trustees bears the ultimate responsibility for ensuring that an organization's financial house is in order.

Today, under pressure from the stock exchanges and the SEC, virtually all public corporations have established audit committees. The conventional role of a corporate audit committee is to meet with the company's outside auditor once a year to hear its report on the company's financial position and control system, as well as the management's response to the auditor's concerns, which the auditor has previously reviewed with the management. At some point, the committee also meets with the auditor without the management present. An effective audit committee is an essential element in the governance of an organization, but the conventional performance of corporate audit committees, while helpful in providing closer financial oversight by the board, in too many instances has not been effective in preventing a breakdown in the corporate control system. Most audit committees simply have not been aggressive enough in scrutinizing the company's financial condition and controls. In an article I wrote in 1994 with Princeton economics professor Burton G. Malkiel, a director of a number of financial and nonfinancial corporations, we concluded that, in the case of corporations, "The 'bottom line' for the audit committee is to shed its reactive mode and become a catalyst in probing for weak spots in the company's internal controls and financial reporting practices."[5]

In the case of exempt organizations, the establishment of a board audit committee is more the exception than the rule. But nonprofits should establish such committees and find one or two trustees with the financial acumen to lead them. Audit committees are especially important for nonprofits, which are not subject to the same kind of external oversight of their financial reporting as businesses whose shares are publicly traded.

As desirable as this step would be, many nonprofits, especially the less prominent ones (which cannot use prestige to attract board members), have a great deal of difficulty enlisting trustees with business and financial skills who have time to play an active leadership role. Thus, boards can help by assuming more responsibility (as I will assert in Chapter 14, "The Foundations of Effective Governance"), but instilling increased financial discipline in the nonprofit sector is going to depend heavily on grantors' conducting genuine scrutiny of potential grantees' financial condition and reporting.

The Relationship of the Independent Auditor to the Audit Committee

A change in the typical relationship between the independent auditor and the organization could do more than anything else to make the auditor an effective agent of the board of trustees. At present, the auditor is effectively chosen—and the fee set—by the management, although nominally the board approves the choice. Instead, the audit committee of the board should select and hire the auditor directly, establishing the auditor's direct responsibility to the board. Moreover, the tasks the auditor is to perform as part of the audit should be discussed with the audit committee and progress reports made to the committee. Under current practice, the auditor typically reviews the audit work plan with the management. The establishment of a direct working relationship between the audit committee and the auditor would give the audit a greater independence from the management and thus enhance the board's oversight of the finances of the organization. In fact, in our article, Malkiel and I recommended the same change in the way auditors are retained for businesses.[6]

There are many specific ways in which an independent auditor can assist the board to ascertain that all the policy issues raised by the financial statements have been brought to its attention and that the organization's control system is sound.

1. The independent auditor should certify to the board that the organization has no unfunded liabilities, whether material or not. In the case of one large exempt organization, its administration began a practice of not including in the financial reports certain liabilities where it was expected that funding would be received or that a subsequent surplus would cover the deficit. Over a four-year period, this practice built up $12 million in unfunded

liabilities—or, in simple language, $12 million in expenses that had not been charged to the operating statement. Then a new audit partner was put in charge of the account and insisted that the amount was material and that the institution begin writing off the liabilities against revenues. To avoid such situations in the future, the finance committee of the institution insisted that the auditor state in writing whether there were any undisclosed liabilities, material or not. This is a practice all institutions should follow.

2. The independent auditor should identify for the board any significant expenditure that has been capitalized rather than charged to the operating statement. Treating large expenditures this way is a form of abuse that can occur in both business and nonprofit organizations, and the board should review and approve decisions to capitalize large sums.

3. The independent auditor should investigate in depth, on a random, rotating basis, one or more of the organization's control systems. This investigation should be conducted with the same intensity as if a major abuse had been uncovered, but with the aim of preventing even the possibility of any such abuse occurring.

4. The auditor should review the manner in which management has organized financial data for board review and should comment on whether the presentation reveals the most important underlying factors influencing the financial condition of the organization.

Auditors should be persuaded to work with the staff in preparing the management's internal financial report and to advise senior management members and the board, albeit informally, whether the report appears to have been prepared in a professionally sound manner and whether, to the best of the accountants' knowledge, any material fact has been overlooked or omitted. The board, in turn, could expressly declare the auditing firm immune from any liability (except for gross negligence), should the management report contain an error of commission or omission. (The object is not to set up the auditing firm for a lawsuit but to get its best help and advice.)

It would also be constructive if the accounting profession went back to basics and examined anew the forms of financial statements it will certify—and the kinds of audit services it will provide—in order to make a more useful contribution to the management of nonprofits.

Conclusions

The principal components of a management information system should address the following areas:

1. Program evaluation

2. Annual operating results

3. Sources and uses of cash

4. Capital condition

5. Risk management issues.

The data related to each of these areas should be disaggregated to the extent necessary to identify the variables that most affect the performance of the organization.

Analysis of these factors, or critical markers, should form the core of a report by the management to the board (a management report). The board, in a formal resolution, should adopt this report as submitted or as amended by the board, or else reject it.

The boards of all nonprofits should establish audit committees to choose the firm's outside auditor, determine the auditor's fee, and review its scope of work and its findings. In essence, the board, acting through an audit committee, should play an active role in scrutinizing the performance and finances of an exempt organization, not merely react passively to information supplied by the management.

The accounting profession needs to undertake a thorough review of the kinds of services auditors should provide to management and to boards. Accounting firms should review how they can be of more practical value to management and the board than they are today.

NOTES

1. A fund is defined as "an independent fiscal and accounting entity with a self-balancing set of accounts recording cash and/or other resources together with all related liabilities, obligations, reserves, and equities which are segregated for the purpose of carrying on specific activities or attaining certain objectives in accordance with special regulations, restrictions, or limitations." Ronald Braswell, Karen Fortin, and Jerome S. Osteryoung, *Financial Management for Not-for-Profit Organizations* (New York: Wiley, 1984).

2. In 1976, the Children's Television Workshop had expended several million dollars of a Ford Foundation grant aimed at enabling it to generate more income and thus become more financially self-reliant. CTW's board decided to invest the remaining Ford money to start an endowment fund. At the same time, the board approved the management's recommendation to set aside a part of revenues, when this was financially feasible, to establish an operating reserve to fund future initiatives and offset future shortfalls. At the end of 1994, the reserve and endowment combined totaled $126 million.

3. Steven A. Ross and Randolph W. Westerfield, *Corporate Finance* (St. Louis: Times Mirror/ Mosby College Publishing, 1988), p. 29.

4. For a review of the role of the board of trustees in overseeing the investment of funds, and the principal options open to it, see Burton Malkiel and Paul Firstenberg, *Managing Risk in an Uncertain Era: An Analysis for Endowed Institutions* (Princeton, NJ: Princeton University Press, 1976).

5. Paul B. Firstenberg and Burton G. Malkiel, "The Twenty-First Century Boardroom: Who Will Be in Charge?" *Sloan Management Review,* Fall, 1994, p. 34.

6. Ibid., p. 34.

SECTION 3

Expanding the
Revenue Base

CHAPTER 10

A Marketing Approach
to Fundraising

One of the most important challenges to the leadership of nonprofit businesses today is to find innovative ways of expanding revenues. As the introductory chapter pointed out, all exempt organizations, other than endowed foundations, are competing for funds in the face of declining government support and the expectation that private giving will not increase much, at least in the near term. This situation makes the task of raising money more formidable than ever.

A successful solicitation of funds from public and private sources of financial support requires a marketing approach. The foundations of such an approach are (1) careful research and planning by expert, highly motivated professionals to identify the specific needs and interests of financial providers, and (2) a solicitation program that communicates how the organization's specific objectives meet those interests.

This chapter looks at effective ways of raising funds from government, individuals, foundations, and corporations. Chapter 11, "Making a Profit for Your Nonprofit Organization," encourages nonprofits to examine their potential for earning income through their activities.

The Sesame Street Funding War

In 1973, Casper Weinberger, President Richard Nixon's head of the Bureau of the Budget, sought to cut the Department of Health, Education, and Welfare's (HEW) recommended fiscal year 1974 budget for funding the children's television programs *Sesame Street* and *The Electric Company*. He wanted to slash the show's funding from $9 million to $6 million. It was unclear at the time why these sums, which formed a relatively insignificant part of the federal budget, would draw the attention of anyone in the Bureau of the Budget or why any federal official would want to go after the funding for two of the most popular and acclaimed educational television programs for children in America.

It was particularly unlikely that Casper Weinberger would have done so. He was an astute politician who moved quietly and smoothly along the corridors of executive power, wielding his influence skillfully. He was also a political realist and not in the habit of stirring up publicly visible conflicts that would cast him in a poor light; miscalculation was not part of his style and certainly not useful to a man such as Weinberger, who had clear ambitions to attain even higher positions in the government.

The Bureau of the Budget's proposed reduction in the *Sesame Street/Electric Company* appropriation was eventually defeated by Congress. Children's Television Workshop (CTW) had so many friends on Capitol Hill that Congress overrode the Weinberger cut. However, within a few months after CTW won the battle of the budget with Weinberger, HEW announced that it would audit CTW. In retrospect, it seems obvious that forces within the HEW bureaucracy were intent on getting CTW out of the budget. At issue was the fact that the series were funded by the agency's tiny Office of Technology and consumed a good part of that office's small budget.

As soon as the audit was announced, CTW realized that it needed to reinforce its position with Congress. After CTW had conducted intense lobbying on the Hill, under David Britt's shrewd direction, the House and Senate reports for fiscal year 1975 contained a statement of expectation as to the level of funding to be provided for *Sesame Street* and *The Electric Company*. This event turned out, however, to be merely a temporary advance for CTW in the funding war, not a decisive victory.

One of the special qualities of the permanent government bureaucracy is its ability to pursue an objective over a very long time and despite persistent setbacks. If one avenue is closed off, the bureaucracy will find other routes to pursue its aim. CTW learned this in its 1978 contract negotiations with the Office of Technology. These negotiations, in the byzantine fashion of federal funding, actually related to the reimbursement of CTW for money it had advanced to produce shows that had already been broadcast.

The federal government's fiscal year ends on September 30. Any funds not legally obligated to be spent by this date are lost to the funding agency and revert to the Treasury. By mid-September of 1978, CTW still could not obtain a draft of the fiscal year 1978 contract to reimburse CTW for its funding of *Sesame Street*. Persistent inquiries to the Office of Technology drew the evasive response "We're working on it." Then, on September 19, Representative L.H. Fountain of North Carolina dispatched to HEW Secretary Joseph Califano a letter alleg-·ing malfeasance in the use of federal funds by CTW over a long period of time. The letter also questioned the propriety of providing further government funding for *Sesame Street* when, in the representative's view, the series was financially self-sufficient as a result of the revenues it derived from the merchandising of Sesame Street products. (The series was not self-sufficient financially if one took into account the administrative costs associated with the show as well as its direct production costs.) In addition, the letter claimed that HEW auditors had taken exception to "financial transactions totaling hundreds of thousands—perhaps millions—of dollars." In fact, the audit had challenged $310,000 in CTW expenditures as not eligible under the terms of the federal grant, but no malfeasance was alleged. Moreover, at the time of the Fountain letter, HEW auditors had not responded to CTW's sharp rebuttal. Eventually, the dispute was settled for $171,000. Since the audit report had not been released publicly, it was obvious that its contents had been leaked, undoubtedly in exaggerated form, to Fountain's staff.

Indeed, it was evident that certain HEW staff members had plotted the whole carefully timed scenario. Fountain admitted to Representative Lindy Boggs, one of the numerous friends of *Sesame Street* on the Hill, that he was not at all familiar with the contents of the letter. He had no animosity toward *Sesame Street*; coming from tobacco-growing country, he was after Secretary Califano because of the latter's antismoking campaign.

CTW mounted a fierce counterattack, knowing it had fewer than 10 days to get a signed contract, or the funding would be lost. The Workshop roused its friends in Congress and in Jimmy Carter's White House, and it pressed its case with two high-level executives in HEW with whom it had prior relationships, Califano's chief deputy and his executive secretary. In addition, CTW tapped public broadcasting representatives in Fountain's home state as well as community groups that it worked with in North Carolina as part of its ongoing national effort to encourage children of low-income families to view the program.

Once again, CTW won a pitched political battle to preserve *Sesame Street* funding. Califano gave the go-ahead, and the contract was signed a few hours before midnight on September 30. However, as a notice to CTW that the war was still not over, in December of 1978, the allegations in the Fountain letter were published by Washington columnist Jack Anderson, who ignored CTW's rebuttal.

After the dust had settled on the fiscal year 1978 contract, Fred Bohen, Califano's executive secretary, took me aside and said, "Look, you won this one but you had everything going for you. Next time you are not likely to have so many friends in the right place."

"You are implying, Fred, that there will be a next time?"

"More than implying," he responded. "The technicians in the bowels of this place don't like *Sesame Street*. They don't get any public credit for the show—that all goes to their bosses—and they are tired of having so much of their budget locked up in one show. Sooner or later they will get you."

I recognized that Bohen was describing the reality of CTW's situation with HEW, so I proposed that the agency phase out our funding over a four-year period, which would give us ample time to adjust to the loss of government support for the show. Bohen liked the idea, and in due course an agreement was reached. Over the next four years, our funding was phased out in a smooth transition without further incident.

The ultimate loss of federal funding by an enterprise with all the political clout and public stature of *Sesame Street* shows the dangers of relying on institutional support, whether from the government, a private foundation, or a corporation. Institutions have a way of changing their agendas. Unless an exempt organization has diversified its sources of revenue, it is very vulnerable to such shifts.

Assessing the Potential to Raise Money

The starting point in any effort to raise funds from any source is to recognize that funding sources are typically inundated with appeals for support, and that getting their attention takes skilled planning and execution.

In fact, such a profusion of messages is unleashed on the public today that it is hard for any single enterprise to be heard. A torrent of advertisements for commercial products and services, campaigns for political candidates and issues, and appeals for worthy causes flood the communication channels. To be noticed at all, one has to create a sharply differentiated and powerfully delivered message.

A marketing approach to fundraising will be premised on a realistic assessment of the potential of the organization to raise money. Past efforts of the organization, results achieved by comparable organizations, and sounding out of prospects will inform the judgment as to how successful a campaign is going to be. Fundraising goals will not be defined solely by the cost of the programs the organization wishes to conduct. Rather, program aspirations must be tempered by a realistic assessment of the market potential for raising support.

Fundraising, whether directed at individuals or at institutions, must also be seen as involving an exchange: value is given by a donor in exchange for value received from the fundraising organization. For instance, government agencies look to advance programs that further their political interests; foundations seek organizations that implement their objectives; businesses give research grants because university-based researchers can often do the work less expensively than the company's own staff; corporations want to advance their public relations goals or even get help with sales promotions; and private donors tend to seek enhancement of their self-esteem.

While not every gift involves such motives, an organization seeking money has to think about—*and carefully research*—what will motivate a funding source to contribute, as well as the right time and place to make the pitch. As Philip Kotler writes in *Marketing for Nonprofit Organizations*, "Donations should not be viewed as a transfer but as a *transaction*."[1]

Positioning Your Appeal

A marketing approach begins, then, with a conscious calculation of an organization's potential appeal to various possible fund providers ("market segmentation"). This analysis will seek to identify a particular segment of fund providers to whom the organization may have a stronger appeal than those of other fund seekers. The single most important decision in devising a marketing campaign is this positioning.

Edward L. Nash asserts in his book *Direct Marketing: Strategy, Planning, Execution*:

> The essence of strategic product planning requires . . . a commitment about what your product or service is and how you want it perceived. You can't have it be all things to all people. It can be the best or the cheapest, traditional or innovative, entertaining or educational. To try to be everything at once is to be nothing.[2]

To position an organization in the fundraising market, then, a careful definition of the organization's appeal is required. Often, the organization's internal description of its services has to be recast in broader, more basic terms to appeal to potential contributors. For example, the American Film Institute's campaign to preserve old film negatives from physical deterioration is presented to potential donors as a program to preserve an essential element of America's cultural heritage.

Communicating Your Appeal

In a well-conceived marketing effort, careful research is conducted into the motives that prompt funding sources to give, as well as their stated criteria for gifts. The form and content of appeals is then tailored to the interests and nature of specific funding targets. In every case, the form and manner in which the appeal is communicated to the donor are as crucial as the content of the message.

For instance, if alumni loyalty to a school is seen as the primary motivator of giving, an educational institution will organize a system whereby selected alumni raise funds from their peers. In other words, an alumnus or alumna of each class (i.e., a class agent) is appointed to conduct a mail solicitation of funds from classmates. This effort is backed up by phone calls from the agent and other volunteer alumni or, occasionally, by current students. Cultivation of very wealthy alumni for major gifts is handled by personal visits from university officers, generally the president.

Nonprofit institutions without a core of loyal supporters may solicit funds from targeted segments of the public by using volunteer door-to-door canvassers; this method usually requires publicity in order to succeed. Appeals may also be cast in the form of invitations to expensive theater benefits or dinners honoring a well-known figure, both of which require a reliable list of upscale potential ticket buyers in order to attain their goals.

If the best potential fund providers are foundations or government agencies, a skillfully written grant application is usually required. But carefully planned personal contact with officials is also important in helping the nonprofit organization to become familiar with the funding source's interests as well as its criteria and process for making awards.

Coordination and Diversification

The fundraising effort should be centrally coordinated in order to avoid solicitation of the same potential donor by more than one department. An attempt should also be made to diversify the sources of support so that an organization is not beholden to one or even a handful of powerful benefactors. Wherever possible, vulnerability to the inevitable volatility of government and foundation funding should be minimized by the solicitation of private support. Indeed, a prudent nonprofit institution that obtains foundation or government support will anticipate from the outset that such aid will be phased out someday and will plan for alternative sources of funds.

Market Feedback

A marketing approach to fundraising is a two-way system. It involves planning and formulating the institution's appeal for funds to potential donors, but it is also an important source of information as to how well the institution's product is being received in the marketplace and to changes in that marketplace. A marketing network thus serves as an intelligence system.

Tom Peters and Robert Waterman, Jr. point out in their *In Search of Excellence*:

> Excellent companies are better listeners. They get a benefit from market closeness that for us was truly unexpected, that is, until you think about it. Most of their real innovation comes from the market.[3]

In sum, marketing is a deliberate and conceptual approach to raising funds; it is a disciplined managerial process involving analysis, planning, and execution. It is an *assertive* process; it sees a nonprofit organization as *earning* the support it receives by conferring important benefits on funding sources rather than simply appealing to the goodwill of benefactors.

The four major sources of funding are government, foundations, corporations, and individuals. Each of these sources can be regarded as a separate donor market with its own special characteristics and requirements.

Government: A Special Relationship in Jeopardy

In today's economy, it is a way of life for private organizations, whether for-profit or not-for-profit, to seek contracts from the government. Exempt organizations are providers of social goods, and government is by far the largest purchaser of such goods. The government is thus a natural partner for many nonprofit institutions in their efforts to carry out their social missions.

Indeed, for some nonprofit activities or projects, there is no alternative except to seek government support. The scale or nature of a particular project, for example, may dictate government funding as the only available resource. For example, take the case of a research project like Princeton University's Plasma Physics Laboratory, where the practical payoff, if any, in harnessing hydrogen fusion to provide energy won't come until after the year 2000, more than 30 years after the start of the project. The annual cost of this basic research is close to $100 million. Industry won't pick up the tab. The only realistic source is the federal government.

At one time, the government was perceived as a natural ally of nonprofit organizations, not only funding many of them but also sharing their concerns and policy agendas. The advice of nonprofit leaders and professionals was regularly sought by government agencies and legislative committees in dealing with issues and in the design of new programs.

In the "post-government era" we are now entering, the relationship between the nonprofit and government sectors may undergo a transformation. Clearly, fewer dollars will be available for many nonprofit programs, given the trend of the budgets now being put together in Washington and many state capitals. The decline in government support appears to have set in before the 1994 election tidal wave that swept Republicans into control of both houses of Congress. In 1994, the exempt organizations categorized by the *Nonprofit Times*[4] as the 100 with the largest revenues suffered a sharp 23 percent decline in federal and state funding compared to 1993. The decline was the first in three years.

More fundamentally, the special rapport that once existed between the government and nonprofit sectors may fracture. The real danger is that the new political agenda driving government today may provoke a more generalized negative attitude toward nonprofits on the part of government. The efforts of Congressional forces to bar nonprofit organizations from representing their interests before Congress, even with nonfederal funds, are one sign of the new attitude that may be taking hold. Another is the increasing rigor with which government regulations in various areas are now being applied to nonprofits, adding significantly to the organization's expenses. Even if the most dire possibilities do not materialize, nonprofits are going to have to work both "harder" and "smarter" than ever before to maintain their traditional special relationship with the government sector. Indeed, the national leadership of nonprofits needs to turn its attention to this issue in order to mount efforts to preserve the relationship.

The following discussion refers not to maintaining the special relationship between the government and nonprofit sectors but to the ordinary day-to-day hazards of seeking government support.

Government Funding: Special Costs and Risks

As the "*Sesame Street* Funding War" illustrated, the continued availability of any form of government support is inherently uncertain as political priorities change over time.

Another drawback of government funding is the frequent need to obtain funds from a variety of government agencies with conflicting program priorities and requirements in order to raise enough money to support a single program. A classic illustration of this is the way public broadcasting is funded by the federal government. The Corporation for Public Broadcasting (CPB), the government institution charged with channeling funds to public television stations and helping them to develop programs, has nowhere near the amount of funds required to finance programming for the system. One year, CPB's entire budget for developing new programs was $8 million. The stations, even with their own efforts to tap public support, must marshal additional sources of funding in order to pay for programming.

In contrast, the commercial television networks in the country provide "one-stop shopping" for program producers: if a network wants a program, it can and will pay the costs of its development. (Commercial television budgets are traditionally much larger than those in public broadcasting.) The result is that producers for public television must not only sell a show to the stations, but they must work very hard to find some combination of government agencies and private corporations willing to help fund the program. This kind of search is not only frustrating and expensive to conduct, but, even when it is successful, it often involves trying to balance the conflicting goals of the various funders, shaping and twisting a concept to please diverse interests. The wonder of the public broadcasting system is that somehow so many quality programs are produced in spite of it.

The difficulties and costs of raising public money for television are by no means unique; rather, the cited problems plague a wide range of social efforts dependent on government support.

Success in obtaining government money also poses its problems. There are subtle and not so subtle dangers in living on government funding. Government funding poses the following risks:

- Distortion of the institution's true interests to conform to government objectives.
- The creation of "have" (government-funded) and "have-not" (non-government-funded) departments in the same organization.
- The establishment of a special class of personnel whose only connection to the institution is their work on a government contract. For instance, for many years the Plasma Physics Lab at Princeton University, with more than 200 employees, had only two university departmental faculty members associated with the project. The vast bulk of lab employees became a special class of employees who sought salary arrangements different from those of other university employees, creating all kinds of problems and tensions.
- Detailed, far-ranging government audits that threaten the heart of an institution's freedom and are expensive to respond to, even if the organization can eventually refute all claims. For example, the 1974 audit by the Department of Health, Education, and Welfare (HEW) of Children's Television Workshop's *Sesame Street* series recommended government review of CTW executive compensation policies even though no salaries higher than $30,000 a year were charged to the government grant. The 1974 audit also recommended greater reuse of show segments to reduce costs, which constituted government influence on programming decisions. In the same audit, HEW staff members also recommended that CTW submit to competitive bidding the segments of the *Sesame Street* series performed by the famous Muppet characters Big Bird, Ernie, and Burt! To government auditors, these marvelous and unique puppets were as replaceable as nuts and bolts.
- The imposition of requirements that are unrelated to the substance of the funded project but further the funding sources' collateral aims. For instance, HEW required CTW to caption *Sesame Street* for the deaf, at a cost to CTW of $150,000.
- Voluminous reporting and review requirements that absorb so much of a nonprofit organization's time and energy as to distract it from its main tasks.

The frustration of dealing with a stream of red tape is often compounded by the efforts of many bureaucracies to cloak their staffs in anonymity, precluding grant recipients from identifying the individuals who are responsible for adverse actions.

The moral here is not that government funding inevitably poses unacceptable risks, but rather that government funding is not for the unwary and unsophisticated. A nonprofit's management must therefore assess the extent to which the operation of an institution is vulnerable to the reduction or cutoff of the flow of government funds. In particular, it should examine in advance whether a potential reduction or cutoff would affect

- ◆ Core programs;
- ◆ Critical, hard-to-replace personnel; or
- ◆ Indirect costs that have been allocated to government projects and that can not be eliminated even if funding is lost.

If it is at all possible, such program commitments and costs should be funded, at least in part, with nongovernmental money so as to minimize the damage that would occur to an institution if its government funding were curtailed.

Building an Organization to Seek Government Funds

An entity that must regularly approach government sources for significant support needs a professional staff with experience in dealing with public agencies. This staff should process applications for funds; coordinate different departments' search for funding; maintain contacts with officials of key funding agencies, and with the legislators who play decisive roles in controlling such agencies' funding or overseeing their operations; ensure compliance with government regulations; and stay abreast of shifting government priorities and interests. Where necessary, the staff must also learn how to pierce a bureaucracy's veil of anonymity and find ways of making the agency more responsive. A nonprofit organization must be as professional in seeking government funding as the treasury department of a large corporation is in raising capital from Wall Street.

In particular, the staff must master the nature of the government appropriation process. An understanding of the process—and the key players in it—is required in order to support the efforts of a friendly executive department or set of legislators in securing funding from the legislature and to plan for when the actual funds are going to be available. The risk of delay in getting funds from the government has to be taken into account in planning the cash-flow of an organization.

Nonprofit institutions playing the government funding game must be prepared, on occasion, to mount a political campaign to protect their interests. In order to be able to mount such a campaign, an organization has to develop over a period of time a political base it can call on. It has to cultivate relationships with the legislature and within the executive branch, as well as with public constituencies, in order to be able to bring them into play when necessary. The 1970s saw a move in the U.S. House of Representatives to eliminate or curtail the tax deduction for charitable contributions. In the end, the movement was defeated—not by presenting neatly argued position papers (although these were prepared) or by lobbying members of Congress on the bill (although this was done), but by developing grass-roots support for the deduction in every representative's home district. The organizers of this effort received their highest accolade when one member of Congress told them, "You guys are as tough as the unions!"

Foundation Grants

There are some 42,000 foundations in this country, but foundation resources and activity are concentrated in approximately 17 percent of the nation's total foundations. The 18th edition of *The Foundation Directory,* published by The Foundation Center in 1996 lists 7,549 foundations that account for approximately $178 billion in assets, or 87 percent of all the assets of active grantmaking foundations in the United States. These foundations made a total of $10 billion in grants, or 90 percent of all the grants paid out in the year of record.[5]

Foundations vary widely not only in size but also in character and in operating style. A good number of foundations are family foundations set up by a wealthy individual to support activities that are especially meaningful to the donor. Such foundations are typically administered by family members or legal counsel. At the other extreme are the professional foundations that support a wide range of activities according to priorities set by their boards of trustees; these foundations are administered by full-time professional staffs.

Corporations sometimes organize foundations to give away up to 5 percent of adjusted net income, the contribution of which they are allowed to deduct against corporate taxes. Some corporate foundations are administered casually on a part-time basis by a member of the corporate staff, or in some cases by a full-time staff member specially hired for the purpose. In addition to the foundations that make grants to others, there are operating foundations, which use their resources to conduct their own research or to provide a direct service. Obviously, these types of foundations are of little interest to an organization seeking funds for its own programs.

Many people assume that foundations are interested in any good work they hear about. In fact, almost all foundations of any size now have very well-defined program objectives; certainly this is the case for professionally staffed organizations.

As a rule, foundations do not like to provide general institutional support; they prefer to back specific new programs that would not be undertaken but for the foundation's help, and that which mesh with the institution's defined program objectives. Most foundations are hesitant to make grants for endowment or for buildings. They prefer to fund operational programs.

Foundations like to make grants that they are convinced will have an "impact," by which they mean inducing others to emulate the program they have financed. They also tend to favor "leveraging" their funds, by which they mean attracting others to contribute to the financing of the program in which they invest.

As one might expect, the degree of precision with which foundations express their objectives varies widely from institution to institution. For instance, three foundations may all be similarly concerned with helping higher education, but one will announce its goals as "aiding higher education," another as "helping colleges and universities deal with their management and financial problems," and a third as "improving instructional methodology and content, especially projects that cross traditional lines between disciplines." Without specifically inquiring of each foundation, it would be impossible to tell from a simple reading of these statements whether they would all support similar specific programs or have very different aims in mind.

To illuminate how a foundation's program goals can shape its grantmaking, let me review how one foundation developed its program. Lloyd Morrisett, head of the Markle Foundation, explained to me in an interview the rationale he had presented to his trustees in 1969 that led to the redirection of the foundation's program from support of medical school professionals to communications. In our conversation, Morrisett recalled having recommended that the foundation center its efforts on communications because

1. The communications industry was an area of great importance but had been largely ignored by philanthropic institutions. The Ford Foundation was active in supporting public broadcasting, but the entire terrain of commercial broadcasting was largely unexplored.

2. Even a small foundation like Markle could have an impact since the target audience, senior officials in the fields of publishing and broadcast communications, was quite small, numbering perhaps no more than 10,000. The number of people and institutions one had to influence was thus relatively small in comparison to, say, the number of people involved with public schools in this country. Lloyd was convinced that the principal reason for the failure of the foundation project is "undercapitalization financially or intellectually." Thus, finding a universe small enough for Markle to fund adequately with its budget was critical.

3. Government regulation of broadcasting as well as of copyrights, and the Supreme Court's interest in First Amendment issues, would inevitably raise

significant public policy issues. Such issues represent an area where it is relatively feasible for a foundation to fund useful efforts. Moreover, the scope of such issues is more readily definable in broadcasting than in such broad fields as education.

4. Morrisett's own experience before coming to Markle indicated that broadcasting was a good field in which to leverage funds. As a vice-president at the Carnegie Corporation, he had initiated the idea of creating Children's Television Workshop and had spearheaded the assembling of a consortium of foundations and the federal Office of Education in order to provide $8 million to launch the workshop in 1969.

5. The people skills needed for grantmaking in communications involve an analytic orientation, an understanding of economic, social, and legal issues, and an appreciation of the impact of public policy on an industry. These skills are general enough for many people to acquire them relatively quickly, especially in comparison to a specialized area such as, say, pediatric endocrinology.

6. The timing was right. If a foundation's efforts are to succeed, there has to be a receptivity in the larger public, as well as in important institutions, to the foundation's aims. The resources that even the largest foundation can marshal will not have an impact unless the climate is hospitable. As an example, Morrisett cited Children's Television Workshop's initiation of the *Sesame Street* programs in 1969 as a case of "perfect timing." The public was focused on preschool education, and potential friends of such a program were in the right places in government and foundations.

Many foundations, once they have identified an area of general interest, such as communications, will develop a set of more specific objectives. For instance, they may try to foster more effective "children's educational programming" and "informational" programming within the field of communications. Under Morrisett, however, Markle resisted this approach. In Morrisett's view, "If an area is important, I'm not sure I would place many limits on decisions to grant support in the field ... beyond the limits of imagination and available resources."[6]

Many foundations today have as clearly articulated a rationale for their choice of program interests as Markle. Accordingly, a nonprofit's focus in seeking a foundation grant has to be on matching an organization's program goals with those of a specific foundation.

There are many sources of information about foundation activities. A good starting point is The Foundation Center, a nonprofit organization with research libraries in New York, Washington, D.C., San Francisco, Cleveland, and Atlanta. The center issues a series of publications including *The Foundation Directory*, which provides capsule descriptions of the program interests of approximately 7,500 of the largest foundations, and *Foundation Fundamentals: A Guide for Grantseekers.*

Since even the most narrowly focused descriptions of foundation interests are likely to be somewhat elastic, a fund-seeking organization should go beyond published descriptions and study what types of grant awards a foundation has in fact made. The foundation's annual report is a good source for this information, and The Foundation Center's *Foundation Grants Index* may be helpful.

Even with this research, informal contact with the foundations an organization thinks offer potential will save time in the long run. A good application takes effort to prepare; if filed blindly, it may sit for weeks at a foundation that has no interest in it. A phone call, even in a case where no one in the organization knows an official at the foundation, can produce helpful hints as to whether a particular activity is likely to be of interest. A brief letter may elicit enough information to preclude the preparation of a full-blown application that is of no interest to a foundation.

If a preliminary inquiry is encouraging, try to arrange a visit to talk with a foundation official before filing a formal application. Find out what the foundation's internal process is for awarding grants and what criteria it applies in making awards. Learn the timing of its funding cycle and try to ascertain what kinds of things really interest the staff member who will review the grant proposal.

For example, would it help to invite the person to visit your organization? Is there something compelling you could show a foundation representative that would give life and power to what could otherwise be dry words on paper? Is the staff member interested only in the content of an organization's program, or is the overall quality of its management, especially its financial administration, also crucial? Can you distinguish your program in some fashion from those of your competitors? What kind of demonstration might show the officials that a grant will have impact beyond the boundaries of your organization? Is leveraging funds important to this particular foundation?

Finally, nonprofit organizations, if they can afford to, should cultivate potentially supportive foundations on a regular basis, not just when they want to put in a grant proposal. Larger institutions, such as major private universities, will typically assign a development staff officer (an "account executive") to make regular calls on a list of target foundations, partly to keep up contacts and partly to learn of new directions or interests developing at the foundation. The account executive sometimes arranges for a senior officer of the university or a distinguished faculty member to accompany him or her to talk about some aspect of the university, not necessarily one for which funding will be sought.

The point is that success at grantseeking has less to do with the altruism of an organization's aims than the skill with which it identifies a foundation with matching interests and then cultivates this interest.

Corporate Support

Many corporations provide support for charitable activities, as the federal tax code permits such businesses to deduct up to 5 percent of their adjusted gross income for gifts to charities. Some corporations, as I noted earlier, organize their charitable activities in the form of a foundation; some operate quite informally. But some programs of nonprofit organizations may also be funded out of a corporation's regular operating budget, if the programs further a specific business purpose of the company. For instance, the underwriting of a public television series may be charged to the corporation's public relations or advertising budget, while counseling services for chemically dependent employees or job training may be funded by the personnel budget. In considering the potential for corporate support, therefore, nonprofit institutions should begin by analyzing how their program can serve the interests of specific business entities. Initially, in the attempt to narrow the universe of corporations to a prospect list that can be explored in depth, the following criteria may be useful:

Geographic proximity. Corporations tend to favor supporting nonprofit organizations located in the same geographical area, especially where it can be shown that the service provides some benefits to the corporation's employees (e.g., a local health care facility or cultural activity).

Specific benefit to the corporation. Corporations will favor supporting a necessary service provided by the nonprofit enterprise directly to a company, such as counseling the corporation's chemically dependent employees. Other services may be attractive to companies because they have a general need for them, although the benefit to the company from any particular nonprofit organization may be only indirect. For example, engineering schools might seek support from companies that hire large numbers of engineers.

Personal relationships with key officials. Personally knowing someone in the right corporate department, or at least someone senior enough to steer a nonprofit institution to the right person in the corporate structure, is an obvious advantage. Board members of a nonprofit organization, as well as professional staff members, should always review their corporate contacts as part of a fundraising search.

An image fit. A corporation's advertising and public relations efforts may suggest themes or objectives for which the nonprofit institution's program can provide support. An example is provided in the discussion, later in the chapter, of how Children's Television Workshop gained the support of United Technologies Corporation for a new children's television series.

An existing area of interest. A corporation may have previously supported similar programs. For example, the Mobil, Exxon, and Atlantic Richfield corporations are known for their interest in underwriting public television series, so a nonprofit entity with a public television project might consider them as possible prospects. Other companies will be known for their active support of the performing arts, museums, hospitals, and so forth.

These criteria, however, are just a starting point in approaching a corporation for funding. In preparing to approach specific companies, a nonprofit organization must keep in mind that corporate support for nonprofits is prompted by a pragmatic interest in enhancing some aspect of the corporation's goals. Hence, in seeking corporate funds, a nonprofit should be able to explain how supporting its program will in turn further a particular corporate objective.

For example, take United Technologies' $2 million grant in 1979 to Children's Television Workshop to help fund *3-2-1 Contact,* a public television series on science and technology for children between ages of eight and twelve. At the time, United Technologies was a conglomerate spending substantial sums on trying to build a corporate identity as a leader in the technology field. Its public relations department had just added two executives who had been at Mobil Corporation and had worked on that oil giant's active underwriting of public television series. CTW contacted the UT public relations staff informally to see whether UT might be interested in being the sole corporate sponsor of the show. When UT expressed interest, CTW made a presentation first to the public relations department and eventually to Harry Gray, UT's chief executive officer, and his key aides. In pitching its proposal, CTW was aware that in public television an underwriter of a show receives only a brief oral and visual mention of its name at the end of the show, after the production credits are shown. This exposure is minimal, especially compared to the scope of commercials for the much larger audiences attracted by commercial television. How, then, did CTV induce UT to contribute $2 million to *3-2-1 Contact*?

In all its presentations to UT, Children's Television Workshop stressed that underwriting *3-2-1 Contact* could give UT substantial public relations benefits, provided that it vigorously promoted its association with the show through advertising in newspapers and other mass media. Of course, in order to do this, UT would have to spend a good deal of money on advertising in addition to what it would spend underwriting the show. But such advertising would bring wide attention to UT's underwriting regardless of how many viewers actually watched the series on public television and noticed the brief underwriting credit at the end of each show. United Technologies bought CTW's concept.

Just before *3-2-1 Contact* went on the air, United Technologies placed ads in selected major U.S. newspapers and national magazines with the headline, "Will there ever be another show as worthwhile as *Sesame Street*?" That gave United Technologies the double benefit of underwriting a show for children on science and technology and acquiring an association with *Sesame Street,* the most widely known educational children's television show in history.

Tie-in promotions with vendors of commercial products or services are another means of tapping corporations to support nonprofit causes. A tie-in promotion involves a commercial vendor linking its product to a charitable cause.

In business, this is know as "affinity marketing." Long-distance telephone carriers and credit card companies assign a percentage of customers' expenditures to a charity they select. In a twist on the routine, a phone company might assign 1 percent of its annual sales to 30 nonprofit organizations chosen by its customers in an annual poll. Today more and more businesses are utilizing this technique.

Individual Contributors

The vast majority of funds provided to 501(c)(3) organizations entitled by the IRS to solicit tax-deductible contributions are contributed by individuals rather than by foundations and corporations; 80 percent of the $129.88 billion Americans gave to charity in 1994 came from individuals.

Successful fundraising from individuals (including solicitation of gifts from entities they control) is in the first instance a product of an appealing cause, persuasively advocated by senior representatives of the exempt organization who have a gift for donor cultivation and the ability to close a transaction. Like every type of fundraising, it is also very much the result of careful planning and investigation by an expert staff.

Campaigns Aimed at a Cohesive Constituency

Cohesive constituencies consist of individuals who share membership in an institution of civic prestige (e.g., a museum), or in a religious congregation,[7] or have attended the same school, or have shared an experience, (e.g., having been treated in the same hospital), or share a special personal affinity with the exempt organization. If a group is large enough, its size may justify the cost of organizing a campaign specifically targeted at the group and capitalizing on group members' affinity with the exempt organization.

However, as the competition for what is at best a slowly growing pool of private contribution dollars intensifies, more and more individual organizations have to consider whether they can raise more money by appealing on their own for contributions or by joining forces in an umbrella campaign by organizations in the same field. Organizations with a very distinctive and sharply defined mission with which their patrons particularly identify can have a special identity—a brand name, if you will. Such organizations, if located in a large enough community, may well find that maintaining their own campaign pays off. Philharmonic orchestras, operas, and ballets in the country's major cities obviously tend to believe they fall into this category.

At the same time, there are individuals that give generally to the performing arts for public relations or other reasons, and there will thus be a substantial number of common contributors to the performing arts. Would a consolidated campaign— with the potential to gain efficiencies in its administration and thus put more dollars into a broader, more visible, and more effective cultivation of donors—yield more net funds for the participating organizations? Such consolidated campaigns are particularly productive when each of the participants is too small to achieve strong name recognition on its own among contributors. The United Way and the UJA-Federation annual campaigns on behalf of hundreds of smaller agencies are examples of how a consolidated campaign can pay off for smaller entities.

The Characteristics of a Successful Fundraising Campaign

Certain intangible qualities make for a successful fundraising campaign. To paraphrase the American Express commercial, don't start a campaign without them. I call them the *Ten Fundamentals of Constituency Fundraising*.

1. Dynamic and Well-Informed Leadership is Essential.

Before I left for New Orleans and Tulane University in the late summer of 1989 to head, among other duties, Tulane's forthcoming major fundraising campaign, I decided to talk to some people in the East who had been successful at the task. My favorite among those I spoke with was George Hyman, a Wall Street investment banker who was chairman of New York University's highly successful campaign. He had a strong, forceful personality and obviously enjoyed his fundraising role. I still remember his observations on the art of successful fundraising from individuals:

> I love raising money. It's a good cause, and I make people feel good by asking them, because that tells them I think they have accomplished something in this life.

> I never worry about asking for too much; I'm just flattering the prospects by suggesting I think [they are] worth more than they actually are.

> I never call on a prospect unless I know everything about the person—not just what he or she does for a living or his or her probable net worth, but what [the person's] interests are and, in the end, what is likely to motivate [the person] to act.

"Of course," he added, "we have a special asset at NYU: Larry Tisch. It is not just the enormous amount of money he's given but the time he's willing to put into helping us cultivate others. There are some prospects who are going to be really impressed by having lunch with Larry in his CBS dining room, and, if it's important to do that, he does it."[8]

I didn't quite realize it at the time, but Hyman had captured the essence of a campaign:

◆ Be proud of the cause you represent and of asking others to contribute to it. It's good work.

◆ Do meticulous homework not just to identify prospects but to know all that you can about them. This kind of previsit preparation is the key to successful cultivation.

◆ Know what will motivate prospects to give—for example, access to someone they value but could not meet on their own, be it Larry Tisch or a leading faculty scientist or economist; or a chance to offer advice or to have their name on a building. *Do not equate capacity to give with a willingness or readiness to give.*

◆ Above all, the leaders of the campaign must be well known among the organization's constituency or enjoy a strong reputation with the group. They must come across as personally committed, focused, persuasive, and visibly confident in the success of the cause they represent. Certainly, this was the impression George Hyman conveyed from the moment one entered his presence.

2. Not Every Gift Can Be Accepted.   Early in my work at Tulane, I learned another indispensable ingredient to successful fundraising: learning when to say "no" to a gift, hopefully without antagonizing a potential donor.

At Tulane, a leading board member and his wife very much wanted their name on a new building the university was planning. They offered what they considered a substantial gift, but the building's naming was one of the university's best opportunities to raise a very large gift. The offered gift fell short of this standard. Since the largest share of any campaign's contributions comes from a relatively small number of very large gifts, the university could not afford to give away the building name for what, in terms of the campaign's needs, was a modest gift.

Moreover, since this donation would have been one of the campaign's firsts—and by a major figure in the Tulane community—it would have sent the wrong signal. As I learned in studying other university campaigns, if a drive is to start off on the right note, it is critical that the first gifts come from important figures in the community and in amounts that represent a "stretch" on their part. The gifts need not be among the largest of the campaign, but the leaders of the university have to demonstrate that they have gone the extra mile, relative to their own resources, because of the campaign's importance. The goal is to send out a signal to other leaders that this campaign is so important that they are going to be called upon to dig deeper into their pockets than usual.

Since I had been the one to point out within the administration that we could not afford to accept the proposed gift, the president assigned me the task of informing the trustee that his gift had been rejected. The trustee was not at all pleased when I delivered the response, but I went to some pains to explain the logic of the university's position and to stress that the university was very pleased with being offered the gift and would be happy to provide a naming opportunity in a prominent place *within* the building. The prospective donor rejected the alternative, but a few years later he and his wife offered a much larger gift, and the building was named after them.

3. The Majority of Funds Will Be Contributed by a Few Individuals. Peter Edles, a veteran campaign consultant, makes the following observations in his book *Fundraising: Hands-On Tactics for Nonprofit Groups:*

1. Ten percent of the goal comes from a single gift.
2. Approximately 80 to 90 percent of incoming funds are donated by 10 to 20 percent of the membership or constituency.[9]

A similar picture was painted for us at Tulane by our campaign consultant, Marts & Lundy; the initial Tulane Campaign Plan projected that half of the target $300 million would come from 49 donors who gave a $1 million or more, including one gift that would account for 8 percent of the total and nine gifts that accounted for nearly 30 percent of funds raised. (See Table 10.1 later in the chapter for the complete projection.)

4. The Campaign Must Have a Sense of Urgency. Fundraising has a way of taking much longer than one expects unless the campaign staff and leadership are driven from the outset by a strong sense of urgency. When one embarks on a multiyear campaign, it is easy to think there is plenty of time to get things done. But time has a funny way of slipping by if the campaign staff and leadership become overly absorbed in internal meetings and don't "get out on the road." My point is simple: you are not going to raise money by talking to each other; the potential donors are "out there," and you have to start the cultivation process as early as possible.

Prospects can also sense the pulse of a campaign. If they get the feeling that the fundraising organization does not believe its needs are urgent, they are not going to be in a hurry to open their wallets. It's hard for an organization to convince prospective donors that it has a compelling cause if it proceeds to make its case at a leisurely pace.

You also never know when some change in external and internal circumstances will upset a well-planned campaign. For example, the stock market crash of 1987 not only seriously reduced the wealth of some key prospects, it unnerved even people who were not as affected and made them less disposed to part with their personal resources. So, if conditions favor your campaign, don't assume life will always be thus; get going while the circumstances are right.

By the way, in business sales there is nothing like the prospect of getting a sharply reduced bonus because one has fallen behind on one's call schedule to keep a sales force on its toes. I can't see why an incentive system would not similarly motivate the development staff of an exempt organization.

5. Paradoxically, You Can't Rush the Cultivation Process. Even when one is dealing with prospects who have previously made capital gifts and are active in the leadership of the organization, one must be prepared to spend time soliciting their views on the organization. This means listening carefully to them, responding candidly to difficult questions they may raise, taking them into one's confidence to explain the state of the organization and its plans, inviting them to special organizational events, exploring their gift-giving ideas, and offering a range of possible purposes for their gift. It's rare to make a first call on a prospect and have them whip out their checkbook and make the hoped-for gift. Getting a donation from a first-time prospect customarily takes quite some time, just as in business it may take a while to persuade a new customer to buy a product, especially if the product is a new one. (At Prudential, I spent nine months flying regularly to San Francisco to persuade the pension director of a large oil company—which had been only a marginal investor in real estate—to make a major investment in a new real estate product we were offering.)

At Tulane, an alumnus who was prominent in the community told me one day about one of the city's wealthiest and most successful entrepreneurs, who was not a graduate of a Tulane—or of any university—and whom the city as a whole had largely overlooked. This man wanted help from the university with a small matter: he wanted a hotel belonging to him and located near the campus to be listed by university departments as a place to send guests and hold meetings. The university arranged a luncheon with him, and within a week his hotel was listed as he wished. Shortly thereafter, the hotel's business from university guests improved substantially. My wife and I then spent months getting to know the man and his family (and, indeed, became good friends).

The next step came six months after the initial meeting, when we asked the entrepreneur to help mobilize some of the people in the city's hotel and restaurant business to support the university's effort to become a member of a regional athletic conference. Our friend did this with great enthusiasm. Still later, he was asked to become a member of a new committee just established by the board of trustees to oversee one of the university's new business ventures. At no time during this process was the idea of his making a gift to the university broached; our goal was to get him involved with the university in areas in which he could contribute, so that eventually he might be receptive to the idea of making a significant gift.

6. A Well-Managed Organization Is a Prerequisite. The rules and realities of fundraising closely resemble those of raising capital for a business. A fundraising effort should be premised on the idea that contributors will be more receptive to an organization whose track record shows that the organization is well managed and can project and then deliver *specific* results. Donors, as a rule, go for "winners," not failing organizations. If an organization is newly formed, then its leaders need to have a record of experience and expertise, and they must produce a solid plan for both the management of the organization and its campaign.

Donors also want to be told just how their money is going to be used and what concrete results they can expect to see. Once, the dean of Tulane's business school and the chancellor of the medical school were fighting over whose priority it was to cultivate a prominent and very successful graduate of Tulane's business school. To try to settle the dispute, I visited the donor and asked him whether he wanted to make his major gifts to the medical school or the business school. He replied that he and his family preferred to make their contributions to the medical school to support specific research projects by particular physicians, because they could see the outcome that resulted from their support. The donor was thus designated a medical school prospect, and the school was given a year to demonstrate that it could cultivate him to contribute in line with his means.

7. The Cultivation of Contributors Does Not End When Their Money Comes In.
The results of a fundraising campaign should be measurable, and the organization should report to contributors how their money was used and what results were achieved. There is, in fact, no more effective way to stay in touch with contributors and to sustain their loyalty than to report to them regularly on the progress being made with the use of their funds. This kind of communication is particularly effective if it comes from the person or team employing the donor's funds. In the case of major gifts, an appropriate ceremony honoring the donor is in order.

Perhaps most important of all is the organization head's readiness to spend time with a major giver *after* the gift is in hand. The president of a private research university and his wife, for example, spend a long weekend every year visiting the home of the university's largest benefactor, and they regularly accompanied another significant benefactor on a trip. Both of these occasions provided an opportunity for easy conversation about the university and other topics. Note that the subject of further giving by the donor is never raised on these occasions.

8. Keep Broadening the Prospect Base. It is risky to keep mining the same limited group of donors for large gifts. Some major donors are not financially able to keep giving on the same scale; others may develop new interests for their charitable giving (since the odds are that many of your major donors are being wooed by other organizations). Some may hold back until they see others step forward, not wanting to be looked to for yet another leadership gift. Indeed, at Tulane, one of the largest donors to the capital campaign told us that he wanted to see if the university could find others who could give in the way that he had because, unless we did, the university could not expect to increase significantly the amount it raised. Finding new major prospects has to be a top priority of the precampaign planning, and especially of the research staff.

9. A Customer-Focused Culture is Key. It is a formidable management challenge to educate personnel to rethink the way they view their jobs and the people to whom they should direct most of their energy. To do so amounts to changing the organization's culture. But this is precisely the challenge that leaders of many nonprofit organizations must meet if they want to increase the funds they raise from private contributors. Nonprofit employees, like their counterparts in many business organizations, are typically absorbed in accomplishing the tasks assigned to them by their immediate supervisors, and in their supervisors' reaction to their work. After all, it is those supervisors who determine employees' raises and promotions.

Even within development staffs, it is not unusual for employees to focus on gaining exposure to senior officers of the organizations, particularly the head of the organization, rather than on cultivating prospective contributors. Following the familiar routine of pushing papers and attending internal meetings on fundraising issues is less demanding than leaving one's home terrain and addressing the concerns—and attracting the interests—of potential prospects.

A fundraising staff that is too internally focused is the result of an organizational ethos that confers status according to how often one meets with the president or his or her chief deputies, as if one were working in a government bureau where the perception that a person has access to higher-ranking officers is itself a source of power. Such organizations are *bureaucratic* in character.

Changing this kind of culture requires a revamping of both the financial and psychological compensation system so that cultivation of prospects is rewarded. In addition to changing the reward system, senior management—starting at the top—must promulgate for each organizational unit a very clear set of objectives. One universal objective should be that developing the goodwill of prospective donors is part of everyone's job. New values have to be established through clear and consistent communication.

Within every organization, there are numerous opportunities to get across messages as to what the basic values of the organization are. I can remember Bill Bowen, as president of Princeton, emphasizing at every opportunity—in large meetings and in personal conversations—his conviction that a commitment to excellence in every phase of university activity was to be Princeton's hallmark. No one could fail to be aware of the standard of performance expected of them by Bowen.

Part of bringing about a change in an organization's culture is making all employees aware of what is involved in cultivating prospects. Effective cultivation involves more than a call on a prospect; it relates to all the dimensions of potential interaction between an institution and a prospect. It certainly includes getting out fast, accurate, and thoughtful responses to routine inquiries by prospects, as well as listening carefully to issues raised by a prospect and treating the prospect as someone with ideas as well as money to contribute. The countless daily interactions between an organization's staff and prospective supporters need to reflect the priority to be given to these supporters. Nothing infuriates a donor or prospect more than a curt or inaccurate response to an inquiry about the status of his or her past gifts, particularly if the response reveals that the staff has not kept accurate records of how much a donor has contributed or how much of such a contribution has actually been used for the purpose for which the funds were raised. An employee who, rather than providing an explanation, reacts as if the donor's question were intrusive, can obviously have a negative effect.

Cultivation of donors ideally takes place separately in time and place from the actual campaign. As an undergraduate at Princeton, I heard over and over again for four years how important alumni were. Days were set aside to bring the alumni back to the campus in a visible and prominent way, to honor many of them, and to express appreciation for their financial support. To top it off, before graduation, the senior class raised money for a class gift to the university. In marketing terms, the university took advantage of the four-year period during which it had potential future givers as a captive audience, and it drove home its message, albeit in a positive and not heavy-handed way. Princeton today has one of the highest percentages of alumni who contribute to the university. In contrast, Tulane made virtually no effort to convey to its undergraduates the importance of the role that alumni could play in the life of the university after graduation, or to communicate the expectation that alumni should give of their resources to the university. Tulane's percentage of alumni contributors, although rising, is still much lower than those of Princeton and a good many other schools.

It is also very important for the organization's head officer to model the behavior he or she expects of others; word about what is important to the president travels quickly through an office network. If the president never leaves the office, this fact is noted. But the organization will also notice if the president or executive director devotes a substantial amount of time to seeing prospects and listening carefully to the comments of people outside the organization, and shows, by his or her personal priorities, that cultivation matters.

10. A Campaign Never Ends. Labeling a fundraising effort a "campaign" is typically associated with an organization's attempt to raise money for specific projects, programs, and facilities, as distinct from gifts that are not restricted in their use. Both capital or purpose-specific gifts and unrestricted gifts should be part of an organization's fundraising strategy. To heighten interest in capital or purpose-specific gifts, a numeric goal for such giving is announced and a deadline for raising such funds set. The program thus becomes a campaign. But if an organization is able to raise capital gifts, it should do so on a continuing basis, whether or not the effort is publicly labeled a campaign. The staff and resources required to raise the targeted funds should be maintained, and not disbanded simply because the public phase of the effort is over.

The Importance of Planning

To these ten fundamentals of fundraising, one more essential ingredient should be added: *careful planning*. Such planning entails a meticulous process covering a series of steps that build up to actually asking prospects for money.

Before solicitation of donors begins, the following elements must be in place:

1. A carefully crafted *strategic plan* specifying concrete objectives and a year-to-year projection of the amount and type of giving required to implement the plan.

2. A carefully *researched projection* of the level of funds the organization can expect to raise that relates to the cash flow assumptions of the strategic plan.

3. A *specific plan* for raising the targeted amount, including campaign strategies, themes, and organization.

4. A *table of needs* listing specific needs and assigning a target amount to be raised for each need.

5. A well-trained, well-organized, and *highly motivated team*—including an expert research staff—to conduct the campaign.

6. A campaign *leadership group* made up of board members and other prominent people with strong ties to the organization.

Let's break down these elements in more detail.

Balancing Strategic Plan Objectives with Donor Preferences.   The strategic plan should identify the basic priorities of the organization and provide a year-by-year forecast of the amount and types of funds to be raised. Often, projections of funds to be raised do not differentiate between gifts that match basic priorities and those that will not; the forecast is done as one overall figure. The plan, however, should project the level of giving that will be consistent with the organization's needs as well as the amount of giving that will fall outside of its priorities because of donor preferences. In the end, a balance has to be struck between strategic plan objectives and the types of funding it is feasible to raise. For instance, Tulane University's strategic plan gave top priority to a very limited number of objectives; it was understood that convincing grantmakers, corporations, and individual donors to shift their contributions to one of the university's priorities would not be easy or always successful. But the university believed it worthwhile to emphasize its priorities with prospects.

A donor's ideas for a project may be far more grandiose than an organization's. This conflict may represent a difference not only in philosophies, but also in perceptions of what the organization can afford. For example, a museum may envision only a modest improvement of its building, whereas key donors may want to create an entire new complex. Such a complex not only will cost more to maintain over the years but will require a far larger expansion of the curatorial staff and acquisitions budget than the museum's plans call for.

Since potential conflicts cannot always be anticipated, a mechanism has to be established to resolve such issues when they arise.

Arriving at a Researched Projection of How Much Funding Can Be Raised.   The organization's lists of needs cannot by itself determine the expectations of the campaign. A number of research techniques need to be employed to come up with a reasoned estimate of the amount and types of funding that can be raised, year by year.

Among the available means of developing a forecast are

1. *An examination of past campaigns.* Certain rules of thumb can be applied to project the growth in giving that can be expected compared to past efforts; however, one needs to be aware of relevant changes in circumstances relating to the organization or the fundraising environment. It is especially important to determine whether the major contributors to past campaigns can be expected to match or even exceed their past level of contribution. Informal conversations with such contributors or people who know them well can be helpful here.

2. *An examination of the amounts organizations in the same field have raised in the past and/or are planning to raise in the future.* For example, if the state cancer society has in the past raised twice as much money as the state heart association, then the heart association ought to look at the cancer society's campaign tactics to see if better execution could improve the heart association's fundraising. An examination of the cancer society's past campaigns may show that the campaign results are distorted by one or two unusually large gifts and that thus the cancer society's fundraising record does not provide a fair basis for setting expectations for the heart association's campaign.

3. *A demographic comparison of the organization's constituency with that of another exempt organization.* A market research firm can undertake such a comparison and, basing income projections on zip code analysis, draw a comparison of the fundraising potential of the two organizations. Tulane employed Marts & Lundy to do such an analysis. Interestingly, the analysis

showed that Tulane's constituency had more giving potential than those of a number of competitive schools that, in fact, raised more funds.

4. *A screening and rating program* in which the organization's fundraisers talk to people in each community to get their opinion of the giving potential of people they know in the community.

5. *Focus-group interviews* in which a carefully selected cross-section of the organization's constituency in a community is interviewed by a professional experienced in conducting such research. The object of such focus-group work is not to pinpoint fundraising targets, but to learn more about the attitudes and outlooks of the individuals the campaign will approach, in order to develop appropriate campaign tactics and themes.

At Tulane, I resisted the idea of commissioning a feasibility study, over the objections of the development staff and against the advice of our outside consultant. Such a study employs a consultant to interview actual prospects in order to develop a sense of the level of giving an organization can expect and the issues it needs to address in the campaign. The use of feasibility studies assumes that prospects will be more candid with a third party than with an organization's executives and staff. This may well be true. However, in Tulane's case, I did not want our prime prospects to be approached until the university had had time to organize and disseminate to this select group the university's strategic plan and its message for the campaign. We knew that prospects' enthusiasm for what would be a challenging effort had to be developed over time. Moreover, the university was in regular contact with its major givers; the president was meticulous about staying in touch and was very well informed about donors' attitudes. I concluded that a feasibility study, although a staple of most campaign planning, was not going to provide enough insights to justify the cost in this instance. Whether I was right or wrong in this particular case can be debated; my point is that an organization needs to make a careful cost-benefit analysis of all proposed expenditures, regardless of how customary those expenditures may be in campaigns.

All these forms of inquiry should provide the basis for preparing a gift range table. This table shows (1) an estimate of the number and sizes of gifts to be solicited in various ranges (e.g., $1–5 million, $250–500 thousand), and the number of gifts in each range that are projected to be raised; and (2) the number of prospects that, based on past experience or the experience of other organizations, typically have to be solicited in order to obtain the targeted number of gifts in each range. Table 10.1 is an example of a gift range table from the Tulane University Campaign Plan.

Outlining a Campaign Plan. The campaign plan has to deal with a series of elements:

(a) The organization and functions of the fundraising staff.

(b) A gift table projecting the number of gifts of specified sizes that must be raised and the number of prospects the organization is likely to have to approach in order to raise such funds (see Table 10.1).

Table 10.1. Gift Range Table from Tulane University Campaign Plan

Range	Prospects	Cumulative Prospects	Expected	Donors*	Average Gift*	Total Dollars*	Cumulative Dollars
$25 million	3	3	1	$25,000	$ 25,000	$ 25,000	8%
$10–25 million	6	9	2	12,500	25,000	50,000	8%
$5–10 million	18	27	6	6,667	40,000	90,000	13%
$1–5 million	120	147	40	1,500	60,000	150,000	20%
Subtotal	147		49		150,000		50%
$500,000–$1 million	90	237	30	667	20,000	170,000	7%
$250,000–$500,000	195	432	65	308	20,000	190,000	7%
$100,000–$250,000	450	882	150	187	28,000	218,000	9%
Subtotal	735		245		68,000		23%
$50,000–$100,000	750	1,632	250	60	15,000	233,000	5%
$25,000–$50,000	1,500	3,132	500	30	15,000	248,000	5%
$10,000–$25,000	2,400	5,532	800	13	10,000	258,000	3%
Subtotal	4,650		1,500		40,000		13%
$10,000	many	many			30,000	288,000	10%
Rec'd Bequests					12,000	300,000	4%
Grand Total					$300,000		**100%**

*Dollars in thousands.
Because of rounding, percentages may not add up to totals.

(c) The role of the board of trustees in the campaign and the identity of the trustees, or others closely associated with the organization, who are going to form the campaign leadership committee. This committee oversees the management of the campaign by the staff, sets major policies governing the campaign, and resolves conflicts or issues that arise during the campaign. Customarily, members of this committee share in the work of cultivating major gift prospects.

(d) The essential steps in the campaign and principal tactics to be employed:

   (i) *When to label a fundraising program a "campaign."* The term "campaign" can be misleading to the extent it that implies a one-time effort; exempt organizations, as a rule, raise money every year. Some of their efforts may be directed toward raising grants from foundations and government, and gifts from individuals, that are unrestricted in the purpose for which they may be used. This unrestricted giving—generally termed "annual giving"—tends to be broad-based in the number of contributors, and to be made up of smaller gifts than capital gifts. Annual giving money is very valuable because the organization is not restricted to using the funds for specific purposes, giving it flexibility in deplying the money. Annual grant seeking and unrestricted giving efforts are typically supplemented by an effort to raise "capital gifts"—gifts raised for a specific purpose, program, or project of an organization as set forth in the table of needs (described later in this chapter). In essence, annual giving and capital giving are different modes of appealing to donors. The term "campaign" is often used to refer to both, but in this text the terms "campaign" and "capital campaign" refer to a program to raise gifts for a designated purpose. Paradoxically, such an effort is sometimes conducted without publicly labeling the effort a campaign—at least for a time. Or the label may be applied only as a device to build interest among potential donors of capital gifts. Whether and when to apply publicly the label "campaign" is thus a tactical choice.

(ii) *The character of the campaign buildup.* No institution simply announces one day to its constituency that it would like to launch a capital campaign. First, the groundwork has to be laid to motivate the constituency to support the campaign once it is announced. Precampaign programs usually include communication with the constituency as to where the institution stands with regarding to programming and finances, and why it is considering a capital campaign. When I began my tenure at Tulane, for example, a systematic effort to build ongoing ties between alumni and the university was little more than a decade old, and in many cases alumni's memories were linked to the city of New Orleans, rather than to the university. In fact, for many years, alumni who came back to visit the university did not visit the campus, but returned to the New Orleans haunts they had enjoyed as students. Only in the 1980s did the university recognize the importance of alumni reunions and begin to stage campus programs, built around faculty and outstanding graduates to attract alumni back to the campus.

We recognized that in these circumstances, alumni, especially those living outside Louisiana who had lost touch with Tulane, had to have their affinity with the university rekindled. Many such alumni had little current information about the university and were unaware of the significant progress the university had made in the last decade in gaining stature among American universities. Furthermore, many of these alumni had graduated before the school began seeking significant support from alumni, and thus most alumni could not be approached to contribute to a capital campaign without some prior education. This situation also explained why, in the 1980s, only slightly more than 20 percent of the alumni provided financial support to the university, a far lower figure than those reported by the universities that Tulane regarded as its competitors for students, faculty, grants, and other forms of support.

To deal with this situation, the university launched a *multifaceted "identity" campaign* to reach out to "lost" alumni and bring them up to date on the "new" Tulane. This effort included a series of presentations about the strategic plan to audiences across the country; improved alumni education programs on campus and in cities around the country;[10] mailings (to 15,000 alumni identified as the best prospects) of both a specially edited, colorful version of the strategic plan and a series of letters from the president about various university issues; a redesign of Tulane's alumni magazine, which was mailed to all alumni, to make it visually and editorially more appealing; and invitation of small groups of special prospects to the campus for a weekend.

(iii)   *The nucleus campaign.* This is the part of the capital gift campaign that is conducted before any formal announcement is made that a campaign is underway. The object is to approach the prospects who are expected to make the leadership gifts and see how much money can be raised from this prime prospect list. Here leadership by the full board in making gifts is very important. As a rule of thumb, an institution can expect to raise about three times the amount raised in the nucleus effort. Sometimes the nucleus campaign goes so well that the ultimate campaign target is raised; conversely, the target may be scaled back if the nucleus gifts do not meet expectations. Ultimately, the size and character of the total campaign are determined by the success of the nucleus campaign.

The University of Pennsylvania campaign is worth examining for a moment because it illustrates the importance of setting the campaign target at a level consistent with the image of the university that its leaders wish to convey. Sheldon Hackney, who was president of Penn throughout the campaign, made this point in a conversation: in his view, the university was on the upswing in terms of its perceived stature at the time the campaign was being planned, and it was important psychologically to set a campaign goal that was in line with the level of funds raised by the nation's best universities. Since Stanford University had just successfully raised $1 billion, Hackney believed that Penn could seek to do no less. All the preplanning research and conventional analysis indicated that this level was very ambitious and that $800,000,000 was a more prudent goal. But when alumnus Saul

Steinberg kicked in a $25 million gift during the nucleus phase, other major gifts followed, and the goal was set at $1 billion over five years. In the end, the university raised $1.4 billion as alumni, pleased with the growing recognition of their alma mater's stature, got behind the fund campaign.

(iv) *Integrity and campaign counting policies.* Like many entities involved in sales efforts, exempt organizations sometimes inflate the results of their capital campaigns to encourage further giving and to build organizational morale. But the last thing any organization should do is kid its own management and board; indeed, I would argue that exaggerating results to any constituency will prove a mistake in the long run, for sooner or later the truth will come out and the entity's credibility will be damaged. At a time when misleading figures have been supplied to publications that rate colleges, charities need to sharpen the accuracy of their reporting, whether to their own leadership, to the Internal Revenue Service and state authorities, or to the public. Thus, policies governing how contributions to the campaign will be counted must be set at the outset.

In the case of an entity that raises capital gifts every year, which year is designated as the first year of the campaign? Do pledges of future contributions, which are not always honored, get counted? (Counting them is a bad idea because the institution, in setting its budget, has to know what money can be expended.) Is there any justification for including money that is to be left to the organization as a bequest at a (still living) donor's death? (Since a will can be revised at any time, the answer is no.) What value should be placed on a gift of real property or art transferred in kind?

The answers to these and similar questions must be decided in light of the obligation of nonprofits to assume leadership in accounting for their performance and integrity in their reporting to various constituencies.

(v) *Preparation of campaign themes and materials.* The principal themes of a campaign are usually embodied in the *case statement*. The themes provide the overriding rationale for the campaign, in contrast to the appeal of specific projects listed in the table of needs. A case statement is an externally focused document and has to be shaped to elicit a positive response from the audience to whom it is addressed—the potential contributors to the campaign. The more well thought out the themes of the case statement are, the more useful it is likely to be. Seeking funds to enable an already successful organization to reach a new level of excellence is a familiar theme; another is enabling an organization to expand its program to a broader audience or to enter allied fields. An example of a potentially less appealing cause is Yale

University's plea—among other things—for money to restore campus buildings that it has for years neglected to maintain properly (although Yale has such a large and rich constituency that its campaign may well succeed in any case). Focus-group research can be helpful in determining what kind of case statement is going to have the strongest appeal to an organization's constituency. A capital campaign requires all kinds of materials, from print to video; a decision should be made as to how much the campaign can afford to spend on these materials and which ones to produce. Work should then begin on the preparation of these materials, and, to the extent feasible, the materials should have a common visual identity as a way of reinforcing the message that a campaign is in progress.

(vi)   *Campaign budget.* Regardless of whether an organization is engaged in a campaign or a noncampaign, a fundraising budget must be established that is affordable and ideally that is in line with corresponding expenditures by similar institutions that have successful fundraising programs. A study made in the late 1980s by the Association of Governing Boards of Colleges and Universities shows that member institutions, on average, spend 21.8 percent of total dollars raised on running the campaign. More relevant, of course, are the fundraising expenditures of the institutions that Tulane regarded as its competitors: Tulane found that its expenditures trailed those of its competitors who were more successful in raising funds. The old maxim "You have to spend money to make money" does apply to fundraising.

Some organizations make the mistake of cutting back on their fundraising and staff expenditures as soon as the public campaign goal has been met, only to find that the flow of capital gifts then drops well below the level the organization continues to require. The raising of gifts for special programs, projects, and other identifiable objectives of an organization should be a continuous process, whether or not it is publicly labeled a capital campaign. The level of funds sought may vary from year to year depending on the general environment, constituencies' ability to provide such gifts, and the organization's needs, but there is no inherent reason why seeking capital gifts—those targeted for specific purposes—should cease once a publicly announced campaign has reached its target.

(vii)   *Campaign procedures and organization.* Procedures have to be established to deal with a variety of issues that will arise during the campaign. For example, in a multidivisional organization, in the case of a prospect whom more than one division wishes to pursue, which unit gets first crack at the prospect, and for how long a time period does it have the exclusive "right" to pursue the prospect before releasing him or her to another unit? If a gift falls outside the table of needs, should the organization accept it? If strings are attached to a gift by a donor, are the conditions acceptable to the organization? If early courtship of a prospect by development staff members or divisional officers yields promising results, when should the president of the organization or a trustee be called in to meet with the prospect? It is also important to compare the campaign's progress regularly with projections, and to share information about which approaches and themes are proving to be effective or ineffective and what problems or criticisms fund solicitors are encountering from prospects. It is essential that the key people in the campaign meet regularly to review its progress, as well as the policy issues that arise, and that a clear line of decision making be established. Ambiguity as to who can decide what can prove as deadly in fundraising as in other managerial functions.

Creating a Table of Needs.   A table of needs is a summary of all the purposes for which funding is being sought. The list of needs can be limited to the organization's strategic plan priorities or, to inject an element of flexibility into the campaign, it can go beyond the parameters of the strategic plan. Obviously, the more appealing the list of projects is to donor interests, the more funds the organization can expect to raise. Since it is impossible to define every potential donor's specific interests in advance, providing a diversified list of needs can help draw in the broadest range of contributors. At the same time, an organization cannot simply let donor interests determine its programs; hence the bulk of the projects for which funds are sought ought to be consistent with the organization's priorities. In essence, then, a table of needs is a well crafted list of specific funding needs, weighted in favor of the organization's highest priorities but including some projects that investigation or experience shows donors like.

Still, it is likely that some donor will want to support a project that is not included in the list. The donor's interests should not be rejected out of hand; they may make good sense and have been overlooked in the planning process, or they may be relevant as a result of a change in the organization's circumstances since the list was drawn up. Also, it may be possible to negotiate with the donor to frame the terms of the gift so that the donor is satisfied but the funds can be applied in a way that the organization's leadership believes will serve the institution's interests. But in the end the purpose for which the funds are offered may be so far off base, or the terms on which they are offered may so directly violate the organization's principles (e.g., allowing a donor to select, or have a voice in the selection of, a school's faculty) that the organization has to refuse the gift.

Organizing and Training an Expert Staff.   In the early days of systematic fundraising, many institutions showed a tendency to staff the fundraising unit—or development group, as it is now called—with employees who were not productive in other departments or, in the case of schools, alumni who were not progressing well outside the academy. It quickly became evident, however, that fundraising was a professional business, requiring experienced and expert staff. Over the years, as development has become recognized as a professional occupation, the number of competent development officers has substantially increased, although most administrators of exempt organizations would still agree the pool of talent is not as deep as they would like. The situation will change as exempt organizations continue to emphasize that they want their development office personnel to have the training and experience needed for the level of responsibility assigned to them, and to be paid accordingly.

Fundraising has become too important to be left to "good old alums" or one of the organization's not-quite-so-talented executives; it requires the most expert personnel that can be found. In some organizations there is little difference between the salaries of the executive director and the chief fundraiser. Organizations are now looking in new places for development expertise. Princeton University turned to a business executive, and the University of Pennsylvania chose as head of its capital campaign Rick Nahm, who had been a very successful fundraiser at a small Kentucky school, Center College. Nahm turned out to be as able and well-organized a campaign head as I ever encountered on the college scene. Now, having waged a campaign that exceeded its ambitious goal, he has moved on to become president of Knox College in Ohio.

In fact, as mentioned earlier, exempt organizations should give serious consideration to establishing a form of incentive compensation for development staffs. Virtually every sales force in the business world is compensated based on individual productivity. Why won't the equivalent staff in a nonprofit setting respond to similar incentives? In the university world, I've heard the counter-argument that deans who raise money for their programs don't get bonuses, so why should the development staff? There are two answers to this argument. First, deans do in fact receive salary increases if they are successful in raising a good deal of money for their programs. Second, a dean's goal is to improve the overall quality of a program, and raising money is only part of what is required to achieve that objective. In contrast, raising money is a development staff's only task, and experience shows that most people in this line of work work more effectively when their productivity is financially rewarded.

I've also heard the counter-argument that donors will not want to see part of their gift going to the person who cultivated them. Maybe so, but in fact, part of every campaign's receipts goes pay the expenses of the campaign. This means that the real challenge is to convince donors that the overall expenses of the campaign are reasonable, not to debate how much of funds raised are assigned to paying incentive compensation to the most productive members of the development staff.

If exempt organizations want the quality of people who enter development work as a career to continue to improve, then they need to adopt reasonable incentive formulas.

One other innovation in the organization of a development staff is critically important: building an expert research group. Increasingly, well-organized development units have a research staff, but the practice is by no means universal yet. The basic function of a research staff is twofold:

◆ To identify prime prospects from a wide range of data sources. This information may uncover potential donors already known to the organization, but whose wealth has recently increased as a result of business success or an inheritance. Research may also turn up altogether new prospects whom the organization has lost touch with or is simply unaware of.

◆ To develop a profile of such prime prospects that helps the fundraiser successfully solicit their help. The anecdote at earlier in this chapter about the preparation undertaken by George Hyman, the chairman of New York University's campaign, shows how useful a well-crafted donor profile can be.

In addition, a research unit, if staffed to do so, can conduct useful research into the funding potential of the organization and the themes that the organization needs to stress in order to motivate its constituency. These services can also be purchased from consultants, and so the costs and benefits of insourcing and outsourcing such work have to be evaluated. However, at the least, the research unit should be aware of what kinds of market research are available and which outside firms are the best providers of such work.

A research staff can also be charged with keeping abreast of tactics employed in other organizations' fundraising campaigns that can be adopted in some form by the organization, as well as of the introduction of new and potentially lucrative gift products by other institutions. This is another form of looking at the "best practices" of other organizations advocated in an earlier chapter. Again, good campaign consulting firms can provide this kind of information, drawing on the knowledge they have gained in working on other campaigns, and so the question of whether to perform this function internally or ask a consultant to undertake it has to be examined. Again, the research unit should at least be able to make informed recommendations as to the best providers of such services.

Another aspect of building a solid development organization is to provide better, more extensive staff training than is customary in many nonprofits, including training that goes beyond the narrow focus of a staff member's current assignment and gives all development staff members a broad understanding of the field. Most development personnel I've worked with know what they know only from their previous work experience. Priority should be given to training the development staff in all aspects of fundraising and particularly to acquainting them with modern methods of market research and the legal and tax considerations that affect contributions.

Parts of this training, at least in the area of market research techniques, can be provided through executive programs offered by business schools. Another feasible and cost-effective approach may be to have a school produce and present, under contract, a curriculum tailored to the needs of the organization, or, on the UJA-Federation model, to develop a joint program between organization executives and a business school faculty. Experts from the field or related fields can also be invited to make presentations to the staff. For example, I brought a skilled marketer and banker to wealthy individuals to Tulane to explain to the entire development staff techniques for cultivating prospects, especially ones already converted to customers. One could see the staffers' looks of astonishment as the banker detailed how she had turned out more than 200 personal notes a week to clients and prospects and how she had used all of her activities to expand her network of contacts. Her presentation gave the staff a whole new context in which to think about cultivation. Whatever the formula, educating development staff in its profession and enlarging its skills beyond its particular experience are essential.

Forming a Campaign Leadership Group.   Many trustees of an organization have to make a commitment not just to write a check but to involve themselves actively in the running of the campaign. Such trustee presence is necessary to demonstrate the board's commitment to the campaign, to bring to bear the experience of board members in how best to approach their peers, and to enlist trustees to call on certain prospects in situations where they can exert more influence than anyone else (perhaps because a trustee has supported a prospect's charity, or because the two are peers in the business world, or because of the "stretch" gift the trustee has made). Trustees should also contribute the benefit of experiences they may have had in other similar campaigns.

In choosing a leadership committee, one needs to look for the qualities required by the role such a committee is to play: members should have stature in the community and prior experience in fundraising; they should be major contributors in their own right; and they should have a network of personal associations and a knack for persuading others to follow their example. Committee membership need not be confined to board members; others with the right combination of talents and an interest in the campaign who are affiliated with the organization or its cause (e.g., alumni or volunteers) may make excellent committee members. The head of the capital campaign at Princeton during the time I served as vice-president of finance was not a board member but an alumnus who had been active in raising funds for the university's annual giving drives. As the result of the fine work he did as campaign chair, he was later made a charter member of the university's board of trustees.

After plowing through all this material on fundraising from traditional sources, the reader may be wondering how this chapter relates to Part 2, "Remaking the Organization." In most instances, one cannot remake an organization without increasing the funds available to the organization or, at a minimum, developing more stable sources of funding. An organization that has to scramble every year to find the money to pay its bills is not going to be able to invest much time in organizational reform.

Several common themes run through both parts of this book:

1. Carve out a niche for your organization in which it can achieve a reputation as a leader in the quality of services it provides and in its appeal to a defined segment of fund providers.

2. Get close to "customers" and listen to them, whether they are recipients of services or fund providers. Their voices and views should help shape the organization's strategy and execution.

3. Set clearly defined performance objectives, assigning responsibility for the actions necessary to achieve them to specific units, and periodically measure progress against the plan.

4. Accountability means credibility.

NOTES

1. Philip Kotler, *Marketing for Nonprofit Organizations* (Englewood Cliffs, NJ: Prentice Hall, 1982), p. 427.

2. Edward J. Nash, *Direct Marketing: Strategy, Planning, Execution* (New York; McGraw-Hill, 1982), p. 215.

3. Thomas J. Peters and Robert H. Waterman, Jr., *In Search of Excellence* (New York: Harper & Row, 1982), p. 193.

4. *Nonprofit Times,* November 1995, pp. 33-55. The paper lists organizations receiving at least 10 percent of their total revenue from public support. The 100 organizations accounted for 16 percent of all money donations to charity in 1994, based on *Giving USA*'s estimates of individual, corporate, and foundation giving.

5. *The Foundation Directory* (New York: The Foundation Center, 1996).

6. All comments by Lloyd Morrisett are from an interview with the author.

7. UJA-Federation of Jewish Philanthropies in New York is an organization that raises funds for 120 social agencies serving the Jewish population in New York and for various organizations in Israel.

8. George Hyman, interview with the author.

9. Peter Edles, *Fundraising: Hands-On Tactics for Nonprofit Groups* (New York: McGraw-Hill, 1993), p. 11.

10. Many colleges have found strong alumni interest in presentations by outstanding faculty on professional topics or other areas of interest to adults. Some schools have even held weekend sessions on professional subjects or "alumni colleges" on themes of general interest. All organizations should think about how the areas in which they are expert can be communicated to adults in such a way that listeners feel they are learning something, not being asked for money.

CHAPTER 11

Earned Income: Making A Profit for Your Nonprofit Organization

The text of this chapter is drawn largely from several chapters of Managing for Profit in the Nonprofit World. *On rereading the original chapters more than 10 years after they were first published, I find that, by and large, they are still relevant today. In fact, as noted in the new data described on page 157, relatively few nonprofits generate significant amounts of earned income. An addition to the earlier material is discussion of the rationale and procedures for converting a nonprofit organization into a for-profit enterprise, which is the subject of Chapter 12.*

Consideration of how to cope with rapidly increasing costs is driving many nonprofit organizations to consider a range of options for building revenues. An aggressive and professional fundraising effort makes sense for organizations in a position to undertake one. But not all nonprofit institutions have a constituency that can provide significant financial support. Moreover, more than a few nonprofit institutions have mounted imaginative and aggressive fund drives only to find they still were not able to offset their rapidly escalating expenses. The repeated inflations and recessions of the 1970s, 1980s, and 1990s have created a difficult climate for raising increased sums from contributors.

The Need for New Revenue Sources

Increasingly, not-for-profit entities must consider generating new sources of revenues from their own activities. Such income may be derived either from commercial enterprises or by developing new customers for the organization's traditional services. In either case, the distinctive feature of such revenue is that it is *earned* by the organization rather than received as a gift or grant. Many nonprofit entities do not consider this revenue-generating option, thinking it impossible or inappropriate, and for some it is not a feasible strategy. But a good number have been successful at developing new sources of earned income.

While the primary focus of this chapter is on ways and means of earning income from commercial activities, more aggressive marketing of traditional services to new clients is no less important a way of earning new revenues.

Starting Point: Part of the Value Scheme

How does a nonprofit organization, long dependent on the charity of others, set about finding ways to make money on its own? The starting point is the organization's system of values and its attitudes toward itself and its customers.

An organization that incorporates financial independence into its central value scheme will seek systematically and aggressively to identify and develop opportunities for revenue diversification. An organization that falls prey to the psychology of dependence will miss opportunities to improve its financial future.

Generating income is not inherently alien to nonprofit organizations. Museums operate gift shops; universities, museums, and other institutions invest endowment funds in the securities markets; and other nonprofits sell magazines to earn income. But, typically, such income generation is seen as a byproduct of the organization's efforts rather than as the result of a deliberate focus on how the organization can market its services.

Developing Marketing Orientation

To find new revenues today, nonprofit enterprises must consciously adopt a "marketing orientation" in the same way they need to apply this outlook to their traditional means of raising revenues (as described in the prior chapter).[1] Philip Kotler, in his text on nonprofit marketing, characterizes a marketing orientation for nonprofit institutions as "customer centeredness," meaning that the focus of the entire organization is not on developing products or making sales but on satisfying "customers' changing needs and wants."[2] Indeed, with respect to their entire program, nonprofit organizations need to be in touch with what the marketplace wants, not just their own ideas of what the public ought to want.

Kotler argues that organizations that move toward a marketing orientation take on characteristics vital to their survival, becoming "more responsive, adaptive and entrepreneurial."[3]

The nonprofit organization that consciously seeks to expand its revenues develops, as a business does, a realistic feel for its competitive environment. It recognizes that nonprofit entities compete against each other, not only for paying customers and a share of financial resources, but also for public attention and support. Tom Peters and Robert Waterman, Jr., writing in *In Search of Excellence* about profit-making corporations, describe "customer orientation" as a "way of 'tailoring'—a way of finding a particular niche where you are better at something than anybody else."[4]

As I observed in Chapter 4, "Carving Out a Strategic Niche," a nonprofit enterprise needs a sharp sense of what is distinctive or special about the services it offers, what we call its "comparative advantage."

Capitalizing on Comparative Advantage

A comparative advantage is the edge an organization gains by concentrating its activities in those fields in which it has greater expertise than its competitors. Peters and Waterman refer to comparative advantage as "sticking to your knitting." They assert, "Our principal finding is clear and simple. Organizations that do branch out (whether by acquisition or internal diversification) but stick very close to their knitting outperform the others. The most successful of all are those diversified around a single skill...." The authors add that there is overwhelming evidence that successful companies "have strategies of entering only those businesses that build on, draw strength from and enlarge some central strength or competence."[5]

As I discussed in Chapter 4, "Carving Out a Strategic Niche," a nonprofit organization needs to first plan how best to capitalize on its special advantages and to then position itself accordingly. Such an analysis can identify opportunities to generate new sources of revenue through the organizations's own activities.

Opportunities to Earn Income

A good many nonprofit enterprises have successfully earned significant amounts of income through business endeavors. There is, however, some indication that, in the case of exempt organizations, a flow of earned income is more the exception than the rule. Of the 100 organizations with the largest revenue streams in *The Nonprofit Times Universe*, only 12 had earned income of 10 percent or more; in contrast, 56 of the 100 had no earned income whatsoever, and another 10 percent derived less than 1 percent of their total revenues from earned income.

Three of the 100—the YMCA, the National Wildlife Foundation, and Goodwill Industries—generated more than 50 percent of their revenues from earned income. The venerable YMCA, which had aggressively entered the day-care business, in 1994 generated 78 percent of its total revenues from earned income.[6]

New Markets for Traditional Services

New income can be derived by finding new consumers for an organization's traditional services. For example, in higher education a decline in undergraduate enrollments (when the country produces fewer 18-year-olds) may be offset by the appetite of older adults for education or by offering distant learning. Community mental health organizations can offer corporate employee assistance programs that utilize their staff health counselors, and public television enterprises can extend their work to the audiences that use the new communications technologies (e.g., cable television, computers, and the emerging forms of interactive television transmission).

Many universities have realized that their scientific and engineering discoveries have commercial potential and have initiated programs to capitalize on this potential. These programs, however, have not been free from concerns over faculty conflicts of interest and disputes between university and faculty over ownership rights. Sometimes the potential to generate income from the activities a nonprofit already undertakes is overlooked because the organization fails to examine the possibility, being locked into its conception of itself as a charitable enterprise.

For example, an organization with 20 years' experience in arranging and managing student and adult international exchange programs became pressed to find new funds. Its fees for arranging such programs had been declining as Japan's recession caused a drop in the number of programs it arranged. Forced to look elsewhere for funds, the organization realized for the first time that it had acquired skills and experience that could be marketed for fee income—the ability to attract students from foreign countries to education and training programs in the United States run by American universities hungry for applicants, and the preparation of business executives (both outbound U.S. executives and inbound foreign executives) to cope in a new culture. Because the organization had never before thought of marketing in new fields the skills and experience it had acquired, it had simply overlooked the opportunity to generate new sources of income from its core activities.

Commercial Sales

Nontraditional sources of income can also be derived from the marketing of products or services related to an organization's principal activities. For example, New York City's Metropolitan Museum of Art nets substantial revenues from its restaurants and from the sale of art reproductions, gift items, greeting cards, and other publications in its shops and bookstores.

Nonprofits with access to a very large constituency have also been marketing by direct mail a variety of consumer products—from life and medical insurance to travel packages and automotive services—as a means of earning income. To be successful at this game requires an identifiable constituency of considerable size (since the response rate to any mailing is very low), highly effective materials, and the financial ability to afford the up-front costs of preparing and mailing the materials. The cost of such mailings can be reduced if they can be "stuffed" in a mailing the organization is otherwise undertaking (as credit card companies regularly do).

Full Utilization of Assets

Imaginative use of under-utilized assets can may be a source of increased revenue. For example, Stanford University, and later Princeton University, saw that their vast campus land holdings were far greater than what they could ever use for educational purposes. Both schools initiated large-scale office park developments on some of their excess acreage, appealing to companies that wanted to be located close to a university's unique resources. These universities have now earned handsome sums from what would otherwise be idle, non-income-producing land. In the same vein, a good number of universities whose campus facilities would normally be idle in the summer now produce added income through summer semesters and the hosting of conferences and other special events, including sports camps for youngsters.

New York City's Museum of Modern Art has demonstrated that an institution may have "underutilized land" even though it appears to take up 100 percent of the land on which it is located. In this case, the museum sold the air rights above its quarter-acre building site to commercial developers for $17 million.[7]

Fears of Commercialism

Efforts by a nonprofit organization to generate revenues from its own activities or programs may run into objections that they are inappropriate. In the public mind, nonprofit institutions are devoted to worthy causes and lose money regularly. Their very existence is perceived as dependent on charity rather than vigorous self-reliance. Earning income is seen by some as incompatible with a charitable posture.

To some extent, this tin-cup image is encouraged by the nonprofit sector itself. Many nonprofit organizations hold to the view that to be businesslike—to seek ways to generate funds internally, to diversify sources of income, to stick to a financial plan—is to succumb to a commercialism incompatible with the pursuit of high artistic, scholarly, or social goals. Contrary to such fears, however, nonprofit institutions have been able to carry on commercial activities in ways that are not incompatible with their basic mission or image. Institutions have successfully imposed high standards of quality, as well as conditions designed to protect their image with consumers, without impeding the financial success of commercial efforts.

However, any effort to persuade a not-for-profit institution to seek revenues from a commercial source, and to do so on a businesslike basis, may run into an unexpressed but strongly felt organizational ambivalence about the appropriateness of entering into the commercial arena. Frequently, nonprofit organizations are staffed with people who, for a whole variety of deeply felt personal reasons, have chosen to work in the not-for-profit world rather than the commercial world. In many ways, they are uncomfortable with the environment and culture of commercial endeavors. It is not unusual for such professionals to be quite self-conscious about establishing that they are different from the people who populate the commercial world. Accordingly, the proposed entry into commercial activities may cut against the grain of deeply held feelings.

Typically, the people who run not-for-profit organizations also have been unfamiliar with how businesses are run, although this is less so today than in the past. For the most part, nonprofit professionals have concentrated their careers on social issues and have little training or experience in business. This makes them, appropriately enough, wary of becoming involved in such endeavors. Moreover, in seeking to move a nonprofit entity toward a commercial enterprise, one is dealing with what is still a much debated notion—that not-for-profit organizations can be successful at commercially oriented activities.

Beyond these environmental barriers to commercial activities, there are some genuinely tough policy and operating issues regarding how to mesh nonprofit activities and commercial endeavors within the same organization. These substantive issues are complex and not always susceptible to a clean-cut resolution.

Most of the expressed reservations boil down to a fear that the values inherent in pursuing commercial success are at variance with the values underlying a nonprofit social mission. Profit, rather than product or service quality, is seen as the primary objective of the commercial sector. Therefore, in the minds of some, pursuit of commercial gain inevitably means relegating the organization's mission to a lesser place in the scheme of things, or that program quality will be compromised. This line of reasoning is pressed vociferously by the institutions that are especially image-conscious, such as colleges and universities. On the contrary, a good number of businesses are built on the delivery of very high-quality products or services. The high end of the market is their niche. Thus, superior quality can be as important to commercial success as it is to the mission of a nonprofit enterprise.

Often masked by the debate over quality is the underlying reluctance of nonprofit personnel to accept, as constraints on their actions, financial limits designed to preserve a profit element. People whose driving motivation is linked to the content of their work, rather than its profitability, may find it difficult to balance profitability and artistry. This is true not only of nonprofit staff but also of artisans in many fields. In their minds, art simply should not have to yield to finances. But the balance between returning a profit and maintaining product quality is one that both nonprofit institutions and profit-making businesses can achieve.

A related reservation is that the pursuit of commercial gain will be carried on in a way that is insensitive to important social and ethical considerations. In particular, very real concerns are often expressed about the use of a nonprofit organization's name to endorse a commercial product. On one hand, such endorsements can present good opportunities to earn income where the organization's name carries weight with consumers. On the other hand, the integrity of the organization can be jeopardized if people perceive that it is lending its name to products that do not measure up to the standard the public associates with the institution, or that it is allowing its name to be inappropriately exploited. Case-by-case determinations are, by and large, the most practical approach to resolving such issues.

For instance, Children's Television Workshop's entry into the licensing of commercial children's products was initially opposed by some because of concern about product quality and fears that "hard sell" television advertising techniques might be used to pitch products to young children. The Workshop's solution was to insist on stiff quality review by its own staff and prohibit television advertising of licensed products during hours when young children were watching.

As the CTW experience illustrates, a nonprofit institution's concern for its values can often be made an explicit part of the commercial enterprise, and not necessarily at the cost of profitability. In fact, protecting the organization's image can be important to the success of a commercial venture. For instance, television advertising of CTW's products to preschool and young children might have alienated parents who, after all, are the real market for such products.

Or take the case of Princeton University's development of the Princeton Forrestal Center, the 1,600-acre commercial real estate venture on land adjacent to the school's campus. As part of its development plan, Princeton dedicated significantly more land to the preservation of open space and environmental protection than was required under the then-applicable zoning ordinances for the area. The university adopted stricter standards because of its environmental concerns, but these tougher specifications also enhanced the value of the land dedicated to development. Thus, social commitment and pursuit of profit were by no means incompatible.

Another typical reservation is that profit-making endeavors will lead to a focus on making money rather than on the program of the organization. The corollary to this argument is that commercial activities will bring into the organization a breed of employee who will not share fellow employees' dedication to its mission.

In fact, employees bent on making profits (and reaping the personal rewards of such success) may initially have less understanding of a nonprofit institution's program interests than those hired to administer the program. In some instances this will prove to be the case; in others attitudes may be more a matter of exposure and education than irreversible bias. In any case, the experience of CTW and other nonprofit organizations is that it is possible to find business executives who share the organization's social objectives.

Another frequently raised concern is that commercial success may undercut the willingness of government funding sources and private donors to support a nonprofit enterprise. The argument is advanced that the flow of income from business ventures will make government and charitable support seem unnecessary. The risk of this happening does exist, but there are two countervailing arguments.

First, substituting business income for inherently volatile and uncertain government aid is desirable. (See Chapter 10, "A Marketing Approach to Fundraising.") Second, the fact that a nonprofit organization is earning part of its revenues from commercial endeavors may well encourage private donors, and even government agencies, to think more highly of the organization. At Princeton, much was made to potential alumni donors of the university's skillful management of its endowment and its successful development of the Princeton Forrestal Center real estate project.

Nevertheless, there is a series of well-taken concerns regarding the competence of nonprofit organizations to participate in commercial endeavors. Typically, the most formidable practical barrier to a nonprofit institution's successful entry into the commercial arena is its inexperience in business ventures. As noted earlier, nonprofit staffers tend not to be trained or experienced in business endeavors, and so they have only a limited sense of how to evaluate commercial opportunities or begin to exploit them. To overcome this deficiency, nonprofit organizations that are neophytes in commercial matters had best turn to board members versed in business and to their contacts for advice and assistance. Professional consultants can also be helpful in examining an organization's potential to generate income from commercial sources.

Once a nonprofit institution is determined to participate in a commercial venture, it can hire staff members experienced in the business, and a good number of organizations have done so successfully. But this type of hiring is not a simple task. Often business personnel fear that working in the nonprofit world will stigmatize them if they later seek employment again in private business. (Fair or not, a good many in the business community see the nonprofit arena as a "soft" world lacking the drive and discipline of the profit-making sector.) At the same time, nonprofit organizations tend to be reluctant to provide the type of compensation, especially incentive compensation, that attracts able business talent.

Of course, seeking to meet the financial expectations of profit-making business executives is not without potential complications for a nonprofit organization. (See Chapter 13, "Managing Your Human Resources.") If the compensation offered profit-making personnel engaged in commercial undertakings is higher than that of nonprofit program staff members, there is the potential of internal conflict, especially if the program staffers believe that their efforts are being exploited commercially. Nevertheless, nonprofit institutions can provide, and have provided, compensation arrangements that are reasonably competitive with comparable undertakings in the profit-making world, without tearing their organizations apart.

The potential resentment of higher salaries for commercial personnel can be minimized if the organization carefully examines the compensation offered for comparable positions by business enterprises and also engages in a process of evaluating, from the standpoint of internal equity, the salaries attached to various positions in the organization. (See Chapter 13, "Managing Your Human Resources.") In addition, the organization can tie these higher rewards for commercial staff members, in part at least, to the success of the business venture on which they are working. At the same time, resentment of the compensation paid to profit-making personnel will be lessened if it is made clear to the other staff members that the success of the commercial venture is helping to pay their salaries.

I recall one summer day at Princeton being stopped by a faculty member as I walked across the campus. The professor objected strenuously to the prospect of renting the university's otherwise empty facilities to "outsiders" during the summer. I replied, "Well, we don't have to, but the income we will earn this year will support about a dozen junior faculty members." The professor expressed surprise that the rental program meant so much to the university and wished me luck with it.

Finally, there is the danger that a nonprofit will fail to make clear the ground rules under which it operates a profit-making enterprise, the consequence being lack of clarity as to whether the venture's goal is to make a profit or to advance the organization's social mission. But clarity of objectives can be achieved, especially if the commercial venture is sufficiently separated from the nonprofit organization in terms of policies, personnel, and even location.

In sum, to enter the commercial arena, a nonprofit's management must attract and appropriately motivate competent business professionals, balance and clarify its competing social and profit-making interests, and ensure that all employees, whatever their tasks, are sensitive to the organization's crucial values. In this way, able nonprofit institutions can tap existing business opportunities.

Tax Considerations

Engaging in business activities need not jeopardize the exempt status of public charity organizations, although private foundations are not permitted to own more than 20 percent of a business. The tax law does not bar nonprofit enterprises (other than private foundations) from actively engaging in business activities and even earning a profit, provided the profit is used to support the organization's exempt purposes and does not inure to the benefit of private individuals. In general, as long as the generation of income is a means of promoting the organization's social aims rather than an end in itself, it is an appropriate activity for a nonprofit institution.

However, the fact that an organization (other than a private foundation) may freely engage in business activities without jeopardizing its exempt status does not mean that the income from such endeavors will necessarily escape taxation. As the following discussion shows, certain kinds of income earned by nonprofit organizations may be subject to taxation.

Legal Forms of Profit-Making Activities

The structure of the profit-making component of a nonprofit organization can take varied forms: a working group, a division, or a separately incorporated subsidiary, which can be either nonprofit or profit-making in form. Of course, by definition, the separately incorporated profit-making subsidiary will pay corporate income tax on any net profit it earns.

In the case of a group or division organized within the not-for-profit corporation or a nonprofit subsidiary, the excess of the component's revenues over its expenses—that is, its profits—may or may not constitute taxable income. If the revenues are generated by an activity that is *related* to the organization's exempt purpose, they will be exempt. (For example, Children's Television Workshop, producer of *Sesame Street* and other educational television series for children, also publishes an educational magazine for children. Income from this endeavor is tax-exempt.) If the income is generated in a manner that is *unrelated* to the organization's purposes (e.g., if a university owns a factory), the income will be subject to federal income taxes with certain classes of exceptions—generally passive income in the form of dividends, interest, rents, and royalties. This holds true whether the component is organized as a working group within the nonprofit division or as a nonprofit subsidiary.

The determination of whether to classify a profitable activity as unrelated (and therefore subject to federal income taxation) or related (and therefore exempt) should *not* be made solely on the basis of tax regulations. Such determinations rarely involve black-and-white situations. The financial gain from claiming tax exemption needs to be compared with certain intangible benefits of profit-making status. Establishing an activity as profit-making may be very important in setting the tone for the enterprise. Moreover, a nonprofit enterprise that engages in a highly visible commercial endeavor but claims that the income is exempt from taxation can generate criticism from for-profit businesses in the same field.

These risks are much greater if the enterprise is competing with tax-paying business firms. In numerous instances, such firms have complained that they are facing "unfair competition" and have triggered investigations by the Internal Revenue Service or provoked the concern of legislators. Simply put, an exempt organization must consider carefully the real potential for public criticism if it generates significant income from active participation in profit-making enterprises, yet pays no tax at all on such income.

Operational Considerations in Organizing Profit-Making Activities

More aggressive marketing of traditional services to new customers should not, as a rule, present formidable problems for a nonprofit, but the operation of a business enterprise by a nonprofit institution is a complex managerial challenge. In the first place, as noted earlier, it is difficult to attract and appropriately compensate people with the skill and mind-set required to run a business enterprise for a nonprofit institution. People who care about making money in their work tend to be drawn to profit-making organizations. Moreover, people who can generate profits want to be rewarded for their success. This means paying them additional compensation over their base salary if they meet their financial goals. The tax law does permit nonprofits to pay incentive compensation if it is reasonable and normal for the position. However, what the IRS may consider "reasonable and normal" may not be enough to attract top-notch business professionals. A way around the problem, as discussed earlier (page 163), is to form a for-profit subsidiary.

Perhaps more serious than the problem of staffing, profit-making activities present the subtle but clear risk of confusion of purpose. The cultural values of nonprofit and profit-making enterprises are quite different. Typically, profit maximization is the overriding goal of a business venture. The single-minded clarity of this objective is an important force in guiding business operations; the value structure of nonprofit enterprise is more diffuse. At its center is the nonprofit organization's mission, which is the chief value that attracts personnel to work for the institution and external sources to give it support. The mission also shapes the enterprise's priorities. But financial survival is also important. Thus, a not-for-profit entity is an organization with fundamental duality of purpose— social mission and financial well-being (the latter being, of course, a far more limited objective than the goal of profit maximization that drives profit-making enterprises).

This duality of objective makes it difficult for a nonprofit institution to manage a commercial business well. Simply put, it is not likely to have the clarity of *business* purpose essential to an effective profit-making operation.

For example, assume that an activity, closely related to an organization's main purposes and offering the potential of producing income, fails to turn a profit. Should it be discontinued, or does its social value justify its continuation?

The mere possibility that such an activity may be continued, even though it is running at a loss, can undermine the necessary focus on creating profits. If profit making is not central to an enterprise, then even those working on a profit-making venture may excuse themselves from the pressures of trying to produce a profit. If earning a profit is not the supreme value, then one can be more relaxed about meeting the budgets and timetables that are necessary to produce a profit, but that impinge on the effort to turn out the highest possible quality product. In a nonprofit environment, perfectionism may indeed substitute for a bottom-line orientation.

Accordingly, where both nonprofit and profit-making activities coexist within the same enterprise, there is a strong risk of confusion of objectives and operating style between the two components. This is not to say that nonprofit institutions cannot insulate profit-making activities from those nonprofit values and operating styles considered inimical to the success of a profit-making venture, but special care has to be taken in organizational design to achieve such insulation.

The Princeton Forrestal Center of Princeton University provides a model of a successful profit-making enterprise undertaken by a nonprofit organization; the reasons for its success within a nonprofit environment now, in retrospect, seem fairly apparent. The center was launched in 1973 with twin objectives. They were:

◆ To convert idle university-owned land into income-producing property with a rate of return at least comparable to that of the successful return earned by the university's endowment; and

◆ To upgrade the quality of development rapidly taking place in the vicinity of the campus.

It is clear that the center has achieved both of these objectives. In fact, the project significantly exceeded its financial goal, and a series of factors may be isolated that account for the success of the center's development.

First, the concept of developing university-owned land commercially was initiated only after exhaustive consideration of various alternatives in a series of wide-ranging discussions with the administration, key faculty members, local community leaders, and the board of trustees.

Second, university officials with pertinent skills teamed up with outside real estate professionals to organize and lead these inquiries. The team did its homework, and its presentations were thoroughly professional.

Third, during the formative stage of the development, a senior university officer close to the president was actively involved in overseeing the development and ensuring that it had the necessary support within the university and the local community. The project was staffed with outside professionals experienced in real estate development, but they were not burdened with the task of winning the ongoing support of the university. That role was played by the senior officer, who was specifically designated by the president to handle the assignment. The senior officer was involved in oversight of the project's management but continued to play his regular institutional role within the life of the university. He served as a knowledgeable champion of the development, dealing with the politics, anxieties, and nonprofit mind-set of the university community.

Fourth, the president fully comprehended the financial and institutional risks involved in the development. He understood particularly the pressures such risks might create for him (e.g., external or internal complaints about the concept of the venture or its manner of execution).

Fifth, the day-to-day development work was carried out by the cadre of professionals from the commercial real estate world. They not only provided the needed skills but also established a profit-oriented environment for the project's management.

Sixth, the university's officials and its outside professional team limited their development efforts to planning the site, obtaining government approval of the plan, and then finding, and leasing land to, companies wishing to build offices or to develop the hotel/conference facilities or housing units planned for the site. By restricting its development role, Princeton avoided the complexities and risks of building and leasing finished space, and thus limited its business efforts to areas in which the university team had clear competence and experience.

Seventh, at the outset a contract was established with the outside professionals that tied the bulk of their compensation to the financial success of the development, and that provided them with the opportunity to earn a profit on their efforts comparable to what they could earn in a similar development launched by a profit-making enterprise.

Eighth, it was established from the outset that policy decisions about the development, including whether to initiate it, were to be made by the board of trustees and, within the board, by a committee made up entirely of trustees with relevant business backgrounds. The committee quickly established that the development was to be treated as a business: it understood the risks involved in the development, did not flinch from backing the venture with university funds during the start-up phase, and at critical moments provided active personal assistance to the project team.

Ninth, the project team was housed away from the university campus and in its day-to-day activities rarely mingled with the university community outside of meetings specifically related to the project.

Tenth, the center's financial goal was quite explicit: to provide a better return on the assets utilized in the development than was being received from the university's endowment. While the center was also charged with attaining a high level of quality that would influence the caliber of development in the region, there was no ambiguity about the priority of its profit-making goal.

The Princeton Forrestal Center is not unique in the nonprofit world. For instance, Harvard University's endowment funds and real estate assets are managed by a university-owned corporation of full-time professionals located in Boston, rather than at the university campus in Cambridge; this unit works under compensation arrangements comparable to those of similar professionals in the profit-making world. The group reports to the treasurer of the university, who is a fellow of the Harvard Corporation. (The treasurer is a part-time official drawn from the professional investment world.)

The point here is that the creation of a successful profit-making component within a not-for-profit environment—the building of a culture within a culture, so to speak—is a difficult business. The chances of successfully doing so will be enhanced if

- The for-profit component is, from the outset, clearly labeled as such, and its different objectives and need for a different operating style are recognized from the start;
- The profit-making component employs its own set of professionals from the profit-making world;
- Separate compensation policies are adopted for the component that provide appropriate incentives for profit-minded professionals;
- The relationship between the component and the institution is managed by a senior executive of the nonprofit who is charged specifically with championing the project and insulating it from inappropriate interference by the institution's staff;
- Ultimate responsibility for the project is vested unequivocally in a group of the institution's trustees, who themselves are experienced participants in the profit-making world; and
- The component is physically separated from the institution.

In short, the greater the separation in terms of format, staffing, oversight, and location, the greater are the chances that the profit-making component will be able to function with the clarity of purpose and operating style appropriate and necessary to its objectives.

Financing Self-Generated Revenues

When it comes to financing a new business activity, a variety of financing options are available for nonprofit organizations. The real art is to understand exactly what role financing can play in furthering that business. Each financing option can make a different contribution to a business beyond simply providing money. A nonprofit organization needs to establish what it wants from a financial source beyond money before it can really determine where to go in search of financing.

Financing Options

A nonprofit organization may raise financing

◆ From funds generated by existing revenue-producing activities. Unfortunately, few nonprofit enterprises have sufficient resources available to fund a new endeavor.

◆ From venture capital or other conventional public and private financing sources available to fund qualified new businesses. Such financing may take the form of either equity or debt, or some combination of the two, depending on the business's needs and financial condition. If the new business is not strong enough to attract funding in its own right, the nonprofit organization may put its credit on the line to secure capital. The terms of financing would be the same as those granted to a profit-making organization of similar resources launching a similar venture.

◆ By licensing a commercial profit-making company to develop the business in exchange for a royalty based on sales, net profits, or some in-between standard. Under a licensing arrangement, the commercial firm typically provides all the capital and oversees the active management of the business. The nonprofit organization confines its role primarily to exercising quality control over the licensed product. Where the nonprofit organization receives a royalty based on sales revenues rather than on a share of profits, the income will be exempt from federal income taxation. Moreover, most alert nonprofit institutions avoid royalties based on anything other than gross revenues in order to avoid getting involved in the morass of another company's accounting practices. To be in a position to negotiate a royalty arrangement, the nonprofit organization must have a name or other property elements that can enhance the sale of a product.

◆ By forming a joint venture with a commercial company to develop the business. The joint venture can take the form of a partnership, a stock corporation, or a contract between two entities to develop a business jointly without forming a new legal entity to operate it. The relative amounts of capital and know-how contributed by the nonprofit organization and the commercial company will vary from case to case. If the organization's name or other intangible assets are of enough value to the business, the organization may be able to negotiate for an ownership share without having to invest its own funds in the venture.

Each of these options offers a different combination of control and risk. For instance, the nonprofit institution will have the greatest control over a venture financed entirely with its own funds, but it will also bear the complete financial and management risk. The least risk exposure is offered by the licensing route, but this route provides the nonprofit organization with the least degree of control over the business.

At the same time, each of the options offers a different range of support for a new undertaking. To determine the kind of support that will be most valuable, an analysis should be made of (1) the skills and resources the nonprofit organization brings and does not bring to the proposed venture, (2) the availability within the proposed commercial financing source of the particular skills and experience necessary to execute the proposed business, and (3) the goals the nonprofit organization is seeking to achieve through the venture.

Such an analysis will help to determine what type of financing and financing source make the most sense for the intended business. Failing to undertake this analysis seriously increases the risk of seeking the wrong type of money from the wrong source.

For instance, a nonprofit organization may have an opportunity to generate revenues from a commercial venture, and the organization's name, trademark, or affiliation with the business may be important to the exploitation of the opportunity. But the organization may not wish to expose itself to the financial or managerial risks of undertaking a business venture. It may also have few skills to bring to the development of the business. In such cases, the appropriate strategy is probably for the organization to license another firm to exploit the particular commercial opportunity in exchange for a royalty based on the revenues generated. Note, too, that the tax law treats passive royalty income as tax-free to the organization. Active involvement in a business thus has to offer a handsome return in order to provide more net after-tax income than tax-free royalties.

Licensing

Children's Television Workshop decided years ago to license a series of established commercial firms to produce toys, games, clothing, and other items under the *Sesame Street* trademark. CTW wanted to earn nonbroadcast revenues from this uniquely valuable trademark. But the Workshop did not have the capital or desire to invest in manufacturing and distribution businesses, nor did it wish to generate taxable income. Moreover, it was concerned that active involvement in an intensely competitive nonbroadcast business would divert management attention and focus from CTW's primary mission of producing educational television shows for children. Accordingly, licensing others to produce and market *Sesame Street* toys, books, and clothing made the most overall sense for CTW, even though the Workshop's control over the manufacture of products bearing its name was limited. When a product is licensed, the nonprofit licenser retains the right to approve the quality of the product (CTW also had rights to approve advertising and marketing plans), but a right to approve quality does not provide the same power over the shape of the ultimate product as an active role in its creation.

Joint Ventures

Of course, licensing may not always be feasible or desirable. A nonprofit organization may find that the product or service it wants to market commercially is so new that creating the product will require a genuine act of invention, or that the organization's reputation will be so closely linked to the product or service that it cannot delegate responsibility for its production to others. It is one thing to license the use of a nonprofit institution's name or properties to help market a product whose characteristics are known; it is another thing to do so where the product must first be invented. In such cases, the institution may well decide to play an active role in the development of the product or service. This can lead to the institution's either undertaking the venture on its own, with a combination of its own capital for equity and conventional lending sources for debt financing, or entering into a joint venture with an established commercial firm. The joint venture can allow the nonprofit institution to play a strong role in product development. At the same time, such an arrangement can give the institution access to the expertise of a commercial partner that complements the institution's own talents, as well as make available the commercial firm's equity capital and credit resources.

For instance, using its own funds over the period of a year, CTW conceived of an educational play park attraction for children (which ultimately came to be known as Sesame Place), in which children play with a unique set of play elements, science exhibits, and computers. The park was projected to cost some $10 million. The park is different from the ride-oriented, passive entertainment of traditional theme parks, and CTW wanted to be an active participant in the creation of this new concept. It also believed that a series of parks would be built and would, in the aggregate, offer a very attractive return to an equity participant, especially compared to a royalty. At the same time, the Workshop recognized that experience in park construction and in the operation and marketing of amusement parks would be crucial to success. Furthermore, CTW was in a position to invest only a small part of the total equity capital required to build a series of parks, and it lacked the needed credit to obtain the debt-financing necessary for multiple parks.

CTW decided to reject offers of funding from venture capital groups and turned instead to the theme park division of Anheuser Busch to form a combined venture to own, build, and operate jointly proposed parks. CTW looked to Anheuser Busch to provide not only the bulk of the equity capital for the parks and the credit for the necessary borrowing but, just as important, the personnel required to construct, operate, and market the project in conjunction with CTW's creative team. Anheuser Busch thus played a role in the development of the parks that no purely financial institution would have been willing or equipped to undertake.

However, despite the array of complementary talents provided by the joint venture—and the strong appeal of the attraction to young children—it has never attained the hoped-for financial success. Construction cost overruns in the case of the initial park and a poor location choice in the case of the second facility are among the reasons for the financial shortfall. However, none of these failings can be attributed to the form of the enterprise; they were errors in execution, in which I was a full participant. I also advocated the joint venture format over the objections of some senior staff members who wanted a royalty arrangement with Anheuser Busch to avoid risking CTW's limited capital on an untested concept. Their judgment proved correct when the actual cost of building a park skyrocketed beyond our estimates. When it became evident that the cost of building the parks would be higher than expected, CTW renegotiated the contract with Anheuser Busch to provide for royalty payments.

The Business Skills of Financing Sources

As part of the process of determining what contributions are needed from a financial source, a realistic assessment needs to be made of the limits on a nonprofit organization's ability to implement a business. Organizations—profit-making as well as nonprofit—tend to overestimate the transferability of their competence from one field to another, and thus they often forgo the opportunity to find a partner that can supply the skills and assets they may lack.

In contrast, Princeton University recognized from the outset its limitations in developing the 1,600-acre mixed-use real estate development on holdings adjacent to its main campus. The university determined that it had expertise in planning and developing the uses of land, processes in which it was regularly engaged with respect to its campus and adjacent holdings, but not in designing, building, or financing commercial structures, which it had never done. Hence, the university decided to sell or lease land to developers and private companies, enabling them to build their own office, research, and housing facilities, and to limit its role to land planning and development and to design and quality review. This strategy not only confined the university's role to its area of knowledge, it also reduced the capital the school had to advance and limited its financial exposure.

Shared Values

As part of the process of defining what contributions a financial source can make to a venture, it is useful to compile as specific as possible a list of the characteristics desired in a financial partner (e.g., expertise in managing construction, operations, marketing). The list should also detail the less tangible characteristics wanted in a partner—for example, an appreciation for the values and culture of the nonprofit institution, a shared commitment to producing a quality product (even at the expense of forgoing some short-run profitability), and recognition of the importance of the public's perception of the quality and integrity of the organization.

In short, it is necessary to determine a whether the partners share a common set of values. If they do not, they will eventually become antagonists, however much both may want to realize a profit from the venture.

In the end, whatever financial approach or internal structure it adopts to develop a business, the nonprofit organization will have to acclimate itself to the culture of the commercial world. This is never easy for organizations driven primarily by the desire to advance social goals rather than by the profit motive. However, to achieve its diverse aims, a modern not-for-profit must be a hybrid: a classic charitable organization in purpose, and a successful business in raising revenues. Where these two values co-exist in proper balance, one can expect to find a viable, vibrant not-for-profit organization.

Another important source of income (for those institutions fortunate enough to have one) is an endowment. First-rate endowment management can make a major difference in the resources available to an institution.

In *Managing for Profit in a Nonprofit World,* there is a extensive discussion of the principles that should govern the administration of an endowment fund, including the important role of the trustees in establishing the policies that guide the fund's investments, in particular its risk and return objectives.

The policies set by trustees remain of overriding importance to the fund's success. The level of return to be sought, the degree of risk to be tolerated, the allocation of the fund among different asset classes, and the nature of the investment strategies to be pursued will ultimately have a more profound bearing on the level and stability of return earned by the fund than will the individual securities selected for investment.

Since I wrote *Managing for Profit in the Nonprofit World* 10 years ago, there has been an expansion in the nature and range of investment strategies and techniques available to endowment managers as well as knowledge about the risks and returns involved in such areas as real estate, international investment, small cap stocks, and derivatives. These have been the subject of many other texts and journal articles, and so I will leave the reader interested in this subject to find information from the plenitude of other sources.

NOTES

1. Philip Kotler and Sidney J. Levy, "Broadening the Concept of Marketing," in Philip Kotler, O. C. Ferrell, and Charles Lamb, eds., *Cases and Readings for Marketing for Nonprofit Organizations* (Englewood Cliffs, NJ: Prentice Hall, 1983), pp. 3–4.

2. Philip Kotler, *Marketing for Nonprofit Organizations* p. 22. Thomas J. Peters and Robert H. Waterman, Jr. (in *In Search of Excellence,* New York: Harper & Row, 1982, p. 14) characterize a marketing orientation in private companies as being "close to the customer" with a focus on providing "unparalleled quality, service, and reliability."

3. Kotler, *Marketing for Nonprofit Organizations,* pp. 24–27.

4. Peters and Waterman, *In Search of Excellence,* p. 182.

5. Ibid., p. 293–294.

6. *Nonprofit Times,* November 1995, pp. 33–55.

7. "Real Estate Transaction," in *The Buck Starts Here: Enterprise on the Arts,* A Conference for Nonprofit Organizations on the Legal Aspects of Making Money (New York: Volunteer Lawyers for the Arts, 1984), p. 65.

CHAPTER 12

Converting to a For-Profit Enterprise

The rationale for organizing an enterprise on a nonprofit basis rather than as a for-profit business once seemed fairly simple: If one's *basic* purpose was to advance a humanitarian, cultural, or scientific goal, then one formed a not-for-profit entity pursuant to the requirements of the Internal Revenue Code. If one's primary purpose was to make money and enjoy the other fruits of ownership, even while serving a public interest, then one organized the entity as a for-profit enterprise. In most circumstances, motive dictated the form of organization.

But today motive alone may no longer be a foolproof guide to the form of organization to create. Moreover, the initial decision to form a nonprofit can be reversed at a later date. Organizations that, instead of depending on gifts and grants, generate substantially more revenue than their overall expenses (i.e., to earn a respectable profit) have the option to convert to a for-profit form.

This chapter examines the range of considerations that shape the initial choice to create a nonprofit organization as well as those that may later influence a nonprofit to convert to a for-profit.

There are a variety of tangible and intangible benefits to organizing a nonprofit. The label "nonprofit" tends to suggest to the public mind a commitment to advancing the public welfare, rather than private gain, and this favorable image enhances access to people and institutions in a position to help the organization. Status as a 501(c)(3) organization also enables such organizations to raise capital through tax-deductible contributions. Assuming an organization is not designed to engage in revenue-producing activities, nonprofit status is the only practical way to raise funds, because nonprofits can access the capital provided to charitable organizations by foundations, corporations, and individuals as well as by government funding targeted for programs of the character nonprofits operate.

Nonprofits, which under IRS rules and regulations qualify for tax exemption, do not pay taxes on the revenues generated by their mainstream activities and activities related to their primary mission. The latter exemption has been interpreted as enabling an organization to be exempt from taxes even on a profit-making activity carried on in a commercial manner in direct competition with for-profit firms (e.g., operation of a museum gift shop).[1]

A nonprofits' favorable image and the public recognition it receives may also enable it to generate income by merchandising products that bear its name. In this era of brand and designer marketing, a well-known name or logo that has a favorable public image can be a valuable marketing asset. The sale of products can be enhanced by the image and name recognition of a powerful brand name. For example, the automobile manufacturer Jeep now licenses clothing bearing the Jeep name; similarly, the magazine *House and Garden* now licenses Wal-Mart Stores to sell garden furniture bearing its name. And every college in the country sells in its bookstore and athletic stadiums T-shirts and other clothing and merchandise designed not just for its students, but for everyone attracted by its name.

Nonprofit status has certain negative aspects, in the form of constraints imposed by the Internal Revenue Service. These constraints warrant careful review and weighing against the strong positive aspects of the nonprofit form. At the same time, changing conditions in the field in which a nonprofit operates can cause it to revisit its original decision to adopt the nonprofit form of organization. For instance, a number of nonprofit organizations compete in certain industries with for-profit companies and are as vulnerable as for-profits to the trends affecting those industries.

The health care field is one where nonprofit and for-profit institutions compete head to head in the same market for the same customers. In the health industry today, a sweeping consolidation is expected and in fact is already well underway. Nonprofit institutions, like for-profits, will be under pressure to acquire or be acquired by other organizations, or else to consolidate operations. In addition, with the staggering growth in the capital costs of operating health care facilities, many nonprofit institutions will have to turn to the capital market for funding, which will entail converting to for-profit status.

This kind of consolidation has already begun in the health services field. The nation's 68 independent Blue Cross and Blue Shield plans, which insure about

65 million people, represent the biggest group of nonprofit health plans. The "Blue Cross–Blue Shield" trade name is perceived as valuable in attracting participants to a health plan; combined with the existing Blue memberships, this makes "Blue" organizations attractive candidates for acquistion by private plans. In the summer of 1994, the Blues National Association reversed its long-standing commitment to nonprofit status and authorized individual Blues to convert to for-profit institutions.

One of the byproducts of such conversions may be the creation of an array of new foundations, since, under the law as interpreted in many states, a nonprofit that converts to a for-profit organization must contribute to charity the value of its assets in order to compensate for the loss of public benefit provided by the nonprofit form. In some cases, the dollars flowing to charity can be substantial. In California, for example, a very large health plan, Wellpoint Health Networks, 80 percent of whose stock is owned by the nonprofit California Blue Cross, has signed an agreement to acquire Health Systems International, another large plan. The combined company will become the first for-profit company to use the Blue Cross name and logo, which will be transfered from Blue Cross to the new company. Because of Blue Cross status as a nonprofit, it will donate $3 billion in cash and stocks to two new charitable foundations. Their combined endowment of $3 billion will be larger than that of most foundations in this country.

The transaction has not gone uncriticized. Nonprofit Blues carry certain public policy obligations such as providing low-cost insurance for low-income people. Some observers fear that the foundations funded by the transaction will not act to help poor people get insurance, but rather will devote their resources to aiding health maintenance organizations (HMOs). One proffered solution is to appoint to the new foundation boards truly independent trustees with no ties to maintenance organizations, especially the ones whose merger led to the creation of the twin foundations.

An existing nonprofit can change its status to that of a for-profit, but neither the decision to do so nor the process required to obtain approval for the change is easy. Take the case of Engineering Information, Inc. (EI).

EI was organized in 1934 as a not-for-profit organization under the laws of the State of New York. The purpose of the organization was to disseminate by various means engineering, scientific, and technical information to libraries, educational institutions, industry, governmental agencies, and the engineering and scientific communities.

For a long time, libraries were the primary consumers of EI's product. Then, with the downsizing embarked on by many institutions, libraries began to scale back their purchases of EI products. Under the leadership of a new CEO, John Regazzi, who joined EI in 1988 from H. W. Wilson, a private for-profit publisher, EI reversed the downward slide in its profitability; but this was a short-term victory brought about by a combination of cost cutting and the introduction of new products with strong appeal.

In April of 1993, the five-year business plan presented to the board of EI set aside some $500,000 for product development—about enough for the first year of the plan—but contained no provision for further funding of new product development and left open the question of how additional product development funds could be raised. The plan thus put squarely on the table the issue of how to finance future capital needs.

After the presentation of the five-year business plan by Regazzi, I was asked as an outside observer to offer comments to the board. Regazzi had told me beforehand that, a year earlier, the board had sidestepped the issue of converting to a for-profit enterprise, and that there was a lot of understandable resistance within the company to abandoning EI's nonprofit status after nearly 60 years.

In talking with the board, I offered the following observations:

> The challenge facing EI, stated most simply, in the words of the business plan, is to "Transition and diversify EI's products and services to broader-based corporate and end-user markets, while maintaining a market leadership position in existing core markets. Library expenditures and budgets are shrinking. The only way EI can prosper in the library market is to expand its market share. Such a strategy would be difficult for two primary reasons: first, it's expensive; and second, it's an attempt to gain market share in a declining market.

> EI undoubtedly will need to protect its position in its core markets, and it may very well need to expend significant dollars to maintain this position. In the long run, however, EI will be better off to diversify, seeking to reach the mass market of engineers and engineering students who now have the technology to seek information on their own and are increasingly aware of the value of the information they need.

> The plan recognizes that EI must embark on customer-oriented, market-research-driven development of new products for new consumers—new both in that they are end users, not libraries, and that they are practitioners, not research-oriented engineers in industry and academia.

It was obvious to everyone at the meeting that EI would have to develop a new marketing system aimed at reaching directly the actual consumers of information.

All these actions would require more money than EI could expect to generate from its present operations. In addition, most of EI's competitors in providing engineering information are businesses that can invest, and have invested, significant funds in equipment and facilities. EI's borrowing capacity was limited, and thus it had to find ways to raise the type of capital that invests in profit-making ventures.

EI had a number of options available in terms of organizational structure to facilitate the raising of capital for product development and new modes of distribution.

1. It could retain its status as a nonprofit and establish for-profit subsidiaries to undertake the development of new products, inviting investors in new ventures to invest capital in exchange for stock.

2. It could retain its status as a nonprofit and establish for-profit joint ventures with other for-profit firms that together would develop new products and/or develop a distribution system to market products directly to the consumer. In fact, EI had already entered into a number of such joint development ventures with private companies.

3. It could convert its entire organization to a for-profit organization and raise capital in exchange for stock in the new company. Under this scenario, EI would have to donate to a charitable entity the fair market value of its assets.

The first two alternatives contemplate a twofold structure: a nonprofit entity that carries on EI's basic business but also owns an equity position in one or more for-profit corporations. The nonprofit's percentage of ownership could vary from a minority position—entailing giving up management control—to ownership of up to 100 percent of the voting stock (with the outside investors receiving one of several forms of a nonvoting interest—for example, preferred stock, which enjoys a right to participate in profits before payment of a dividend on the voting stock).

While such arrangements have their place, neither of the first two alternatives made sense for EI, for several reasons.

First, the two alternatives required dividing the organization into two classes of personnel—those working on a for-profit basis and those working on a nonprofit basis—when all EI employees were engaged in essentially the same business. This arrangement would have created two cultures and two sets of goals within the same enterprise.

Second, the twofold structure implied different compensation systems, one for those employed by the for-profit subsidiaries and one for those employed by the nonprofit parent, even though the two groups would be engaged in parallel activities. While nonprofits can establish incentive compensation under IRS rules, the incentives cannot be as large or as directly linked to profits as in a for-profit company.

Third, the twofold structure meant that outside partners would share in the control of the for-profit subsidiary and thus could produce a management system at complete variance with the management of the nonprofit parent.

Fourth, the nonprofit status of EI did not appear necessary to the accomplishment of its objectives, nor did it offer to EI any concrete benefits, such as the ability to raise large amounts of funds through contributions.

The establishment of for-profit subsidiaries can be an effective means for a nonprofit to tap into the private capital markets, or to form partnerships with private interests, when the business to be pursued by the for-profit entity is distinct from the mainstream activity of the parent organization. The twofold structure can enable the parent to maintain its access to funding sources that traditionally support nonprofit organizations while also raising for-profit capital. Under such circumstances, having a separate culture, management, and compensation system for a for-profit subsidiary is easier to justify to employees of the nonprofit parent and is thus less likely to prove a divisive factor in the operation of the nonprofit parent.

Moreover, the incentive compensation and, in all likelihood, the higher pay of for-profit employees can be offset by providing other benefits to the nonprofit employees. For example, a better medical plan and a pension plan that—because it is offered by a nonprofit—is the only portable pension plan in the United States. (See Chapter 13, "Developing Your Human Resources.")

In deciding on a course of action for EI, Regazzi needed to consider the most effective means of raising capital; but equally important was the fact that Regazzi wanted to shape his organization's culture to be responsive to the changing world in which EI was now competing and to provide incentives that would motivate his staff to compete effectively with EI's for-profit rivals. Ultimately, the twin considerations of raising capital and restructuring the organization to deal with its competition in a new marketing environment led to the decision to convert all of EI into a for-profit company and to create a foundation to which EI would donate the fair market value of its assets.

Although the board took no formal action that day in 1993, its outlook had changed, and John Regazzi was allowed to go ahead with the preparatory work of establishing a formula that the State of New York would accept for converting EI to a for-profit and locating the capital to fund such a transaction. Obtaining approval of the conversion would ultimately require resolving certain tax issues and meeting requirements established by the attorney general and the courts of New York State.

EI knew that it would have to contribute the value of its assets to a new nonprofit entity, but two critical questions arose: What valuation would prove acceptable to New York State authorities, and where would the funds to be transferred to a new for-profit come from? An additional problem was that Regazzi wanted the employees to own the bulk of the new for-profit enterprise through an employee stock ownership plan (ESOP). This meant finding a source willing to put up the capital the new for-profit needed to transfer to the nonprofit foundation, and willing to advance the funds without acquiring an ownership interest in the new business venture. Raising equity directly for EI as a for-profit, with its long track record in the same business, might not have been hard, but channeling the needed capital through financing an ESOP would be no small feat.

The conversion plan also required establishing the fair market value of EI's net assets as a going concern. An early decision was made to leave EI's $2 million in cash and marketable securities with the foundation. The valuation problem was thus limited to EI's publishing assets (including its lease). The appraiser had to be chosen from a list prepared by the New York State attorney general's office.

With respect to the tax issues raised by the possible conversion, EI sought an opinion from the law firm of Sullivan and Cromwell (S&C). As an alternative, EI could have sought a private ruling from the IRS, but such letters can take a long time to obtain. The S&C letter made the following points to the board:

The Internal Revenue Service has ruled privately that a sale of property by a Section 501(c)(3) organization will not violate the prohibitions against private inurement and private benefit if (i) the property is sold for a price determined on an arms-length basis and at least equal to its fair market value, (ii) the sale is generally in furtherance of the organization's exempt purposes, and (iii) the net proceeds do not inure to the benefit of any private individual.

S & C, in support of this statement, pointed to IRS Private Letter Ruling 8234084 (May 27, 1982) relating to the sale by a nonprofit organization of its hospital and research facility to a limited partnership created by the organization's board of directors. The IRS ruled that the sale did not result in private inurement or benefit because the sale price was set at fair market value, as determined by an independent appraisal, and because no loan abatements or other special concessions were given to the directors in their capacity as the purchasers and operators of the hospital. Negotiations were conducted on an arms-length basis, and the transaction documents were prepared and negotiated by independent counsel for each party. The sale was considered necessary because the charitable entity did not have enough resources to expand the hospital (as required by the growing needs of the community) and also continue its existing research and educational activities. The sale proceeds were used to further the organization's research and educational activities.

Two years later, however, the directors partnership sold the hospital for $21.3 million more than the purchase price. The state attorney general successfully sued the directors for breach of their fiduciary duty, and the IRS recommended that the organization's tax-exempt status be revoked. (See Private Letter Ruling 9130002, March 19, 1991.) S&C pointed out that this later ruling did not attack the transaction per se or the procedures followed by the organization, but instead demonstrated the importance of a good appraisal.

Similarly, S&C told the board that in IRS Private Letter Ruling 8838047 (June 28, 1988), a hospital had sold its real property to a partnership formed by its employees, subsequently leasing the property back from the partnership. The sale-leaseback was necessary to enable the hospital to repay outstanding debt and expand medical services. The IRS ruled that no private inurement or benefit had occurred because the sale price was at fair market value, confirmed by a declaratory judgment action brought by the hospital in state court naming the state attorney general as defendant.

EI would be consistent with the above rulings in selling its assets at their fair market value, as determined by its board of directors on the basis of an appraisal prepared by a qualified independent appraiser using several valuation methods. The sale proceeds would be added to the foundation's investment assets and used to make grants in furtherance of the foundation's charitable purposes.

Payment by a charitable organization of reasonable compensation to "insiders" would not result in private inurement. Whether or not compensation was reasonable must be considered in light of all relevant circumstances. The fee that the foundation proposed paying to the for-profit corporation for providing certain administrative services was substantially less than what the foundation would pay a third party to perform such services.

S&C concluded that, in its opinion, the restructuring would not result in private inurement or private benefit jeopardizing the foundation's tax-exempt status. S&C went on to observe that the restructuring should not result in the foundation's being found to have "excess business holdings." Section 4943 of the Internal Revenue Code imposes an excise tax on private foundations deemed to have excess business holdings. A private foundation, together with disqualified persons, may own no more than 20 percent of the voting stock, profits, interest, or beneficial interest in a business enterprise. If the business is effectively controlled by a third party, the foundation and disqualified persons may own a 35 percent interest in the business [I.R.C. SS 4943(c)(2)].

After the restructuring, the foundation was to own only 10 percent of the voting stock of EI. The only other stockholder, the ESOP, would not be a disqualified person, and thus its holdings would not be aggregated with the foundation's holdings.

On December 30, 1994, Regazzi was ready to act, and a lame-duck deputy attorney general of the State of New York signed off on the transaction just one day before he and his boss—who had lost his bid for reelection—left office. If the transaction had not been ready for signature while the deputy attorney general was still in office, EI would have had to start all over again with educating a new attorney general and his or her deputy and trying to persuade them to approve the transaction.

According to Regazzi, the staff's reaction to the change has been very positive. A series of seminars were held with staff members to discuss what kind of an organization EI had been before the restructuring, why the restructuring was being undertaken, and where EI was headed. The seminars proved to be very constructive.

EI has not yet sought outside capital, but expects to do so in the near future; gaining this ability was one of the reasons for the conversion. In the minds of EI executives, reshaping the organization's culture was another important reason for the conversion. As one officer commented during the first year after conversion, "We are learning to be a for-profit company." In fact, Regazzi believes the organization has benefited from increased employee productivity as a result of its new for-profit orientation, and thus has acheived one of the goals of conversion. One senior staff member observed: "Since the conversion, everyone is more conscientious about [his or her] role in the company, and there is a higher level of productivity. No question but people now feel, 'My career is at stake here.'"

Perhaps most significant of all, in light of the current flurry of mergers of nonprofit health plans into for-profit insurers, the EI conversion was carefully structured to protect the public interest. That is, there was an independent appraisal of the assets of the exempt organization and a transfer of equivalent value made to a foundation which will serve the original charitable purposes of the nonprofit EI. The foundation will not function as a back-door for supporting the new for-profit enterprise, and the conversion itself did not enrich EI executives. The potential for individual enrichment has to be realized through the performance of the new for-profit entity.

NOTE

1. See Paul Firstenberg, *Managing for Profit in the Nonprofit World* (New York: The Foundation Center, 1986), pp. 162–164.

PART 4

The Human Dimension

CHAPTER 13

Managing Your Human Resources

One of the pivotal advances in management practice in the second half of the twentieth century has been learning how to use fully the talents of all the people in an organization. The idea that people are a resource rather than a cost has transformed the way organizations are run.

The concept of human resources has displaced the notion, which once dominated American business, that all wisdom was vested in the senior leaders of an organization—and that subordinates' task was to do exactly what they were ordered to do by top management. It is now widely agreed that the task of the senior management is to create an environment in which all employees are stimulated to contribute to how the business is run.

The concept of human resources also implies that talented subordinates will be given the autonomy they require to accomplish the objectives they have developed in concert with the senior management. This, in turn, has meant that fewer layers of management are needed to monitor the work of subordinates.

Lawrence A. Bossidy, chairman and CEO of Allied Signal, in explaining the steps he took to revive the fortunes of the company, stresses over and over the importance of giving workers a sense of ownership. In an interview with the Harvard Business Review, sounding more like a sports coach than a business strategist, he asserts: "I think you don't change a culture. I think you coach people to win. Basically, people want to be successful. They want to go home at night and feel they've made a contribution."

Bossidy also points up the change in managerial style that the new era requires, observing:

> *The day when you could yell and scream and beat people into good performance is over. Today you have to appeal to them by helping them see how they can get from here to there by establishing some credibility, and by giving them some reason and some help to get there. Do all those things, and they'll knock down doors.*[1]

More than ever, then, people are recognized as an enterprise's prime resource, and maximizing their talents as a critical management task.

This chapter is organized as follows:

Today's World of W
ork

- ◆ *Less Stable Careers*
- ◆ *The Lure of Private-Sector Pay*
- ◆ *Overlooking the Intrinsic Value of Work*
- ◆ *Women's Entry into the Work Force*

How an Organization Can Respond Affirmatively to the New World of Work

- ◆ *Recognize the "New" Pressures on Employees*
- ◆ *Recognize the Diverse Values That Motivate Workers*
- ◆ *Provide Affirmative Leadership at the Top*
- ◆ *Set Clear Expectations*
- ◆ *Offer Constructive Performance Appraisals*
- ◆ *Provide Reasonable and Equitable Compensation*
- ◆ *Administer Compensation Fairly*
- ◆ *The Role of the Trustee Compensation Committee*

The Recruiting Process

Developing Talent

How to Discharge Employees in an Era of Downsizing

Today's World of Work

Profound changes are taking place in the nature of employment and in the work environment that impact both for-profits and nonprofits. To maximize the productivity of an organization's staff, the management has to be aware of the new forces at play in the work life of its employees.

Less Stable Careers

In the 1990s, it became evident that a profound change had occurred in the nature of the implicit contract between employer and white-collar employee. Many of us entered the world of work on the assumption that our employer would continue to employ us, giving us progressively more responsibility, as long as the organization was doing reasonably well and we did our job well. However, a tidal wave of corporate downsizing has breached this contract and has made it evident that from now on a new concept will govern employment.

Widespread executive downsizing began in response to the recession of 1990–91, which for the first time saw more white-collar workers laid off than blue-collar workers, as organizations sought to become more efficient at the managerial level. However, downsizing did not end with the recession; as profits rose, many companies continued to lay off employees. In 1994, corporate profits rose 11 percent, and in 1993 they rose 13 percent, according to DRI/McGraw Hill. Meanwhile, corporate America cut 516,000 jobs in 1994, according to an outplacement firm cited by *The Wall Street Journal*—far more than in the recession year of 1990, when 316,047 jobs were eliminated, and almost as many as the 555,292 discharged in 1991, at the height of the recession.[2]

Companies that are discharging employees as their profits take off maintain that they have to continue to work at being lean to keep up with fierce global competition. Workers, however, see such cuts, amid record profits, as mean and arbitrary, as eroding employee loyalty and creating tension and stress that undermine teamwork and productivity.[3]

The result is a growing recognition by employees that they have to view their career as an exercise in self-employment in which they may work for a particular company for a while, but not necessarily in an enduring arrangement. Like a business, they must anticipate the possibility of change and continue to develop the skills and experience that will enable them to find new sources of livelihood if their employment with one company hits a dead end or is terminated. In fact, in thinking about their career, people have to do more than examine the fields that most interest them. Just as a prudent investor seeks to diversify its portfolio to reduce risk, they have to determine how to prepare for multiple careers. They also have to accept the chance that they will have to uproot themselves and their family in order to move to where new work can be found.

These conditions represent profound changes in the career pattern that prevailed through most of the twentieth century, and their effects will not be fully visible for some years to come. I do not mean to imply that the effects will all be negative; developing a more self-reliant work force could be a positive outcome. But all employers, for-profit and nonprofit, ought to reflect on how these changes affect their ability to attract and hold on to talented employees.

A case in point is the experience of law firms, where talented partners, even whole departments and their clients, jump from one firm to another in response to offers of higher earnings, upsetting the profession's tradition of stable legal partnerships and continuity of service to clients.

Investment banking firms, too, have fissured when a department is not paid as well as the corresponding department in another firm, and when the department in question has performed well, even though the firm as a whole may not have. Wall Street employees tend to ask themselves: did *I* reap as many dollars as my peers at other firms? If people in the mergers and acquisitions department at another firm got a bigger bonus than I did at my firm, even though our production was the same, then I'm going to walk down the street to someone who will pay me more. Salomon Brothers, once one of Wall Street's leading firms, adopted a compensation program that weighted heavily the overall results of the firm and not just individual performance. The plan was adopted at the instance of Warren Buffet, the firm's largest shareholder, who came to rescue the firm from the effects of a scandal in the treasury bond field. The result was massive defections by senior executives who, when the firm as a whole did not have a good year, did not take home the same bonus as their competitors across the way.

It may not be much of an exaggeration to say that the concept of "free agency" is not limited to professional sports but has penetrated all professional endeavors. Turnover, of course, costs employers a great deal—in time lost in finding a replacement, in the actual cost of recruiting a replacement or replacements (who typically prove to be more expensive than the staff member[s] who left), and in the incalculable cost of the disruption to the unit from which an employee or employees departed.

The Lure of Private-Sector Pay

After retiring from his post as president of Harvard University, Derek Bok wrote *The Cost of Talent: How Executives and Professionals Are Paid and How It Affects America*.[4] Bok is a labor lawyer who was first a member of the Harvard Law School faculty and later the school's dean before being named president of the university. He is obviously deeply concerned that the compensation provided in the private sector is having an adverse effect on the professionalism of our lawyers, doctors, and other practitioners and on the flow of talent to occupations that pay less well. He concludes flatly:

> Many practitioners in the private sector are overpaid, some egregiously so. The distribution of talent seems heavily skewed to the benefit of the private sector even though much of the work of government and the public schools is increasingly important to the nation and cries out for able people. Incentives are often warped in ways that lead executives to take an excessively short-term view while tempting lawyers and doctors to provide more services than their clients and patients truly need.[5]

Bok attributes the preference of the nation's most able students for private-sector work at least partly to "unwarranted differences in compensation."[6] He notes that between the early 1970s and the 1990s, the gap between the starting salaries of graduates of leading law and business schools who chose to go to Wall Street and the pay of those who went to work for the federal government or became teachers, widened dramatically. In the early 1970s, there really was no significant pay gap between starting salaries in the federal government and those of lawyers and MBAs headed to Wall Street, although the latter's salaries were twice those paid to teachers. By 1990, Wall Street starting salaries had grown to double the entry-level salaries in the federal government and four times those of beginning teachers.[7]

Bok ends his book by asking rhetorically "whether a preoccupation with material gain can produce either a deeply satisfying existence or a life that we look back upon with pride."[8]

Ideally, everyone attracted to work in the nonprofit sector would identify with Bok's outlook. Unfortunately, for nonprofits, the pressure exerted by private-sector pay levels is particularly acute. While many nonprofits could offer better pay, there are real limits on what exempt organizations can pay their employees. These limits are derived from the organization's financial condition and, fair or not, the public perception of what is appropriate compensation in organizations that enjoy tax exemption and raise tax-deductible contributions from the public to further their charitable aims.

Overlooking the Intrisic Value of Work

The following observations are perhaps less a description of a change in the workplace than a cautionary note that as nonprofits move to adopt the mechanisms of modern management, as this book urges, the appeal of the nature of their work not be lost.

Driving intensity, sharp focus, and meticulous attention to detail are qualities essential to outstanding performance; students start to learn this in school and on athletic fields. In adulthood, these qualities tend to determine who achieves goals and who falls short. But these same forces, carried to an extreme, can be counterproductive, producing a zealousness in pursuit of an objective that even dedicated coworkers find oppressive. I once knew a supervisor whose energies fueled him seven days and nights a week. He could not restrain himself from calling subordinates at home at all hours, summoning people away from recreation and family activities, and holding long telephone conferences on weekends. There is no question that his zeal to produce better results took hold in the organization. But so did resentment that reached a point where his ability to shape the spirit and direction of the organization was compromised.

The fierce determination to best a competitor can, if not bound by limits, push some to engage in unethical and illegal behavior. As Derek Bok writes in *The Cost of Talent,* "When competition grows too intense, it can demand a level of effort out of proportion to the benefits achieved, just as it can cause people to violate the law and undermine professional norms."[9]

Bok makes the point—which will resonate with many of those who have chosen a career in the nonprofit world—that, for many, work is *one of the ways* in which people seek personal fulfillment. Discussions that focus only on "how to pay people enough money to attract them in sufficient numbers and motivate them to perform properly" reflect a view of work that Bok describes as "sadly incomplete." He concludes:

> Building on organizational culture that inspires commitment . . . does not involve manipulating rewards to align acquisitive instincts with organizational goals. Instead, it seeks to change the attitudes of executives and professionals and cause them to perceive a greater meaning in their jobs. Rather than alter the pay people receive for their work, it tries to change the value of work itself.[10]

Lest the reader disregard Bok's thoughts as hopelessly idealistic and out of touch with the real world, let me relate a personal anecdote about him. Some years ago, one of my classmates from Harvard Law School arranged for Bok, then the active president of Harvard, to meet with a small group of New York City lawyers who were very disturbed by the strife among different ideological factions of the law school, strife that had spilled over into the print media that afternoon. Bok looked, in my opinion, much more refreshed and composed than the highly successful lawyers sitting around the conference table. Before he began his explanation of the situation at the law school, I asked Bok, as one of the longest-serving presidents of an American university, what accounted for his longevity in the job. He paused a moment and then, with obvious sincerity, said simply, "I enjoy what I do."

Women's Entry into the Work Force

A combination of factors have moved women into the work force in great numbers over the last several decades. The trend has been fueled in part by economic necessity, as families increasingly find it hard to achieve the quality of life they desire—or, in too many cases, simply to survive. High rates of divorce have been another factor: two people living apart each need more money than if they lived together. If we add the fact that alimony has virtually become a thing of the past (except in a handful of very long-term marriages), and factor in the fact that a good number of fathers default on their child support obligations, then we have another group of women who have no choice but to go to work.

But economic pressure is not the only reason why so many women now work. As a result of the women's movement, our culture now accepts that women and men have an equal right to enjoy a career. This cultural factor probably accounts for the fact that half, and in some cases more than half, of the students at most of our best business and law schools are women.

The generation of men confronted with adapting to this influx of women was largely white and over age 40 when the number of women in the workplace started to become substantial. Some of their prejudice is overt, some more subtle but no less injurious. It is hard to accept that the 1990s have seen gender discrimination as blatant as that documented in some court cases. Clearly, prejudice against women still runs deep in our society. In most institutions, one can see barriers to women's success simply by comparing the numbers of highly ranked women and men that organizations employ.

One also can see less blatant but still potent expressions of gender prejudice in many workplaces; e.g., penalizing women in terms of advancement or compensation because they are not only professionals but also bear the primary responsibility for the rearing of children. Men can fail to take into account the multiple roles women play in our society and to make adjustments to this reality in the work culture they have created. I remember a senior colleague adamantly refusing to keep on his payroll a very talented woman who, following the birth of her baby, wanted to work three days a week. The employee pointed out that there were plenty of assignments which did not require her presence in the office five days a week, or extensive overnight travel. My colleague then protested that, if the employee was only obliged to work three days a week, it might be impossible for her to attend certain meetings. She countered that everyone juggled meeting dates all the time to accommodate male executives. Still my colleague refused to bend.

A young woman who was a partner at a law firm and had a child once explained to me that if she did not bill the same number of hours as her male counterparts, she was penalized financially, whether or not the quality of her work was better than theirs and whether or not she was highly valued by clients. And, lest the reader jump to the conclusion that law firms often get business by burning the midnight oil and turning out work fast in a crisis, let me add that no one had ever accused this woman of not being available in such a situation. But in the world of hourly billings, she was penalized financially for not having the same totals as men of her age and experience, without regard to the relative quality of their output or the differences in their situations.

Sexual discrimination can also take the more direct form of sexual harrasment. Male colleagues and supervisors can make female employees' compensation or even their employment status contingent on sexual favors. Male coworkers can create what the courts call a "hostile environment"—one in which the remarks made by males, and the attitudes they display toward a woman colleague, are so hostile as to make it impossible for her to work in the unit. Anyone who doesn't believe that such situations continue to exist should go to a law library and read some of the cases.

How an Organization Can Respond Affirmatively to the New World of Work

For an employer—be it a profit-making business or a nonprofit organization or a mix of the two forms—the issue is how to address the changes that have taken place in the work world in a way that enables the organization to continue to attract and *retain* able personnel.

Recognize the "New" Pressures on Employees

The first step is to recognize the special pressures the modern employee faces and appreciate the fact that such pressures can undermine an employee's productivity. In fact, companies that develop intelligent responses to today's issues will enjoy an advantage over companies that do not. Joan Ganz Cooney, the founder and first CEO of Children's Television Workshop, would observe that CTW tended to attract the best women in their fields because they saw a woman as president and believed—correctly—that the organization did not impose limits on women's progress.

For competitive reasons, a number of companies have begun to consider how to keep their talented women executives without making motherhood an impossible burden for them. For years, many organizations, at their own initiative, provided unpaid leave for an employee to take care of a newborn child. Now this practice has been written into law and broadened to cover certain health-related family emergencies. The Family and Medical Leave act of 1993 provides that employers that have 50 or more employees must provide 12 weeks of unpaid leave not only for employees with a newborn child but also for employees with a sick relative whom they are caring for, and for employees who are themselves ill.

Also, more and more employers have recognized the business will not collapse even if an employee, female or male, is not forced at the last minute to stay late at the office when that employee has a child or children at home for whom the employee is the primary care provider.

Granting unpaid leave in certain situations is but one step toward retaining employees, especially female ones. Organizations ought to put high on their senior management and board agendas the issue of how to create a work environment that is attractive to their employees, including women of child-bearing age. For instance, organizations might consider

♦ Providing work assignments and training that broaden employees' career options in the event that one day they become victims of downsizing.

♦ Providing flexible work hours to male and female employees with young children or sick relatives for whom they are the primary care provider, and to employees who are undergoing or recovering from an illness of their own. Unpaid leave is not an option that every employee can afford; part-time work or a flexible schedule may be a better response.

♦ Arranging help for employees with emotional problems or drug or alcohol addictions.

♦ Appointing an official whom employees can approach to explain a problem with a supervisor or with work, or even to report wrongdoing on the part of others. Access to such a person must be provided without giving employees reason to fear that their position or future in the organization will be compromised.

Recognize the Diverse Values That Motivate Workers

In referencing Derek Bok's comments about the negative side-effects of excessive financial compensation and of overemphasis on beating the competition, I did not mean to imply that financial rewards for good performance are not important and legitimate motivators and that competition within appropriate boundaries is not a vital, healthy force in an organization. For many, work is about the amount of money that can be earned and the independence that accumulated wealth can bring. For others, work provides a means of measuring oneself against others. Our compensation systems have to recognize these very human drives. But they are not the whole story, certainly not for all people in all occupations. For some, the motivating force is the nature of the challenge to be met, be it working out a new intellectual concept, or designing a new or better product, or rendering service to better the lives of others. Such people are animated by the satisfaction they derive from the substance of their work, although this does not necessarily mean they are indifferent to their pay or how it compares with that of others in their field. Organizations, be they profit-making or non-profits, should recognize the values that motivate such people and should make these values a part of their culture, identifying quality performance in and of itself as a justifiable source of pride.

Provide Affirmative Leadership at the Top

An anecdote from my own experience is the best way to make the point here. A new CEO held his first meeting with the top executives of one of the world's major corporations. His lean and severe looks were accentuated by his thin black hair, combed straight back, and his wire-rimmed glasses. As he stood behind a podium, he appeared stiff and ill at ease, his facial muscles drawn tight. It took a long swallow of water to get him started speaking. He read from a prepared text, his strained voice catching in his throat. As he read, he did not use hand gestures to punctuate his points; his eyes left his text only rarely and never made contact with those of his audience. He did affect his audience, however, although not as he had intended. The message that his most important colleagues heard loud and clear was that he was not confident in his new role; indeed, he was visibly anxious about how to fill it. Years later the inability to be visibly in charge in a crisis undid him. A scandal that had happened before the start of his presidency exploded publicly during his term and became the cause of his downfall when he could not seem to rise above it. The chief executive of an organization must inspire confidence, especially when an organization faces a severe challenge.

Top leadership needs, first, to choose the right people for a particular assignment and then motivate them to do their best. The starting point is to select people with the right talent and temperament for the job at hand, people who will work together to enhance each other's personal qualities and skills and will be energized by the organization's basic purpose, be it earning the greatest possible profit for a business or achieving the objectives of a tax-exempt not-for-profit organization.

Then, with the best possible team in place, the organization's leader has to offer a clear, consistent, and well conceived vision of the entity's mission, its principal objectives, and the standards of performance expected of all employees. To top it off, the leader must work continually at motivating all employees to live up to those expectations, drawing on a system of tangible and intangible rewards, and must demonstrate the ability to hear the opinions and needs of others and to respond to them. At the same time, the CEO must be *actively* responsible for ensuring that adequate controls exist to prevent employee misbehavior.

Such leadership is hard to find in any sector of life—governmental, business, or charitable. One of the things that makes such leadership so difficult is human nature. We don't all react the same way to the same stimuli, we don't all express ourselves with equal clarity, and we are all vulnerable, in various degrees, to different demons. All the management practices outlined in this book—or other books, for that matter—aren't worth much unless they are applied under the leadership of a person who has mastered the human equation.

Powerful leadership can, however, be negative or positive. Tactics such as being highly critical of subordinates (especially in front of others), reacting with a temperamental outburst to bad news or the discovery of an error, constantly urging people to work faster, being impatient with employees who don't get your message right away, or directing fury or ridicule at those who mess up an assignment, can be temporarily effective in pushing people to work harder and longer. But such an approach is eventually very costly. Few people thrive in such a contentious atmosphere, and the additional stress imposed on them ultimately results in poorer performance or inhibits their willingness to speak out, especially to the supervisor who is the source of their anxiety. The result is that few ideas for innovation or change reach the top, so that the supervisor becomes doubly convinced that he or she alone is focused on what has to be done, and consequently drives subordinates even harder. Ultimately, the best employees may leave to find other opportunities. The resentment and anger of those who remain will seriously undermine the organization's productivity.

Infusing personnel with a sense of pride in their skills, and in the high quality and value of the organization's work (not just the money it makes), is an *affirmative* approach to motivating employees. My experience is that people respond better to having their sights lifted than to having their heads bowed.

Set Clear Expectations

Any organization, for-profit or nonprofit, inevitably creates a set of expectations for employees. The range of possibilities is broad: hard work, skilled execution, and individual initiative may be valued highly; or, at the other extreme, it may be acceptable to work only the minimum number of specified hours, to do exactly what one is told, and to expect promotions to be based strictly on seniority rather than merit. Compensation policy and how that policy is administered play a critical role in shaping such expectations. (See the discussion later in this chapter.) It provides one way of inspiring employees to outstanding performance and initiative taking rather than leaving them content to be mediocre performers of a rigid routine.

A range of nonfinancial means are also available for shaping employee attitudes. The behavior of senior officials, superiors' praise of subordinates' initiative, the nature of the people included or excluded from important organizational decisions, and training to upgrade staff skills are among the obvious ways of influencing employee performance.

Clarity in setting expectations, from the highest to the lowest level of management, also affects employee performance. At the highest level, the board needs to discuss with the CEO precisely what it expects him or her to accomplish, and to reach agreement on priorities. In turn, the CEO must spell out his or her expectations of senior managers, and so on down the line. Serious problems can result when this doesn't happen. For instance, assume that some members of the board want the CEO to concentrate on raising funds and building the external image of the organization. Others, however, expect the focus to be on cutting costs and improving day-to-day operations. No consensus is reached; perhaps, as is often the case, the agenda of the CEO is not even reviewed with the board. Under these circumstances, the CEO's performance very likely will disappoint some trustees and produce a tension that ultimately can undermine the chief executive's ability to perform effectively. Moreover, the confused signals given to the CEO by the board are likely to be reflected in the directions passed on to the staff.

Lack of clarity in setting expectations can shape employee performance at the most elementary level of an organization. The following anecdote illustrates the point: A stenographic pool in an organization was the object of widespread complaints from users about the typists' high error rate. An investigation revealed that the typists had been instructed only to increase their speed; apparently, no attention was paid by superiors to work quality. When asked how the errors would be caught, one typist said, "Oh, we all count on the authors to do that. We're only interested in getting out the work as fast as possible."

In short, a range of factors affect employee performance: the role models created by senior management; the organization's financial and nonfinancial rewards system; and the policies communicated to employees. Managerial acts of omission, as well as of commission, will influence employee attitudes. The manager who makes no effort to shape employee performance reinforces prevailing behavior through neglect. Consequently, managers who want better employee performance have to work at getting it, instead of simply taking employee attitudes and expectations for granted.

Offer Constructive Performance Appraisals

No task is more important in affecting employees' work than providing employees with constructive performance appraisals. Such an appraisal needs to be in writing, whether it is outlined in a letter or memorandum, or in some other form. A written appraisal that clearly states the supervisor's points ensures that an employee will not go home afterward and misremember or even distort what the supervisor had to say. Similarly, it discourages the supervisor from telling an employee that performance did not live up to expectations, without being able to explain why that is the case.

An effective evaluation lists the pluses and minuses of an employee's performance. Once the employee has had a chance to read and digest the evaluation, the employee and the supervisor go over the evaluation together, and the supervisor tries to help the employee understand the minuses and what can be done to overcome them. The point is to help the employee accept his or her weaknesses and not shrug them off as the mistaken perceptions of a superior. The power of people to rationalize their shortcomings or to deny their existence is formidable. A supervisor is not being helpful if he or she does not make an effort to break through the employee's defenses. The worst result is to find all of the minuses still on the list at the employee's next performance appraisal. Some organizations find that a constructive way to achieve results from performance appraisals is for the supervisor to engage in a dialogue with the employee before committing the observations to writing.

Provide Reasonable and Equitable Compensation

The efforts of nonprofit organizations to upgrade the caliber of their professional staff have led to increasing awareness of the role that well-conceived and well-administered compensation programs play in attracting and motivating able personnel. In the view of executive recruiters with whom I have spoken, as nonprofit salaries have gone up in recent years, so has the quality of people ready to be employed in the nonprofit sector.

Lack of resources is a factor in the pay typically provided by nonprofit organizations. But also at work is the long-held view that people in the nonprofit sector ought not to make what might be perceived as a healthy salary. Some nonprofits maintain that they don't want to employ anyone who is interested in the organization because of compensation. Attractive pay is seen as inconsistent with the values of a nonprofit organization and its mission to benefit others. In some cases, this attitude toward compensation is a heritage from the past, when nonprofit work was done largely by well-intentioned volunteers and the need for professional management was not recognized. Not very long ago, all nonprofits were thought of as "charities" in the sense of religious charities, and working at a cleric's pay was seen as in keeping with the spirit of the work.

In my experience, such attitudes sharply limit the pool of available qualified candidates. Indeed, over the 10 years since I wrote *Managing for Profit in the Nonprofit World,* there has been a growing recognition that quality management is essential in the nonprofit sector and that the gap between what such talent earns in the private sector and nonprofit pay levels needs to be narrowed. As one veteran executive recruiter who specializes in nonprofit placements explained to me, "I listen to twelve people sit around telling me all the things they want in an executive director, and then I ask them, 'Do you think you can get such a person for what you have said you are willing to pay?' Many times they adjust upward what they are willing to pay." The recruiter added, "The people coming from the corporate arena, or with skills and credentials to work in the private sector, want some degree of comparability."

Another factor in attracting quality employees, in the recruiter's view, is the establishment of pension plans in organizations that have heretofore not offered them. My own experience in working in four different nonprofit organizations, as well as several business organizations, has made the nonprofit portable pension an extremely valuable asset. Virtually no private company offers a portable pension—that is, one in which employer contributions made to the plan belong to the employee regardless of the length of his or her service with an organization and which may be added to the pension contributions earned. At other nonprofits the pension is also held in a tax-deferred retirement vehicle, insulating the employer contributions from taxation on investment gains until the funds are actually withdrawn. In contrast, private business invariably requires a combination of a lengthy period of service—typically 20 to 30 years—and the attainment of a certain age before any part of the employer's contributions becomes an asset of the employee. Someone can work for a private company for as long as 15 to 20 years and then leave, either voluntarily or involuntarily, and lose all that the company has contributed to his or her pension. The availability of a portable pension can be useful in attracting qualified people to the nonprofit world.

Administer Compensation Fairly

Whether a compensation program serves its intended purpose depends not only on its design but on how it is administered in practice. One day, a friend who is a senior officer of one of the nation's most important urban cultural institutions was comparing notes with me about various nonprofit organizations' approaches to compensation. I learned that practices considered standard by compensation professionals were not followed by my friend's organization or, doubtless, by many other nonprofit institutions. The cultural organization of which my friend was an officer

- Awarded all professional employees the same percentage salary increase every year, regardless of whether their performance was stellar and lackluster.
- Established no yearly individual goals for employees as part of the compensation process, leaving employees without a clear sense of what specific accomplishments were expected of them.
- Neither established salary ranges for each professional position nor conducted surveys to determine the salaries paid by other organizations for comparable positions.

In effect, the organization failed to use compensation policy as an important tool for inspiring good performance and making employees accountable for the quality of their work. The organization's approach also failed to recognize the importance of compensation policy in setting institutional priorities.

In setting compensation policy, there are three overriding objectives:

- Competition with the external market;
- Provision of internal equity; and
- Provision of differentiated compensation increases based on performance (i.e., a performance-based compensation system).

All three are complex to administer, but, as in so many areas of management, communication lies at the heart of effective process. One should never tire of explaining to staff members what compensation policies are being followed and how they are being administered. Following is an examination of each of these three objectives.

Pay Competitive with the Market.   What is the relative competitive market? How, for example, to judge someone who comes to a nonprofit organization from the academic world, but whose future may lie with the profit-making world (a computer scientist, for example)? Or, in the case of a nonprofit television producer, is the relevant competitive market commercial television or public broadcasting? Salaries in these two worlds are quite different.

How to measure what the market is paying? An outside consulting firm can assess the competitive external market for each job position. The review should be done annually, because the market changes from time to time. The firm will survey what people in similar positions are paid, but the system is very imprecise. Positions in other organizations are hard to compare with positions within one's own institution, and some positions simply are not comparable to positions in other organizations. Furthermore, reliable data on pay in other institutions are often hard to come by.

Nevertheless, as imprecise as the process of determining competitive pay may be, it needs to be implemented so that employees will believe that the organization is trying to live up to its commitment to pay competitively with the marketplace, and that there is an objective basis for pay levels.

Internal Equity. This means that positions of comparable importance within an organization are comparably paid.

At one nonprofit organization, the process of establishing internal equity starts with having staff members rate jobs according to specific criteria (e.g., required knowledge, skills, complexity, scope, and impact). The job, not its occupant, is rated. The rating can be done intuitively or using an elaborate weighting formula; it is critical to have broad staff participation in establishing comparability of jobs. After all, since the comparison will not be scientific, consensus and a sense of fair process are crucial to its effectiveness.

When internal equity and market factors are in conflict, external market considerations should normally prevail. But in any given case, if a sense of equity is critical, internal equity can be given more weight than market factors.

Performance-Based Compensation. Too often the policy in nonprofit institutions is to give everybody the same percentage raise. This approach rewards mediocrity and penalizes talent. The compensation structure in the not-for-profit world ought to reward performance.

A performance-oriented approach forces managers to differentiate between ordinary and extraordinary effort. This is possible if, at the outset of the pay period, one establishes clear performance objectives that are understood and accepted by the employee and manager. The delineation of such performance goals also becomes a prime tool for setting the direction of the company.

To induce managers to make compensation recommendations based on performance, central management needs, at a minimum, to review the salary increase distribution patterns of departmental managers and to question the practices of managers who do not show a reasonable spread between superior performance and ordinary performance in awarding salary increases. Also useful is a centrally administered bonus pool from which funds are allocated on petitions from particular managers on behalf of particular employees.

The review of "performance relative to objectives" in connection with compensation awards is, as I noted earlier in the chapter, probably the most important function any manager performs, and yet it is generally the function performed with the least care and attention. Central management needs to educate managers how to do this.

The Role of the Trustee Compensation Committee

Given the importance of compensation to the morale of the organization and its sensitivity to public criticism, a committee of the board of trustees that has no affiliation with management should review and approve the organization's compensation policies as well as its procedures for administering such policies.

The formation of such a committee should follow the precedent established for publicly traded companies by the Securities and Exchange Commission, which requires the compensation committee of the board of directors to report annually to the Commission explaining the basis on which compensation is awarded to top executives.

The compensation committee of a nonprofit ought to review periodically

- ◆ The organization's overall program of compensation for all employees, including salaries and benefits;
- ◆ The system by which raises and any bonus or incentive awards are granted; and
- ◆ How the organization's compensation compares to that of comparable organizations. To do this, from time to time the nonprofit may have to commission studies by outside consultants to evaluate how the organization's compensation for specific positions compares to that of other nonprofits in the same field and of comparable positions in business. One important question to examine in such a review is how much the organization would have to pay to *replace* its key executives; often the answer to this question produces higher compensation figures than a study of comparability of pay.

In addition, the committee should annually review and approve the compensation to be paid to the organization's senior executives and should then prepare a report to the full board explaining the basis on which such awards were made.

The Recruiting Process

Plainly, the key to an organization's future lies in the quality of the hiring it does and how well it nurtures good talent once it is recruited. In the not-for-profit world, this is frequently another of the least-considered aspects of management.

"Every person chosen right," the head of one of the nation's most efficient transportation companies once observed, "can have the most singular impact on productivity." Ironically, in many nonprofit organizations the process of recruiting talent is done well for program employees and haphazardly in the case of administrative workers. Universities, for example, have relatively well-developed processes for recruiting new faculty members and yet search in a random, casual way for administrative talent. The point is that a successful nonprofit enterprise must make a major investment in recruiting and nurturing *all* of its employees.

There are a number of mechanisms for recruiting people:

◆ Advertisements
◆ Word of mouth
◆ Walk-in applicants
◆ Recruiting by executive search firms[11]
◆ Search committees.

No method necessarily promises better results than the others. The most critical factors in making good choices are

◆ A clear sense of organizational purpose.
◆ Clear job descriptions including carefully delineated necessary qualifications for candidates.
◆ A good internal screening process, so that both the candidate and the organization get a real chance to become familiar with each other. It is important to screen applicants for their psychological as well as their skill-related compatibility with the organization.
◆ A careful review of references relating to the employee's prior record. (State laws relating to reference checks can now make checking references a more complex task, but this obstacle can be overcome by asking candidates to authorize such reference checks.)

There are no shortcuts to this process. Staff members have to spend time interviewing candidates, contacting people who have worked with the candidates earlier in their careers (ideally these should be independent sources, not just the candidates' handpicked references), and, when feasible, examining samples of their work. My experience has shown that, at least in filling important positions, it is worthwhile to have an interviewer skilled in reading others' psychology explore candidates' emotional fit with both the organization and the particular position for which they are being considered.

Still, hiring is a percentage business, and some poor choices will inevitably be made. Hence, a manager must have the nerve to fire an employee as soon as it becomes apparent that a poor hiring choice has been made.

Developing Talent

Beyond selecting good talent, there is a need to develop the talent once it is on board. The identification of such promising talent and its development is not something that can be done only by subordinate managers; it must be a prime concern of higher management. The critical factors in developing talent are:

◆ compensation policy that especially rewards outstanding performance rather than all employees equally;

◆ active identification by top management of the superior young personnel in the company, and ensuring that they are being moved along a path that is interesting to them and gives them an opportunity to develop;

◆ making sure such employees are aware they are considered outstanding prospects and know of their opportunities for growth.

High employee turnover costs an organization severely. It clearly pays today to develop systems that attract the best employees, actively help them to develop their talents, and find meaningful opportunities for them to apply their energies. The best inducement for good people to stay with an organization is the chance to expand their talents though challenging assignments.

A real problem in many nonprofit organizations is that there is not a great deal of room at the top. The organization that has only a very few jobs at the senior level can stifle opportunities for its younger staff. One antidote is to make sure that when good people reach a bottleneck, the organization assists such people in finding outside jobs. This will help the organization gain a reputation of being a good place to work because it gives a boost to an employee's career.

How to Discharge Employees in an Era of Downsizing

In *Managing for Profit in the Nonprofit World,* I wrote:

> One of the skills that is very rarely discussed in business or management schools, but that is critical in managing an organization, is how to fire people. It's distasteful, unfortunate, and a very severe blow to an employee, but it is a necessary part of organizational life. Doing it well can be critical to the success of the organization and, certainly, to minimizing the damage and pain to the affected employee. In fact, firing people well is as critical as hiring people well.

> From my own experience, the best way is to be as clinical and surgical about it as possible without being brusque or seeming unsympathetic. Being let go is a powerful form of rejection, and anyone being discharged is going to feel deeply hurt. Elaborate

details, explanations, hesitation, indirection, and indecisiveness all make the situation worse. Don't beat around the bush. Get to the point quickly. Be sure to give a specific reason for your action. Be candid, too. In the long run, a discharged employee will handle the truth more easily than circumlocution. And make the explanation short, simple, and easily understood. Then, quickly get beyond the discharge to what's going to be done to cushion the blow to the employee. For example, spell out what the severance benefits are, what kind of out-placement counseling is available, and what other kinds of help you are willing to offer, including what you will say to people who might call for references about the person. These are the life and death questions that discharged employees face.

As an employer, you have an obligation to help an employee you have let go make a transition to a new job. This is true even when the employee is being discharged because of unsatisfactory performance. After all, if the employee is not right for the organization, it is partly your fault. You made the decision to hire that person in the first place, and you had a better idea than the employee did of the kind of environment he or she was entering and what the expectations and the requirements of the position were. (Obviously, I am not talking here about situations in which an employee has engaged in wrongdoing or abused his or her position in some way.)

Accordingly, in discharging an employee, an employer should, within reason, support the person's effort to find new work. Indeed, it is in any organization's interest to develop a reputation as a thoughtful and fair employer in the circumstances where a discharge is involved.

Large-scale executive layoffs have made the problem of how to fire people far more acute and organizations' exposure much greater. The U.S. Bureau of Labor Statistics reports that 10.1 million workers were "displaced" or lost their jobs between 1989 and 1992, 35 percent more than in the previous four-year period. At the same time, the number of discharge-related complaints filed with the U.S. Equal Employment Opportunity Commission has risen 33 percent since 1990. This figure does not take into account the number of lawsuits filed for wrongful discharge and the millions of dollars that companies have paid out in jury damage awards in recent years.

The need to handle mass employee discharges in a sensitive and legally appropriate manner is by no means unique to the business world; nonprofit institutions are under similar pressure to cut their staffs in order to bring their budgets into balance, and this pressure is likely to grow in the years ahead as government support declines and resources become scarcer.

Downsizing an organization can be done in a way that mitigates the pain employees will feel when they lose their jobs and the anxiety of those who survive a round of cuts. Genuine efforts by the company to help employees cut loose in a downsizing to find new employment should be seen as an obligation, one to be taken very seriously by the employer and not palmed off on just any outplacement firm. The employer should either choose the firm carefully—and closely monitor its work—or, if it can not find a firm that will do the job well, establish its own operation. Such an approach is in the employer's interest, because the employees who remain will get wind of how their former colleagues are being treated. If the organization seems indifferent to the fate of laid-off employees, the news will reach the staff. Moreover, an organization is ill-advised to dump a large number of employees into the marketplace in a way that leads the discharged employees to become vocal critics of the organization.

An employer can provide help beyond assisting in a job search; for example, discharged employees can receive training in running a small business, or in how to work as self-employed professionals, or in buying a franchise. Such forms of assistance may be more appropriate responses to the opportunities available today to employees who are laid off. When a significant number of layoffs is planned, it is useful to appoint a senior executive to oversee the process until most or all of the laid-off workers have found new employment.

At one nonprofit with several thousand employees, when significant cuts in the administrative staff became necessary, the president decided early on to try to cut deeply enough the first time so that the exercise would not have to be repeated. He knew that unit executives tend to underestimate their budget gaps when they know staff cuts are in the offing, with the result that round after round of layoffs becomes necessary. His directive was, "Let's do this once and do it thoroughly so we can tell people honestly that, barring unforeseen developments, this is it." Repeated "restructurings" and "downsizings" will shake the credibility of any organization with the rank and file and provoke resistance to further change.

The president also appointed one of the most senior officers of the organization to develop procedures for the layoffs, including reexamining the severance policy, which had not been drafted with this kind of situation in mind, and being personally responsible for the administration of the program. The officer was widely perceived within the organization as sympathetic to the rights and needs of employees and was also the leading advocate of affirmative action—an important consideration since complaints of racial, gender, and age bias are inevitable in connection with a downsizing program.

Obviously, financial arrangements that cushion the blow to laid-off employees are useful mechanisms. So are special severance or retirement packages, when an employer can afford to use these to induce people to leave voluntarily. In particular, provision for extended medical coverage is very important to those losing their jobs. But special retirement programs can backfire when people whom an organization wants to retain jump at the package offered and leave.

While there are limits to the benefits that organizations—especially nonprofits already strapped for funds—can afford in this regard, it is important to reduce the projected savings from layoffs by the cost of severance packages for discharged employees.

One step an employer can take without spending money is to have top managers instruct supervisors to give priority to inquiries from potential new employers about former employees' performance. In addition, at a small cost, an employer can establish an office through which firms interested in hiring former employees can obtain confirmation that the discharge was for economic reasons and not related to employees' performance, and where they can be given a full and fair picture of employees' performance, based on the organization's records. Such a "reference office" helps laid-off employees in a number of ways: by confirming that they were not let go because of poor performance; by ensuring speedy responses to inquiries from potential employers; by sparing potential employers the necessity of talking to several supervisors if the employee has worked for more than one person; and by serving as a surrogate in the event that the employee's former supervisor is no longer available to provide a reference.

NOTES

1. Noel M. Tichy and Ram Charan, "The CEO as Coach: An Interview with Allied Signal's Lawrence A. Bossidy," *Harvard Business Review,* March–April 1995, pp. 71–73.

2. Matt Murray, "Thanks, Goodbye: Amid Record Profits Companies Continue to Lay Off Employees," *Wall Street Journal,* May 4, 1995, p. 1.

3. Ibid.

4. Derek Bok, *The Cost of Talent: How Executives and Professionals Are Paid and How It Affects America* (New York: Free Press, 1993).

5. Ibid., p. 247.

6. Ibid., p. 242.

7. Ibid., p. 242.

8. Ibid., p. 297.

9. Ibid., pp. 262–263.

10. Ibid., p. 294.

11. An executive search firm is retained by the management and recruits at its request. Regardless of who finds the person who, in the end, fills the job, the firm collects its fee. A standard search firm fee is about 30 percent of the candidate's total first-year compensation. An employment agency searches on behalf of employees and gets paid by an employer only if the employer hires a candidate presented by the agency.

CHAPTER 14

The Foundations of Effective Governance

Myles Cane, chairman of the board of Skidmore College, has the understated demeanor of a wise counselor: a restrained speaking style, a calm visage, a good ear, and obvious intelligence. The words that leap to mind immediately among people who know him are "meticulous" and "thoughtful." However, beneath the unruffled surface is a hard-driving and passionate man, continually seeking new challenges.

Cane earned his law degree at the University of Virginia, where he was an editor of the law review. As a practicing lawyer, he worked in the corporate finance and real estate fields. He also built a small New York firm into a midsize powerhouse. Now he has reinvented himself as an investor and deal maker. His passion, however, is Skidmore College. He is not an alumnus of the college but was recruited in 1978 to join the board after his stepdaughter graduated from Skidmore. He thus brings nearly 20 years of experience as a board member to his role as chair. He is also a board member of several foundations, served as a director of Planned Parenthood from 1978 to 1986, and is the director of several for-profit organizations.

Cane devotes about 25–30 percent of his time to his role as board chair. He sees his responsibilities as threefold: (1) the care and feeding of the president, (2) the selection of board members, and (3) the building of the college's endowment. Three times a year, he presides over a two-and-a-half-day meeting of the full board; he also devotes times to committee meetings, fundraising cultivation, and speaking engagements. In addition, he talks to the president of the college at least once a week and reviews key correspondence of the president and other university papers.

Three or four times a year, Cane attends meetings of the Conference of Board Chairs, consisting of the board chairs of 40 private liberal arts colleges. Founded more than 10 years ago by Eugene Lang (when he chaired the Swarthmore board), the group reviews issues common to all member institutions, in meetings that broaden the perspective and understanding of its participants.

Cane's leadership of the Skidmore board represents a model of the businessperson as a highly effective trustee, sympathetic to the aspirations of an institution, insightful about the nuances of its culture, and able to see how his own experience can assist the organization.

Defining the Role of the Board

Boards have a natural inclination to support management; management has an actual persona that trustees interact with and form relationships with. The board's and management's shared experience of working through problems builds mutual loyalty. Still, it is possible for a board to achieve an independent stance without creating an antagonistic and confrontational relationship with management.

A starting point in strengthening the board's independence is to define expectations of what it is reasonable for trustees to accomplish. For instance, it is wishful thinking to expect trustees to be more clairvoyant than operating executives in setting strategy for an organization. Trustees should not so much be faulted for lack of foresight as held accountable for the quality of their hindsight: did they take appropriate and timely action once they knew, or should have known, that the organization was off course—that its level of effectiveness was demonstrably not what it should be, that its mission was no longer responsive to a changed environment, that its financial underpinnings were in jeopardy, or that its internal financial controls were inadequate? Where there are objective warning signals that management is not performing in accordance with the policies and specific expectations set by the board, then the board is obliged to conduct a thorough inquiry into management's performance.

Board members should be able to:

◆ Discern inconsistencies between management's announced outlook and objective evidence of the realities of the organization's condition.

◆ Understand the risks and potential rewards of a strategy as well as recognize when management has not formulated one.

◆ Evaluate the quality of operating management and spot flaws in either individual senior executives or major managerial systems.

◆ Test, with the aid of outside auditors or consultants, the adequacy of financial controls and reporting systems.

◆ Design and supervise compensation systems that provide incentives for outstanding performance without undermining the basic values of the not-for-profit form of organization.

◆ Identify and frame policy issues that for one reason or another may not be receiving the degree of attention they deserve from management.

◆ Evaluate—and where necessary improve—the quality of management's decision-making processes. Under the pressure of day-to-day events, management may be inclined to move too quickly, or it may stall and avoid tough decisions. Without necessarily trying to second-guess management, boards should be satisfied that critical decisions are being reached through sound processes and in a timely manner.

◆ Support specific policies and objectives before public and government authorities. Trustees who are able to speak out on behalf of an enterprise can be a valuable asset.

◆ Have the confidence to take unpleasant actions that their judgment indicates are necessary.

Given all that a board can contribute, a strong board, fully aware of what its role is and what it is not, is a major asset to any enterprise and a source of unique support for management.

A strong, effective board will have a sense of cohesion, will act based on of its own independently formed judgment, and will not subordinate itself to the CEO. The board will be capable of holding management accountable rather than simply acquiescing in exculpatory accounts of management's stewardship. The board will trust its informed instincts and not, out of an ingrained reflex, simply defer to management's wishes in all cases. Such a board will also transform its meeting into a forum in which both management and trustees can freely put issues on the table.

Accordingly, if the character of governance is to change, the culture that prevails in many boardrooms must also change. But changes must be crafted to meet each organization's particular needs and situation. Given the widely varying nature of exempt organizations, uniform rules and practices would not make sense.

Improving the Effectiveness of the Board

In the business world, the role of the board is being transformed, largely under pressure from large institutional shareholders, which now own roughly half of U.S. corporate shares (a percentage that has risen sharply over the last decades, as stock holdings have increasingly become concentrated in large pension funds). Institutions have found that, because of the size of their ownership position, it can be costly to sell their holdings in a company, or that a sale would alter a portfolio designed to track the composition of a market index. In such circumstances, pressing the company to improve its performance or change its strategy is seen by some investors as a more productive step.

At the same time, the Securities and Exchange Commission has taken a number of actions to facilitate shareholders' taking a more proactive role in the affairs of portfolio companies. Add to the picture the growing number of lawsuits against directors and the voluble criticism of board performance not only in academic journals but in the business press; the sources of pressure for changes in the governance of business corporations are obvious.

However, no similar sources of pressure exist in the nonprofit world, which has no shareholder-owners and no national regulatory agency with broad oversight of the governance of nonprofit organizations. The U.S. Internal Revenue Service does have national jurisdiction with respect to nonprofits, but this jurisdiction pertains to the specific provisions of the tax code rather than to the effectiveness of the governance of exempt organizations. Because such forces are absent, nonprofit boards must act on their own initiative to become effective overseers of management.

The current literature regarding corporate governance of for-profit institutions is filled with specific recommendations for making boards more effective in governing companies and for the role that shareholders should play in overseeing the performance of companies in which they have invested. This literature includes an article I co-authored with Burton G. Malkiel, professor of economics at Princeton and a director of a series of public corporations.[1] Besides drawing on this piece, I have also taken advantage of William G. Bowen's insightful *Inside the Boardroom: Governance by Directors and Trustees*.[2] I have drawn on this literature as well as personal experience in identifying the building blocks of effective governance of an organization. Note too that governance reform is not about shifting power from management to the board but about combining the forces of the two entities in support of the organization.

Here, then, are seven fundamentals of effective governance.

1. Giving control of the nominating process to outside trustees.   In my view, this is the ultimate foundation of an independent board. While the CEO should be consulted by the nominating committee, the board should be the final judge of its own membership. When such an independent nominating process exists, the board has a good chance of being an independent entity, not an instrument of management.

Vesting nominating power in the board does not preclude it from allowing members of the organization or its volunteer workers or, in the case of a school its alumni, to elect a specified number of board members.

Care must be taken, however, to ensure that the nominating process does not fall under the control of a clique of trustees. An insular board made up of a tight group of like-minded trustees that does not reflect the diversity of the organization's interests can prove as unfortunate to the long-term health of the enterprise as a board consisting of the CEO's cronies.

One possible safeguard is to require that membership on the trustee nominating committee be rotated among the full membership of the board. In addition, board members can be required to step down from the board after a specified number of years, with the proviso that after a certain period of time they may be reelected to the board. This form of term limit can also provide a way to deal with board members whose performance has not been satisfactory.

2. Shaping the board's agenda.   What issues are brought before the board, how much time is devoted to them, how issues are presented and discussed, who is heard, and what supporting materials are required are matters that the board should decide after consultation with management. In short, the control of the substance and form of board meetings should lie with the board.

3. Providing access to independent sources of information.   If a board is to arrive at its own assessments, it cannot depend entirely on the information provided to it by management. Board members must be free to consult with members of management (in addition to the CEO), outsiders with whom the organization deals, and experts in a given field. While this concept of access to information may threaten some CEOs, a number of private corporations, such as General Motors, provide for regular consultation between the board and managers other than the CEO, so that such meetings are not automatically perceived as a sign of lack of board confidence in the chief executive. Some companies go even further. For example, Home Depot requires its outside directors to visit stores regularly to interview employees and customers, believing that such visits not only guarantee a well-informed board but also a new source of information for management.

4. Establishing a committee on governance.   As I noted earlier, one of the principal shortcomings of many boards is their failure to examine what their role ought to be and what procedures should govern the conduct of the board and its relationships with others inside and outside the organization. For this purpose, a governance committee should be created and its conclusions debated by the full board and made available for comment by other people with a stake in the organization—employees, volunteers, and major sources of continued funding.

Opening up the governance process is another protection against domination of the board by a small, insular clique of trustees or by the CEO. The guidelines should thus be reviewed periodically.

5. Holding board meetings without management present.   In order to permit free and open discussion among board members, and to develop a sense of cohesiveness among them, the board should meet from time to time, on a scheduled basis, without any officers of the organization present, even when there is no crisis on the horizon. If such meetings are scheduled periodically, they will not be taken as a sign that something is necessarily amiss.

6. Choosing a leader of the board.   An issue that in the corporate world is perhaps the most sensitive of all—whether to appoint a board chair other than the CEO—is not typically a problem in nonprofit organizations. The appointment of a trustee as chair is fairly commonplace. In the business world, vesting the title of chair of the board in a board member is seen as undermining the authority of the CEO, and so the concept of a "lead director" has evolved as a compromise. Whatever title is used, the board of a nonprofit does need to choose a leader who can administer the affairs of the board, be accessible to other board members, and interact with management and outsiders.

7. Empowering the audit committee.   This concept is discussed in Chapter 9, "Depicting Performance and Financial Condition."

Business Executives as Trustees

In the nonprofit world, there are many dedicated and highly competent boards that play an active role. I have worked with boards made up of people of uncommon accomplishment, insight, and judgment who took a very active interest in the workings of their organization. Even so, it is true that nonprofit organizations have difficulty attracting people with business expertise who are willing to serve on boards in an active and informed way, rather than just passively lending their name to a good cause.

William G. Bowen, a careful and precise scholar and commentator, observes in *Inside the Boardroom* that "it is true that well-regarded representatives of the business world are often surprisingly ineffective as members of nonprofit boards." Bowen continues:

> Although it would be hard to devise a rigorous empirical test, I suspect my initial, harsh-sounding proposition questioning the effectiveness of nonprofit board members from the business sector holds with surprising frequency. Having now checked this perception with a variety of individuals, I can report that it is widely shared.[3]

One can only speculate why this should be the case, and Bowen devotes 10 pages of his book to trying to put his finger on the cause or causes. My hunch is that a good many business executives join nonprofit boards because of the prestige of the organization and/or as a way of lending their name to a good cause. In lives already burdened with commitments, if something has to give, it is the time board members devote to learning and following the business of the exempt organization.

How to make board members take a more active interest in the affairs of exempt organizations? I put this question to Frances Hesselbein, former head of the Girl Scouts of America and now director of the Peter F. Drucker Foundation. Hesselbein sits on both for-profit and nonprofit boards. To my question, she replied, "That's the job of the CEO. He or she has to pay personal attention to board members and to spark their interest."[4]

There is a lot of truth to Hesselbein's comment. When I first joined the Children's Television Workshop board, one of the reasons I looked forward to meetings was that Joan Cooney, as CEO, began each meeting with a half-hour overview of the organization, where it was headed, and how developments in the world of commercial broadcasting and politics could affect its future. It was a fascinating half-hour. My interest in board meetings was also heightened by the quality and diversity of my fellow board members; their stature in their fields and their insights into CTW made them stimulating company.

What I am driving at is simple to write, although by no means easy to put into practice: if you want an active and talented board, then make board meetings lively and interesting; don't overcontrol the meetings; give board members ample time to ask questions and deliberate; and, above all, put the most challenging issues that face the organization before the board for its input, and, where appropriate, decision. In short, treat the board as a valuable partner and not a necessary evil.

It is also useful to ask board members to undertake specific assignments relating to the formulation of organizational policy and strategy, or even to have them solve specific problems, particularly in areas where their professional expertise or problem-solving skills can supplement or complement the staff's talents.

In addition, exempt organizations should be realistic about the trustees they seek to attract. People who have attained a great deal of personal prestige through their own professional accomplishments are likely to be heavily obligated to others already. Nonprofits, particularly smaller or newer ones, should consider recruiting younger executives and professionals who have skills and valuable experience but may not yet have risen to the top of their field. Such individuals are typically not besieged with requests to join corporate or nonprofit boards and may respond quite enthusiastically to the opportunity to serve.

Exempt organizations have a natural tendency to recruit trustees who have the capacity to make substantial financial contributions and to solicit their peers to contribute. Board members' ability to contribute significantly to the start-up of a capital campaign can in fact determine how successful the campaign will ultimately be. Richard T. Ingram, president of the Association of Governing Boards of Universities and Colleges, has advised that a board's fundraising record should ideally show 100 percent of the members giving the largest gift they can afford, and that in major campaigns their donations and pledges should constitute 30 to 40 percent of the nucleus fund.[5] According to Ingram, trustee giving on the whole falls short of these goals.

It is dangerous to overemphasize the wealth of individuals in choosing board members. The risk is that the largest contributors will have a disproportionate say in the running of the organization, and that, indeed, they may have a pet program that they push at the expense of equally, if not more, worthy objectives. It is also possible that one or two major donors can take effective control of the board, dominate its deliberations, and, through chairing the nominating process, determine the make-up of the board. Other board members will defer to them for fear of alienating them and losing their contributions. That is obviously not a healthy situation. Ability to give cannot, therefore, be the sole criterion by which the composition of the board is determined.

Maggie Mahoney, in her final annual report as president of the Commonwealth Fund, observed, "Responsible boards are not born. They are composed carefully." In her view, board members should be chosen because of their personal characteristics, their qualities of mind and spirit—competence, integrity, intelligence, judgment, and empathy—and because of their actual accomplishments, "not just issues of age, geographic distribution, and gender."[6] Ms. Mahoney has hit the nail on the head.

NOTES

1. Paul Firstenberg and Burton G. Malkiel, "The Twenty-First Century Boardroom: Who Will Be in Charge?" *Sloan Management Review,* Fall 1994.

2. William G. Bowen, *Inside the Boardroom: Governance by Directors and Trustees* (New York: Wiley, 1994). This slim but informative volume deals with both for-profit and nonprofit institutions.

3. Ibid., p. 132.

4. Frances Hesselbein, interview with the author, April 1995.

5. *Chronicle of Higher Education,* May 19, 1995, p. A-37.

6. The Commonwealth Fund 1994 Annual Report, p. 5.

CHAPTER 15

Leadership:
Bundy, Bowen, and Cooney

At the center of every outstanding enterprise is a highly effective leader. The qualities that make a personality a leader are so varied and subtle that they do not lend themselves to neat categorization. Moreover, the character traits and behavioral style that make a person a leader in one environment do not necessarily make that person effective in an entirely different context. For example, there are very successful business executives who have been unable to master the politics by which one governs an academic institution or a government organization.

Still, although I recognize the dangers inherent in trying to generalize, it seems to me that effective leadership of exempt organizations has certain general characteristics. These include the ability to

- *Develop a vision of the organization's purpose and to instill that sense of purpose in others;*
- *Inspire other individuals to avoid the path of least resistance and instead strive to grow;*

◆ *Communicate to others that they are engaged in an exciting enterprise, rais-ing their interest in and energy for their work; and*

◆ *Project an aura of being firmly in control and ready to act decisively, re-gardless of doubts the leader may be experiencing or the degree of adversity the organization is encountering.*

At the root of effective leadership is a passion for the enterprise that is evident in the leader's words and deeds and in his or her ability to inspire others.

I have encountered such exemplary leaders in three nonprofit organizations. Each was as different from the others as one could imagine. But all three had sharply defined personalities that remain as vivid in my mind today as when I worked for them quite a few years ago.

These relationships developed within the period from 1970 through 1983, a 13-year stretch during which I worked consecutively for three nonprofit organiza-tions, first heading the Ford Foundation's new program-related investment program during McGeorge Bundy's presidency, then serving as financial vice-president in Princeton president Bill Bowen's initial administration and as Chil-dren's Television Workshop's first executive vice-president under its founder and president, Joan Ganz Cooney.

In the following three sketches, I try to capture what it was about these indi-viduals that made them so memorable. That is not to say they didn't have flaws or slip from time to time. Indeed, I doubt whether one can be effective as a leader if one has not suffered some adversity. Unless people have been proven wrong or have been challenged by a force beyond their control, they tend to be intol-erant of others' foibles and to underestimate the cost of being wrong, because they don't really believe they can be wrong. Furthermore, people who have es-caped adversity may not appreciate to what extent random factors influence our lives. But, having said that these three CEOs have their vulnerabilities and short-comings, let me now share my impressions of the personal qualities that make them such vivid figures.

McGeorge Bundy

> "He possesses one of the keenest intellects I have encountered and he was by far the ablest National Security Advisor I have observed over the last forty years."
>
> *Robert S. McNamara*[1]

On July 28, 1995, the ABC television network broadcast, in prime time, a thought-provoking program on America's use of the atomic bomb against Japan

50 years earlier. One of those most prominently interviewed on the program was McGeorge Bundy, then 75 years old. The former national security adviser to Presidents John F. Kennedy and Lyndon B. Johnson spoke with undiminished acuteness, his manner of speech so crisp and taut it admitted of absolutely no excess verbiage.

Bundy appeared on the program because, at the age of 26, he had worked with Henry L. Stimson, who had been secretary of war during World War II, on the statesman's biography. Stimson was one of a handful of government officials who knew about the bomb's development and was deeply involved in the plans for its use. A nominal Republican, Stimson was actually part of a small core of distinguished Americans who were dedicated to serving Republican and Democratic presidents alike as foreign policy advisers. Bundy, whose father knew Stimson well, was likewise a nominal Republican and was raised, and schooled at Groton and Yale, to serve in the same tradition as Stimson.

During World War II, Bundy had gained admission to the Army by memorizing the eye chart in order to foil the test that would otherwise have disqualified him because of his poor vision. On D-Day, he was on the bridge of the cruiser *August* as Army aide to Admiral Alan G. Kirk, who was in charge of landing the American troops on Normandy's beaches.

As I watched Bundy responding on the program with the crispness and incisiveness for which he is renowned, I thought to myself: What a remarkable career this extraordinary man has had! He has been at the center of American affairs from World War II though the Cuban Missile Crisis and the Vietnam War, the drive for racial equality and the attack on the nation's areas of structural poverty. In the 1980s and 1990s, Bundy remained active in public affairs, becoming a leading proponent of taking steps to reduce the risk of nuclear war. In the spring of 1982, he joined with veteran diplomat George Kennan, a leading authority on the Soviet Union; Gerard Smith, former arms control chief; and Robert McNamara, in urging the United States to adopt a "no first strike" policy whereby it pledged to use nuclear weapons only in response to their use by others.[2] As recently as 1993, Bundy co-authored with Admiral William J. Crowe Jr., former chairman of the Joint Chiefs of Staff, and Sidney Drell, a professor of physics at Stanford University, a series of policies to reduce nuclear danger.[3] By all accounts, he is a man who has been part of the action of his times.

I first began talking with Mac Bundy a number of years ago about his Ford Foundation days. Bundy was working on lower Fifth Avenue in Manhattan in his faculty office at New York University. His secretary, who had been with him in Washington and at the Ford Foundation, was at a desk in a cramped outer office. Bundy was in a room littered with books and files, at work on a long-promised book on nuclear policy. He wore a sport shirt open at the neck, and his tweed jacket was slung over the back of his chair. He had to move aside a pile of books to make room for me to sit down. The setting was a far cry from the elegant, polished surroundings from which he had run the Ford Foundation.

For 13 years, from 1966 to 1979, Bundy had presided over the affairs of the foundation, the nation's largest, with some $3.7 billion in assets and an annual budget of more than $200 million in the 1960s. At the time he became its president, the Ford Foundation's assets were equal to one-sixth of the total resources of all the nation's 25,000 foundations.

Bundy directed the foundation from a spacious, rectangular-shaped office on the tenth floor of the foundation building in New York City. The office was lined with books and utterly quiet, as if it were a library. At one end was a floor-to-ceiling picture window that looked out on an 11-story atrium within the foundation building. At the base of the cavernous atrium was a lush garden.[4] No shades covered the office window, so Bundy was always visible to anyone on the outside.

The president's office at the foundation was an altogether fitting setting for the former dean of the Harvard Faculty of Arts and Sciences and national security adviser to Presidents Kennedy and Johnson. Indeed, Bundy was one of the shimmering jewels of Kennedy's "New Frontier," with an almost legendary reputation for a cool style and a lucid, finely honed intelligence.

During 1970–71, I was a program director at the Ford Foundation. There I knew Bundy as a man who matched his Washington reputation. He had a brilliant, versatile mind and the ability to express the issue at the center of a problem with astonishing quickness and clarity. He would draft a policy paper with just the right balance of simplicity and depth to enable its readers to plunge into a lively debate. His audience would feel sufficiently informed to express its reactions, but also anxious to learn more, rather than intimidated into silence and confusion by too much information.

This skill was coupled with an extraordinary breadth of knowledge and an ability to make judgments and then not waver under fire. These qualities enabled Bundy to exercise strong leadership at the Ford Foundation.

To some, Bundy's manner has always seemed to border on the autocratic, and indeed he has the gift for the sharp retort that one might expect of a sometime Harvard dean. But his manner at the foundation was infused with a certain gaiety, as if he knew the role people expected him to play and played it with relish lest he disappoint them.

Bundy has strong instincts and is given to listening to his hunches. One day in 1971, I reported to him a request from Children's Television Workshop, which Ford helped to launch, that the foundation now finance CTW's development of a cable television system in Washington. I told Bundy that I thought the project was beyond CTW's capabilities, but I added that I was impressed with the energy and potential of this then three-year-old organization, which had startled the television world by producing *Sesame Street* and then *The Electric Company*. I suggested that we find a way, other than by the cable project, to help CTW build its self-generated revenues and reduce its dependence on government funds. Bundy leaned back in his chair, tilting it slightly as he put his hands behind his head. He reflected for a few moments and then asked, "Do you think we'd lose our money if we invested in the Workshop?" he asked. "No," I replied. "Okay," he went on, "then let's give CTW $10 million as unrestricted support."

The whole conversation had taken no longer than five minutes. But Bundy never wavered from the decision of that moment during the next nearly 12 months as he and I and others at the Ford Foundation negotiated to overcome the initially strong objections of the foundation's board of trustees to providing capital to enable CTW to launch business enterprises.

Shortly after The Pentagon Papers were published in the spring of 1971, Bundy announced at one of his customary staff briefings following a trustees' meeting, "The publication of the papers raises in the minds of some questions about my fitness to lead the foundation." He then said that he would shortly hold an open meeting for the entire Ford Foundation to discuss the subject. He did hold such a meeting, and although he gave no ground about the war, he also set no boundaries on the questions asked of him.

Bundy deploys his forceful intellect with great skill and consequently he evokes equally forceful reactions. President Kennedy told his wife Jackie that, with the exception of David Ormsby-Gore, then British ambassador to the United States, Bundy was the brightest man he had ever known. "Damn it," he added, "Bundy and I get more done in one day in the White House than they do in six months in the State Department."[5]

Kennedy told his friend Ben Bradlee, editor-in-chief of *The Washington Post*, "You can't beat brains and with brains, judgment . . . he does a tremendous amount of work. And he doesn't fold or get rattled when they're sniping at him."[6]

Bundy had been appointed Kennedy's special assistant for national security affairs after Kennedy had given some fleeting thought to naming Bundy, then dean of Harvard's Faculty of Arts and Sciences, as secretary of state. The idea was rejected on the grounds that Bundy would look too youthful to the public to serve as head of the state department. Bundy was instead offered the position of under secretary of state for political affairs, the number three post in the State Department. However, after Bundy accepted, the offer had to be withdrawn when it was learned that Chester Bowles, the senior under secretary of state, wanted to concentrate on political matters himself. Under these circumstances the organization of the State Department called for the number three secretary to concentrate on economic matters and Kennedy told Bundy, "I don't think either one of us could get away with that." Bundy spurned Kennedy's next offer—to be under secretary of state for administration—saying that his deanship at Harvard had about exhausted his taste for administrative work. When Kennedy came back with the offer of the position of assistant for national security affairs, Bundy accepted, figuring that working directly for the president, whom he liked, would be a good idea.

Bundy's role under Kennedy is characterized in positive, almost glowing terms by historian Michael R. Beschloss, who writes of Bundy:

> [He] made it his business to supply the loyalty, speed and imagi-
> nation Kennedy felt he could not get from the State Depart-
> ment. . . . He never let off steam or tried to improve his own
> reputation in the manner of later presidential aides by making dis-
> loyal cutting comments about the boss to reporters. His ample
> skepticism and self-esteem prevented him from becoming a yes-
> man. When he challenged the President, he heeded his finely
> tuned instinct about what would cross the line into insolence.[7]

Beschloss also relates anecdotes of the Bundy wit in action, citing examples of the jocular notes Bundy would append in his own hand to documents and cables sent to Kennedy to read—"Shah gives the Secretary the Business"—and quoting from the poem Bundy composed in response to Kennedy's query about whether it would be politically wise for the First Lady to attend the Virginia Horse Show in formal riding clothes—"Shall I let her in the Horse Show/The President was Gloomy/'Will our critics strike a worse blow'."[8]

A caustic, bitter portrait of Bundy is provided by David Halberstam in his *The Best and The Brightest*.[9] Halberstam writes that "the professional Bundy was all steel and work and drive; the smile was hard, almost frozen." The Pulitzer Prize-winning reporter continues, "There was also a lack of willingness to resist a put-down when someone was inept or slowed him down and at times there seemed a certain cruelty about him, the rich, bright kid putting down the inferior." Halberstam, himself an undergraduate at Harvard when Bundy was dean, adds that there was a "feeling of many in Washington that Bundy was in all his dealings too much the elitist." Halberstam, who made his reputation as a *New York Times* correspondent covering the Vietnam War, of which he was a vociferous critic, adds that "the people around Bundy seemed to sense a lack of reflection, a lack of depth, a tendency to look at things tactically, functionally and operationally rather than intellectually."

Halberstam finished his stinging portrait by characterizing Bundy as part of an "establishment convinced it knew what was right and what was wrong for the country. . . . In Bundy this was a particularly strong strain." The Halberstam picture of Bundy certainly attempts to rip all the bark off the tree, leaving in view only his frailties.

Bundy's testimony in 1969 before a Congressional committee investigating foundations is said by some to have angered the committee by its autocratic nature, although it was evident that partisanship led to his being attacked for giving Ford Foundation travel grants to aides of Robert Kennedy after the senator was assassinated.

The man I worked for at the foundation did not put subordinates down for sport; on the contrary, he was welcoming and supportive of the staff. I remember being introduced to him during my interview process, and his comment "You will find the foundation a healing place." That remark was in keeping with the environment of the foundation under Bundy, and the foundation undoubtedly served that purpose for people who, like Bundy, had come to the foundation from the cauldron of high government posts.

Bundy also evidenced a personal concern for his staff at the foundation; this was vividly demonstrated when his financial vice-president, Roger Kennedy, was horribly injured by an ambulance that ran him down from behind while he was bicycling in Central Park. Bundy was a daily visitor at his colleague's hospital bedside until Kennedy was out of danger and his recovery assured.

There is no question but that Bundy was a man of strong convictions; he did not back down easily once he reached a position, even in the face of strong disagreement or even public criticism. But Bundy's strong sense of conviction did not mean that, as Halberstam writes, he always thought he knew what was best. On the contrary, he was open-minded long enough to hear people out, and without his strong convictions the foundation would not have moved in the new and, at the time, controversial directions that it did under his leadership.

Although Bundy was educated at Groton and Yale and later served as dean of Harvard's School of Arts and Sciences, he had a perspective on the importance of being admitted to such institutions. One night, after I had left the foundation to become financial vice-president of Princeton University, Bundy was visiting the Princeton campus, and university president William Bowen invited him, me, and Tom Wright, another foundation alumnus and then university general counsel, to dinner at Bowen's home. After dinner, Bundy challenged Bowen on Princeton's and like institutions' highly selective admission process. "Bill," Bundy argued, "you can claim that 10 percent of your applicants stand out from all the rest and surely should be admitted. And there are probably another 10 percent who plainly do not meet your standards. But, as for the other 80 percent, they are all about equally qualified, and it is really impossible to choose fairly between them."

Bowen responded that his admissions office could draw fine distinctions within this 80 percent and make sound choices. Bundy countered by proposing that it would make more sense to conduct a lottery to select applicants from this category. "Otherwise those who are admitted," he went on, "overvalue their admission, and those who are rejected are unduly disappointed."

Bundy took over as the Ford Foundation's fourth president on March 1, 1966. One of his first actions as president was to establish a major redirection in the Ford Foundation's program priorities. He recalled, "The foundation was only marginally engaged in the most important domestic issue of 1966—the race issue. Getting the foundation trustees on board went very quickly. They agreed I could state that this was our most important interest, and I announced it in a speech to the Urban League."

The new program direction was launched with a series of unrestricted grants to the Urban League and the National Association for the Advancement of Colored People—the first such support the foundation had ever given to a black organization.

Bundy followed up by naming as head of the Ford Foundation's National Affairs Division a man of his own choice, Mitchell Sviridoff, a former trade union leader who had never attended college. Bundy recruited Sviridoff from New York Mayor John Lindsay's administration and then, in January of 1967, brought in Roger Wilkins, a black official in the Kennedy and Johnson administrations, to run the National Affairs Division's Office of Social Development, which was to be the spearhead of the foundation's efforts to support minority groups and communities. A year later, the first African-American was added to the foundation's board: Dr. Vivian Henderson, president of Clark College in Atlanta. Very quickly, the percentage of the foundation's outlays allocated to National Affairs more than doubled, many of them grants for minority voter registration, community economic development, and other politically sensitive objectives.

Bundy's recounting to me of the change in foundation priorities made it sound very simple: the trustees wanted a man with fresh ideas, and Bundy supplied them. One former foundation colleague, an admirer of Bundy, speculates, however, that a business-dominated board of trustees did not necessarily buy Bundy's idea of making the racial issue the foundation's number one priority out of its own commitment to social innovation. In this person's view, the board had probably anticipated that Bundy would make his move in the international area and was surprised at the direction he took. In his view:

> The support for Bundy's racial initiative reflected less conviction
> that Bundy was right than the corporate tradition of deference to
> a new chief executive and of giving him initial latitude to initiate
> his new ideas. Bundy was effective because he had grown up as
> part of the establishment, was always regarded as part of it, and
> was sensitive to the psychology he confronted. . . .

Bundy also took a plunge into noncommercial television, giving the electronic medium a higher budget priority than the foundation's traditional support of the arts. To lead this effort, Bundy recruited Fred Friendly, former head of CBS News. "Walter Lippmann called me," Bundy recalled, "and said 'Mac, you're going up to the Ford Foundation and you ought to talk to Fred Friendly.' The foundation had then a commitment to educational broadcasting, but with Fred we got into being the private banker and counselor to public broadcasting. . . . We were heavily involved . . . that was Fred's style."

This active, interventionist approach to grantmaking also characterized much of the work of National Affairs. In the pre-Bundy era, Ford, like most other foundations, would, when it received applications for grants, review them without extensively scrutinizing the operations or management of potential recipients and then write a check for those it approved, with few strings attached. By and large, recipients were limited to well-established institutions with national reputations.

Under Bundy, the foundation began dealing with relatively new organizations and asking tough questions of and making tough demands on its grant recipients. It got into the details of the recipient's program design and the quality of the people who would be running the programs it financed. And the foundation was by no means shy in insisting, as a condition of its support, that grantees make changes in their programs and their personnel and meet performance tests. Foundation officers and their consultants began digging into the nuts and bolts of grantees' operations, especially their financial management.

Our discussion about the foundation's more interventionist style led me to ask Bundy to make some generalizations about the elements of effective foundation grantmaking. He responded:

> The process begins with a quality staff that can identify the problem and a means of attacking it. And, crucially, there must be something in the environment that makes people ready to respond, a ripeness or readiness for change . . . someone must be interested besides the foundation. . . .

Bundy continued:

> I came to believe in 'knowing issues' and 'staying with the problem.' . . . It is very rare that the best thing to do is make a single grant and go away. . . .

In support of his view, Bundy cited the foundation's controversial decision to fund public interest law firms. "It took years," Bundy noted, "to build relationships with the bar."

However, in a recent conversation Bundy also made a point of calling my attention to the foundation's unsuccessful effort to promote change in the New York City public schools during John Lindsay's tenure as mayor. There was support in certain circles then for decentralizing the management of the city's schools. The foundation agreed to support the Lindsay administration's effort at decentralization, which quickly ran into powerful opposition from the teachers' union and the education department bureaucracy. The ensuing controversy led the mayor to back away from the idea and the foundation became a high-profile target for criticism. Bundy commented, in urging me to reference the foundation's lack of success in reforming New York City schools:

> I believe that a foundation that makes no mistakes is clearly too cautious, and the story of our relation to New York City school reform does at least show that our record was not in the error-free category.

I asked Bundy how a foundation ought to choose its program objectives. He offered:

> There are a lot of good things to do. . . . You have to look at who
> you are . . . what you know . . . what skills you have . . . what
> you are personally interested in . . . one could never say one idea
> is better than anything else . . . one only could say it's worth doing
> and we know how to do it. . . .

Bundy reflected that there were a few cases in which the Ford Foundation had made a major investment in an institution without getting involved in management. He pointed to the foundation's program to improve the viability of theater groups. "We were not trying to meet the immediate crisis in theater companies," he observed, "but to help them position themselves to be able to cope continually with their financial needs. We used the carrot of grants to induce their managements to act in a money-conscious manner and so we developed a roster of consultants who would get into their financial nuts and bolts."

Bundy quickly pointed out that the Ford approach was not necessarily typical of the foundation world. At the other pole, he observed, are foundations that "agree on a purpose with a first-class institution and then let the institution execute the grant without much oversight." "But this style," he added, "won't work where the institutions are not yet fully matured."

Program-related investments (PRIs), one of the very few innovations in foundation techniques for funding programs, were developed early in the Bundy regime. They were consistent with the more interventionist approach taken by Ford toward those it supported under his leadership. The PRI technique involved "investing" Ford Foundation funds in an organization instead of making a grant. The investment, in the form of a loan or equity, was not only to be repaid, the foundation was to earn at least a modest return on its funds.

The object was twofold: First, by expressing support in the form of an "investment," the foundation was making the financial viability of the recipient organization and the economic feasibility of its proposed program subject to review. Second, the fact that recipients were obliged to pay back the foundation investment meant that those repayments could be recycled to support new activities. In a time of scarcer foundation resources, the recovery and recycling of funds was an important consideration.

Bundy seemed clearly the right man at the right time for the Ford Foundation. He had a keen instinct for identifying new foundation priorities that were in tune with the changing agenda of the country, and he had the skills to articulate new directions and persuade trustees to support them.

William G. Bowen

William G. Bowen was 38 years old when he assumed the presidency of Princeton University in 1972. He had spent the first 17 years of his adult life, following college, at Princeton. In 1955, Bowen graduated from Denison University in

Granville, Ohio, an excellent small liberal arts college, and matriculated at Princeton to obtain his Ph.D. in economics. He earned his doctorate in three years, far more quickly than the typical graduate student completes the Ph.D. process. Identified as a brilliant comer, Bowen was promptly awarded a coveted appointment as an assistant professor of economics at Princeton, and by the age of 30 he received tenure.

Bowen published at a furious pace, and in 1966, he and Will Baumol co-authored *Economics of the Performing Arts,* whose analysis of the performing arts and forecast of the sector's growing financial problems received front-page treatment by *The New York Times.*

The book advanced the idea of limitations on productivity gains in the service sector. In essence, it argued, in the arts, education, and other services, costs rise with inflation, because there are not opportunities, as in manufacturing, to make capital investments in parts and equipment that increase productivity. Without such gains, rising costs must be offset by rising prices.

In 1967, Bowen was named Princeton's first provost (deputy president) on the eve of a series of striking changes in the university:

- ◆ The increasingly active recruitment of minority students, and a marked increase in the diversity of the undergraduate student body;
- ◆ The often divisive move to coeducation, which led to the matriculation of the first female undergraduates in 1969;
- ◆ The adoption of the university's first modern and open budgeting process, involving the formation of a priorities committee composed of students, faculty members, and administrators; and
- ◆ The campus unrest and protests stirred by the Vietnam War.

In each of these matters, Bowen played a pivotal role, working closely with his predecessor as president, Robert Goheen, to resolve conflicts and steer the university through the turbulence of the times.

When Bowen was named president of Princeton, he had already won the reputation of being one of the country's leading administrators of higher education. I remember Mac Bundy telling me, when Bowen took office, that to avoid "invidious comparisons" he would characterize Bowen as "the best college president under 40."

Although Bowen and I had not known each other previously, he offered me the post of financial vice-president in his administration. Bundy and others I talked to said I could not afford to miss out on the experience of working for such an extraordinarily talented educator.

Others informed me that Bowen was not only brilliant but also a man of limitless energy, with amazing recuperative powers. As one common friend explained, Bowen was liable to duck out of his office at lunchtime to play an hour of tennis—a sport at which he excelled—and then to return, his energy restored, to work late into the evening. Bowen is simply the kind of person for whom the 24-hour day is not long enough.

Working for Bowen was indeed a special experience. While I had been briefed about the quality of his mind, I was not quite prepared for the range of subjects he could master on initial exposure to them. Once, during the second year of our working together, the university's general counsel and I prepared a detailed, tightly written memorandum about a complex tax issue relating to the commercial real estate development the university was planning to initiate. We had worked on the memorandum for several days with the help of a tax partner at one of Philadelphia's leading law firms. We needed a quick sign-off from Bowen but were afraid that the issue was so intricate and sufficiently outside the realm of his prior experience that it would take some time to make him comfortable with the matter.

We finished the memorandum just in time for Bowen's secretary to include it in the large packet of materials that would be delivered to him when he got off a plane at Newark airport. (Bill was not going to waste the hour it took to drive from the airport to the campus and always had his mail awaiting his landing from a plane trip.) The general counsel and I had sent a message to Bowen through his secretary that the issue was urgent.

As soon as Bowen was back in his office and had handed over to his secretary the tapes he had dictated on the plane and the papers he had reviewed during the car ride back to the campus, he called the general counsel and me in to meet with him. In a few sentences, Bowen stated his understanding of the issue we had posed. His recitation was so crisp and to the point that the general counsel and I looked at each other as if to say, "Are we once again associates standing before a senior law firm partner?"

We both acknowledged to Bowen that he had correctly grasped the issue at hand. Then Bowen looked us straight in the eye and said that it seemed to him that the answer turned on a point we had not sufficiently addressed in the memo. He was right, of course. Bowen had quickly gotten to the heart of the matter and had put his finger on the most critical point. With slightly flushed faces, the general counsel and I proceeded to expand on the memorandum's discussion of the pivotal issue Bowen had identified. Bowen listened and then simply agreed with our analysis and told us to go ahead. The whole meeting had lasted no more than five minutes.

Bowen was also knowledgeable about every aspect of the university. As a faculty member and as provost, he had soaked up an incredible inventory of knowledge about the details of the university's operations.

Moreover, Princeton was his world, and nothing escaped his attention. He was not one of those university presidents who use their position to embark on a series of activities that frequently take them away from the campus. Because his familiarity with virtually every facet of the university's operation was well known, no one presented an issue to him without first being sure of having mastered all the pertinent details.

Bowen's feel for Princeton, however, went well beyond facts and history; he had an uncanny sense of the forces that affected the equilibrium of the institution and of how to deal with sensitive matters in order to maintain the integrity of the university. Where campus peace was at issue, Bowen made it plain that exhaustive planning for all contingencies should be standard operating procedure.

Bowen also understood that the heart and soul of a university is the quality of its faculty. The finest buildings and loveliest campus would not produce a great university unless the school's faculty was superior. He thus faithfully chaired meetings of the Committee on Appointments and Advancements, which met on a grueling schedule to review all the academic departments' recommendations for individual salary raises as well as for promotions. Bowen personally weighed each proposed appointment to tenure as if the university's future depended on it. Whatever the field in question, Bowen would become an expert on what constituted cutting-edge work in the area. He was, as a faculty member who served a term on the committee said, its "key player."

Bowen's concern for maintaining the highest-quality faculty possible extended beyond these review proceedings to personal contacts. A friend of mine on the faculty who was once approached by Harvard with a job offer told me that the most remarkable thing about the whole process was that, within a few hours after Harvard contacted him, Bowen was on his doorstep, both congratulating him and explaining why he should stay at Princeton. My friend did stay, partly because Bowen's intense personal interest convinced him that he genuinely mattered to the university.

Bowen was also conversant with new fields of knowledge that were emerging as important. Early in the 1970s, he understood the importance of molecular biology, which was becoming a fundamental building block of new advances in medicine. Bowen mobilized the resources needed to recruit researchers in the area and build an expensive modern laboratory for such scientists, and he actively recruited the young talent that would mature into leaders in the field. Today, Princeton's molecular biology department is one of the nation's finest, even though many said such an achievement was not possible without the addition of a medical school.

At the same time, Bowen looked at potential new initiatives in the context of Princeton's niche in higher education. Princeton offers an undergraduate education second to none among American universities and is an established leader in graduate research and the production of Ph.D.'s in the core fields of the humanities, the arts, the social sciences, and the physical sciences. Princeton does not have a business, law, or medical school, and its professional schools are limited to engineering, architecture, and the Woodrow Wilson School of Public and International Affairs. It is thus a highly focused institution backed by one of the largest per-capita endowments of any American university and possessing thousands of acres of land on which to grow, should it choose to do so.

Bill Bowen kept Princeton solidly positioned in its niche, working endlessly to maximize the school's potential and recognizing that success lay in the details.

Bowen was always in command in any setting, whether at a full meeting of the board, of the university faculty, or of the campus governance committee (made up of faculty, students, and administrators), or in a one-on-one with one of his key administrators. His encyclopedic knowledge, his razor-sharp mind, and his ability to express himself clearly and forcefully enabled him to manage the flow of discussion, whether with the senior business executives who sat on Princeton's board or in the freshman economics class he regularly taught. As a friend of us both once said to me: "Bowen is the best meeting runner I have ever seen. It doesn't matter whether a hundred or ten are present, Bill runs the meeting."

Joan Ganz Cooney

In the fall of 1969, a new television program for young children was launched on the Public Broadcasting Television Network. At the time, virtually every American household, at every income level, owned one or more television sets, and television was established as the most powerful communications medium of the twentieth century.

The new program was considered so revolutionary in its approach that Jack Gould, the television critic of *The New York Times,* wrote about it on the front page of the *Times.* The program was *Sesame Street,* and it combined the pacing and visual appeal of popular programming and commercials with educational content for preschoolers. Its humor also appealed to adults, so that parents could watch the series with their children. Even more amazing, over the ensuing years, the show has been seen in 130 countries and has been produced in countless languages, from Spanish to Arabic and Hebrew.

The reach of the series and its educational effectiveness continue to be documented. In 1994, researchers' analysis of national survey data showed that the series was reaching between 80 and 90 percent of American preschoolers in virtually every demographic group. Moreover, preschoolers from low-income families who watch *Sesame Street* are more likely to show signs of emerging literacy and numeracy than poor children who do not watch it.

In evaluating the series' impact over time, University of Kansas researchers reported that the series made a significant and lasting contribution to children's cognitive development and played a positive role in contributing to desirable learning outcomes, even in the face of difficult home environments.

Today, some 27 years since it first went on the air, the show continues to mix fast pacing, humor, and visual appeal with educational and socially relevant content, and with both the entertainment and education continually refreshed by new material in tune with the changing times. Whether one evaluates the series in terms of its sheer appeal or its contribution to the development of preschoolers, it is a landmark in American communications.

More than of any other person, *Sesame Street* is the achievement of Joan Ganz Cooney. It was she who in the late 1960s did the original study that conceived of the series and made the case for its potential appeal and educational impact. Cooney's work was inspired and supported by Lloyd Morrisett, then an officer of the Carnegie Corporation, which provided a grant for the study. At the time, Cooney was a public affairs producer in public television who had never produced an entertainment show, let alone one for children. But what Lloyd Morrisett[10] saw in Cooney was not only an arresting intelligence but a rare ability to visualize the format and theme of a show and to communicate that vision clearly to a talented group of artists who would create the program. These talents were combined with Cooney's ability to recognize outstanding creative talent and to work with—indeed, inspire, strong egos, as well as her keen sense of when material would work and when it would not.

Joan Cooney has a drive to keep reaching out for new professional terrain. She gave up a successful and personally satisfying career in public affairs to take on the challenge of trying to create an entirely new broadcast format for an audience television had virtually ignored: young children. This willingness to move in new creative directions marked her leadership of CTW as it ventured into new areas of programming. After *Sesame Street,* the workshop produced the highly successful and acclaimed *The Electric Company,* a series designed to enhance the reading skills of 6- to 10-year-olds.

Then Cooney turned CTW to producing its first programs for adults—a series on health and the miniseries *The Best of Families,* a drama about three different economic and social strata living in New York City at the turn of the century. Neither program succeeded. Although disappointed, Cooney moved on to conceive and launch *3-2-1 Contact,* a series designed to make 8- to 12-year-olds, especially young girls, more receptive to science. Finding the right format for the program was not easy. After a good deal of creative struggle, five pilot shows were produced and tested, using CTW's research methodology, for both their audience appeal and their effectiveness in achieving the show's educational objectives. The testing results were negative. CTW had a lot of money invested in the pilots, but Cooney's reaction was decisive; toss them into the wastebasket and start over. New creative talent was injected into the effort, a new design emerged, and the show was well received when it finally aired.

Part of Cooney's management style in working with strong and successful creative talent was to give people free rein even if she had reservations about what they proposed. Dave Connell, the original executive producer of *Sesame Street* and *The Electric Company,* had his heart set on doing on commercial television an animated version of C. S. Lewis's popular children's stories, *The*

Chronicles of Narnia. Cooney did not warm to the project and doubted whether commercial television would go for it. After all, commercial TV specials for children were all built around established comic strip characters. But she told Dave to go ahead and try to get the show on the air if he wanted to. Eventually, a major sponsor of television programming was willing to back the show, and with the sponsor's support and that of its advertising agency, J. Walter Thompson, one of the largest in the world at the time, CBS agreed to air the show during prime time on a Sunday night. The two-hour animated feature won an Emmy for best children's special and, more relevant in the commercial world, won the largest audience share in its time slot.

However, Cooney's doubts about the project were not completely off base; when it was shown again a year later, the special did not do well in the ratings and it failed to become what many had hoped it would—a long-term classic that would be aired every year.

One of the qualities that draws people to Cooney is that she is a superb listener. Friends as well as staff members turn to her when they are really stumped, either on the professional front or by a personal problem. Cooney *hears* them and often finds just the right answer to turn them around.

Cooney is also in touch with the larger world. She has never lost her interest in public affairs and the people active in that world. A meeting in her office is just as likely to begin with her commentary on a current event or a public figure she has met as with the business agenda at hand. Her view of the world is invariably original.

Cooney is also an unusually articulate person with the ability to make her point in a few words. As I described earlier in this chapter, in 1971 the Ford Foundation was considering a multimillion-dollar grant to Children's Television Workshop to enable it to engage in business activities in order to reduce its dependence on foundation and government funding (a fortunate strategy, given that government support of *Sesame Street* was eliminated at the end of the decade). The foundation's trustees were uneasy about this first-of-its-kind grant, especially to an organization that was only in its third year of existence. McGeorge Bundy, rather than forcing the issue with the board, suggested that board member Bill Donaldson—who was the most outspoken with his doubts—meet with Joan Cooney and express his reservations directly to her. Donaldson was one of three founders of one of America's first post-World War II investment banking houses, the first on Wall Street to go public.

At a long lunch in an elegant private dining room at the Ford Foundation, Donaldson and Cooney sat next to each other, talking quietly while Bundy and I ate our meal largely in watchful silence. At coffee, Donaldson brought things to a head, declaring that he was very uncomfortable that the Ford money would "corrupt" CTW. Cooney shot back: "Bill, you have no idea of the corruption of poverty!"

Donaldson laughed wholeheartedly, and the lunch broke up. A few days later, the grant sailed through. Today CTW is a diversified communications organization with an endowment fund and reserves of more than $125 million.

One of the concerns that boards have about founders is that they will not let go of what they have built and will stay in control longer than is good for an organization. Several years ago, Cooney named her deputy David V. Britt as president and CEO of CTW and became chair of CTW's executive committee. Unlike many founders, Cooney has let go and she does not interfere with Britt's running of the Workshop. Britt had been with CTW for 20 years and Cooney's deputy for nearly 10 years when she turned over the reins of management to him in 1990. The rapport between them, built over a long period of time, established the foundation for a smooth executive transition and positioned CTW to build on Cooney's extraordinary contribution to television programming for children.

In some ways McGeorge Bundy, William Bowen, and Joan Ganz Cooney practiced sharply different styles of leadership. Bowen brought an unparalleled level of intensity and energy to his role as president of Princeton, as well as a penchant for personally scrutinizing every detail of every transaction he considered important. A friend observed: "Bill Bowen was not content to devise the course for the ship of state. He also insisted on running the engine room." And the remarkable fact is that he could run the engine room as well as any of his subordinates. Bowen did not delegate in the sense of leaving to his deputies implementation of his policies; he held them accountable to him regarding how they planned to execute a task, and if he didn't like their plan, he personally revised it and then made sure that it was carried out as he believed it should be. Such detailed oversight requires enormous energy; it leaves little room for time off, and Bowen worked ceaselessly as university president.

Bundy, in contrast, would often step back from the operations of the Ford Foundation. He was intimately involved in crafting the foundation's policy, but he left its execution largely to others. In leading the foundation, Bundy set limits on his involvement; customarily he left work before 6 o'clock—perhaps to attend to one of his many other interests, perhaps for a social engagement. But Bundy was not at Ford to set new records in hours clocked at the foundation. After his grueling years in Washington, Bundy wanted a diversified life, and he conducted his foundation presidency accordingly.

Cooney kept the lightest hand of all on business details. The creation of television shows was her passion, and she was at the center of the creative process. But once a show's concept was set, she gave her producers ample room to deliver the product. Likewise, she was content to set the business and financial directions for CTW and let others work out the details. Her day was a mix of the business of CTW, of the half-dozen corporate boards she sat on, and of the wide network of friends and acquaintances she had in a range of fields. She largely left it to her subordinates to come to her, and they did because they acknowledged CTW to be her creation and wanted her counsel.

The talent most common to these three very different personalities is their gift of expression. Whether employing the spoken or written word, each could get his or her point across in a way that was not only comprehensible but also persuasive. A talent for communicating is an indispensable element of leadership of nonprofit institutions. When you are running a nonprofit organization, it is not enough to be right; you need to make others *believe* you are right.

In business, persuasiveness is similarly crucial to effective leadership, but in a business organization there is not the same attention to the quality of expression as there is in much of the nonprofit world. In a sense, words are the currency of nonprofits, just as profits are the currency of business enterprises.

Of the three people I have profiled, Bundy used words the most elegantly; his sentences, written or spoken, were crisp and clear, stripped of any excess that might clutter the principal idea. But his simplicity was always polished with a turn of phrase that enhanced the clarity of his thought. Bowen, in contrast, wrote as he worked; he almost overwhelms the reader, taking into account every possibility, every contingency, and dealing with it with meticulous thoroughness. Cooney had a flair for closing out a seemingly endless debate with a succinct, sharp observation that cut to the chase, as in the case of her luncheon rejoinder to Bill Donaldson.

What, then, do these three figures—Bundy, Cooney, and Bowen—with their distinctive personalities and management styles, have in common? What accounts for the fact that all were highly effective leaders of their respective organizations?

All the obvious reasons—they genuinely understood their business and what made it work and what could damage it. They were all able to establish an overall direction and a set of values that were well understood. Each had a way of motivating people to do their best, although each employed quite different tactics to do so. The three leaders also had in common the ability to focus their attention on the one objective which they conceived of as pivotal to their organization's success; for Bundy it was shifting the foundation's program priorities, for Bowen it was enriching the quality of an already superior faculty, and for Cooney it was the continuous creation of new television programming. Amid the myriad issues and challenges they faced, they never lost sight of this objective, and they directed their greatest energies and talents to its pursuit. And yet none of these factors really explains the keystone of their leadership. In my view, they led by *the force of their personality*. Each in his or her own way was a formidable person—you *felt* their presence, and your energy and alertness increased when you dealt with them.

I have had superiors in my career who, whatever their professional skills, were too uninteresting to talk about with anyone. But Bundy, Cooney, and Bowen were different. You talked about them to your colleagues and to your friends, not just because you were working for them, but because they were intriguing people and you were involved with them at a time when you shared a powerful common interest.

NOTES

1. Robert S. McNamara, *Reflections* (New York: Times Books, 1995), p. 95.
2. McGeorge Bundy, George Kennan, Robert S. McNamara and Smith, "Nuclear Weapons and the Atlantic Alliance," *Foreign Affairs,* Spring 1982.
3. McGeorge Bundy, William J. Crowe, and Sidney Drell, *Reducing Nuclear Danger* (Council on Foreign Relations, 1993).
4. The dramatic and elegant building was completed in 1967 at a cost of $17.5 million. Intended as an esthetic addition to New York City, it has been a subject of continuing controversy as to its appropriateness and its architectural merits.
5. Michael R. Beschloss, *The Crisis Years* (New York: HarperCollins, 1991), p. 249.
6. Ibid., p. 249.
7. Ibid., pp. 249, 254.
8. Ibid., pp. 249–251.
9. David Halberstam, *The Best and the Brightest* (Ballantine, 1995).
10. Today Lloyd Morrisett is in his 27th year as head of the Markle Foundation, which specializes in the field of communications. He also continues as chairman of the board of Children's Television Workshop, the nonprofit corporation that has been *Sesame Street*'s parent since day one.

Index